Clinging to the rock was a great ice cornice hanging over the mighty Kangshung Face. Under the effects of gravity, the ice had broken away from the rock and a narrow crack ran upward. Nervously, I wondered if the cornice might collapse under my pressure. There was only one way to find out!

Although it would be relatively useless, I got Tenzing to establish a belay; then I eased my way into the crack, facing the rock. I jammed my crampons into the ice behind me and then wriggled my way upward using every little handhold I could find. Puffing for breath, I made steady height—the ice was holding—and forty feet up I pulled myself out of the crack onto the top of the rock face. I had made it! For the first time on the whole expedition, I had a feeling of confidence that we were going to get to the top. I waved to Tenzing and brought in the rope as he, too, made his way laboriously up the crack and dragged himself out beside me, panting for breath.

We didn't waste any time. I started cutting steps again, seeking now rather anxiously for signs of the summit. . . .

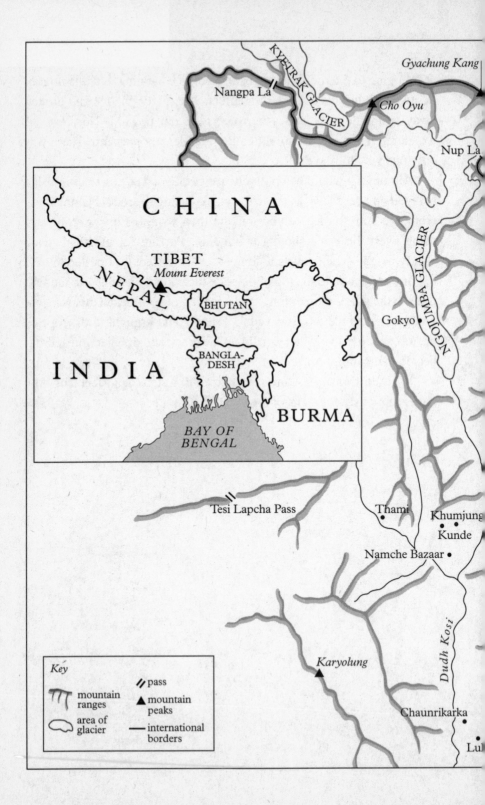

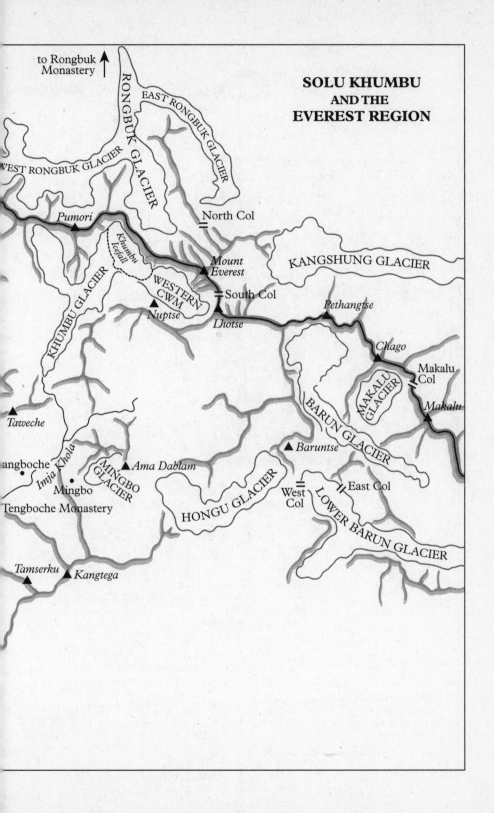

to Rongbuk
Monastery

SOLU KHUMBU
AND THE
EVEREST REGION

RONGBUK GLACIER

EAST RONGBUK GLACIER

WEST RONGBUK GLACIER

North Col

Pumori

KANGSHUNG GLACIER

Khumbu Icefall

Mount
Everest

WESTERN
CWM

South Col

KHUMBU GLACIER

Nuptse

Lhotse

Pethangtse

Chago

Makalu
Col

MAKALU GLACIER

Makalu

BARUN GLACIER

Taweche

Baruntse

angboche

Imja Khola

MINGBO GLACIER

Ama Dablam

Mingbo

Tengboche Monastery

HONGU GLACIER

West
Col

East Col

LOWER BARUN GLACIER

Tamserku

Kangtega

VIEW FROM THE SUMMIT

SIR EDMUND HILLARY

POCKET BOOKS
New York   London   Toronto   Sydney

POCKET BOOKS, a division of Simon & Schuster, Inc.
1230 Avenue of the Americas, New York, NY 10020

Copyright © 1999 by Sir Edmund Hillary

Published by arrangement with Transworld Publishers, Ltd.
First published in Great Britain in 1999

ISBN: 0-7434-0067-4

First Pocket Books trade paperback printing May 2000

10 9 8 7 6 5

POCKET BOOKS and colophon are registered trademarks of
Simon & Schuster, Inc.

For information regarding special discounts for bulk purchases,
please contact Simon & Schuster Special Sales at 1-800-456-6798
or business@simonandschuster.com

Front cover photo credits: Sir Edmund Hillary © Karsh of Ottawa/Camera Press; Mt.
Everest © John Cleare/Mountain Camera; By arrangement with Transworld Publishers,
A Division of the Random House Group Ltd.

Printed in the U.S.A.

Contents

Acknowledgments

There are many people that I should thank for the important part they have played in my adventures and in my aid projects, too. Their assistance has made everything possible and I deeply appreciate their support. But there are too many of them to thank individually here.

Only a few have played a major role in this book and I must express my thanks to them personally:

George Greenfield, my friend and literary agent for forty years, who once again organized my agreement with our publishers; Tom Scott, also a friend of long-standing, whose research has ensured that many anecdotes and stories I might have overlooked or never seen are incorporated in this narrative; Averil Mawhinney whose patient and determined investigations have located many illustrations for the book; my friend of many years, Margaret Body, has played a very important part on the editorial side, as has Joanna Goldsworthy of Transworld.

Perhaps most important of all has been my wife, June, who read every word and made sure that the story was correctly presented, as nobody knows more about my life than she does. She made sure that the pages and paragraphs flowed reasonably smoothly—not an easy thing to do.

To them all I express my deepest appreciation.

INTRODUCTION

THIS IS THE STORY OF MY LIFE, CONDENSING SEVENTY-NINE YEARS of somewhat vigorous activity into a few hundred pages. My views may not always coincide with the stories of my companions, but this is the way I clearly saw things at the time.

I have had much good fortune, a fair amount of success and a share of sorrow, too. Ever since I reached the summit of Mount Everest more than forty-five years ago the media have classified me as a hero, but I have always recognized myself as being a person of modest abilities. My achievements have resulted from a goodly share of imagination and plenty of energy.

As a youngster I was a great dreamer, reading many books of adventure and walking lonely miles with my head in the clouds. I was unaware that many exciting challenges lay ahead of me and that over the years I would receive a host of honors and awards. I have had the good fortune to meet Queens and Princes, Presidents and Prime Ministers, but perhaps more importantly for me I have made close friendships with many people from a variety of cultures.

Achievements are important and I have reveled in a number of good adventures, but far more worthwhile are the tasks I have been able to carry out for my friends in the Himalayas. They, too, have been great challenges in a different way—building mountain airfields and schools, hospitals and clinics, and renewing remote Buddhist monasteries. These are the projects that I will always remember.

Ed Hillary

Sir Edmund Hillary

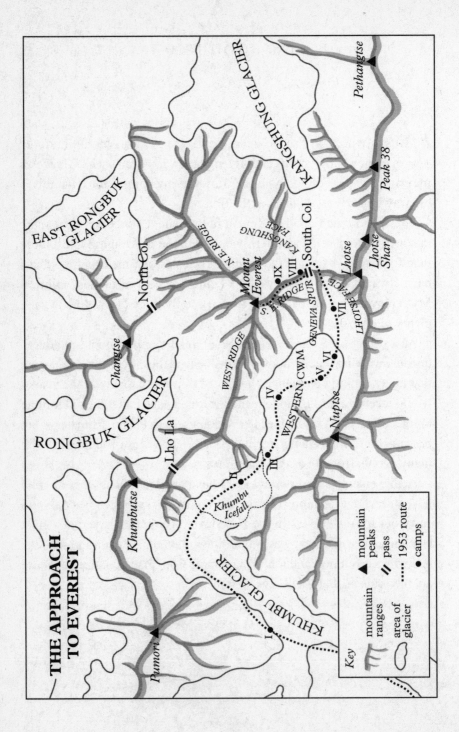

THE APPROACH
TO EVEREST

EAST RONGBUK
GLACIER

KANGSHUNG GLACIER

Pethangtse

Peak 38

North Col

N.E. RIDGE

Mount Everest

KANGSHUNG
FACE

South Col

Lhotse

Lhotse
Shar

Changtse

IX

VIII

S. E. RIDGE

GENEVA SPUR

LHOTSE FACE

VII

RONGBUK GLACIER

WEST RIDGE

IV

WESTERN CWM

V VI

Nuptse

Lho La

III

Khumbutse

Lho La

II

I

Khumbu
Icefall

KHUMBU GLACIER

Pumori

I

Key

▲ mountain
   peaks

‖ pass

····· 1953 route

● camps

〰 mountain
   ranges

◯ area of
   glacier

───── ───

1

Roar of a Thousand Tigers

TENZING CALLED IT THE ROAR OF A THOUSAND TIGERS. HOUR AFTER hour it came whining and screeching in an unrelenting stream from the west with such ferocity it set the canvas of our small Pyramid tent cracking like a rifle range. We were 25,800 feet up on the South Col, a desolate saddle between the upper slopes of Everest and Lhotse. Rather than easing off, the gale grew more violent the longer it went on. I began to fear that our heaving and thrashing shelter must surely be wrenched from its mooring, leaving us exposed and unprotected amongst the ice and boulders. I was braced between Tenzing Norgay and the tent wall with no room to stretch out to my full length. Jammed in tight, just turning over was difficult and resulted in a spasm of panting. The thudding canvas beat constantly against my ribs and whenever my head touched the fabric my brain felt like it had been placed under a pneumatic drill. As a weight-saving device, we had left behind our inner sleeping bags and this was proving to be a considerable mistake. Even wearing all my down clothing I found the icy breath from outside penetrating through to my bones. A terrible sense of fear and loneliness dominated my thoughts. What is the sense in it all? I asked myself. A man was a fool to put up with this! When it came, sleep was a half-world of noise and cold. Then my air mattress deflated, freezing my hip where it rested on the ice. It was the worst night I have ever spent on a mountain.

On the other side of Tenzing my old climbing friend and fellow New Zealander George Lowe and the English climber Alf Gregory were similarly hunched up in their sleeping bags, twisting about in futile search for some position less uncomfortable and for some escape from the bitter cold. We were using the oxygen sleeping sets at the rate of one liter per minute, which made it easier to doze. At this height you dribble a good bit in your sleep, and when your oxygen bottle gives out you wake with a terrible start and your rubber mask is all clammy and frigid. Throughout the endless night I kept looking at my watch, wondering if it had broken, for the hands hardly seemed to move. Finally, when the hour hand crawled around to 4 a.m., I struck a match and read the thermometer on the tent wall. It was −25°C and still pitch black. I gently nudged Tenzing and he was immediately awake and, in his universally helpful fashion, wriggled up and began lighting our primus stove. The tent started warming up a little and I retreated callously deeper into my bag and thought about the events of the previous day. What a momentous day it had been!

The 26th May 1953 had dawned cold, bright and clear. We were at Camp VII, 24,000 feet up in the middle of the Lhotse Face. Overhead a cloud of powder snow was being blown off Everest's upper ramparts, but it didn't look too bad. It boded well for the first assault pair of Charles Evans and Tom Bourdillon. They were at Camp VIII on the South Col and would be going all out for the South Summit this day. Their start would need to be better than ours. At Camp VII it took us ages to get moving. Even simple tasks at this height take an inordinate length of time, as oxygen-starved brains and bodies have little concentration and lack coordination. At 8:45 a.m., after breakfasting on biscuits and lukewarm tea, Tenzing and I, the second assault pair, led off on one rope. Our support team of George Lowe and Alf Gregory followed on a second rope. Behind them were our three high-altitude Sherpas who would help us establish Camp IX on the South-East Ridge. Bringing up the rear were five load-carrying Sherpas who were taking supplies only as far as the South Col. Charles Evans and Tom Bourdillon had been chosen for the first assault because they had developed a successful partnership and were better versed than any of us in using the more experimental closed-circuit oxygen equipment which, if it worked, would allow faster and more economical progress toward the South Summit and, maybe, beyond. If the weather made it a one-dash venture, they were equipped to take their chance. Meanwhile Tenzing and I had established our credentials by being acclimatized and strong, so we would be close behind, awaiting our turn, with the cumbersome but more familiar open-circuit systems.

We crossed a frighteningly unstable crevasse and made our way up the long steep slope of the Lhotse Face. We hadn't gone far before the ever-observant George shouted and pointed up to the distant South-East Ridge, where we could see two tiny figures making their way upward toward the South Summit. It could only be the first assault party of Evans and Bourdillon. Their main objective was to reach the South Summit itself but they could make the decision to carry on toward the top if they thought they could do it. Further down the South-East Ridge we could see another couple and judged this to be John Hunt and Da Namgyal carrying some assault supplies for us as high as they could on the ridge. It was an exciting scene—we were really on the move!

Tenzing and I rushed on ahead and reached the top of the Geneva Spur. We caught glimpses of the first assault team making excellent time up the ridge until they disappeared into the cloud covering the upper part of the mountain. I noticed that Tenzing looked decidedly subdued. We dropped down the 200-foot descent to make our second visit to the South Col. The first had been when we had pioneered the major lift of supplies to the col which had made the attempts on the summit possible. The small group of tents in the camp, bucking in the wind, looked very lonely indeed and we crawled inside one for shelter.

I kept looking out the door and very soon picked up two figures moving down the Great Couloir, and traveling very slowly. I hurried across the South Col to meet them. It was John Hunt and Da Namgyal and they were completely exhausted. They had carried their loads until they could carry no longer and then dumped their supplies on the South-East Ridge. John had left his half bottle of oxygen there too and had come down without it, so was in a desperate condition. I supported him across the col as best I could but he collapsed time and time again. It was only when I obtained some oxygen from the camp and returned with it to John that his energy partly returned and he made it back to his tent and crawled thankfully inside.

By now George and his team had joined us, and he suddenly gave a yell. Through a break in the clouds his sharp eyes had caught a view of the tiny figures of Evans and Bourdillon, still above 27,000 feet, but descending into the Great Couloir. Clouds swept in again and then lifted barely ten minutes later. To our astonishment we realized that our two friends were now at the bottom of the couloir. Obviously they had slipped and fallen hundreds of feet. Only the soft snow at the bottom had saved them from plummeting into a crevasse or down the terrible Kangshung Face. They, too, were completely exhausted, only able to move a few steps before stopping and slumping over. George and I hurried across to join them. They were an astonishing sight—covered in ice from head to foot. It demanded a great effort to get them over to a tent and push them inside with John Hunt.

With numb lips they told their story. Right from the start they had problems with their powerful but experimental closed-circuit oxygen equipment. When all went well they made excellent speed. High on the South-East Ridge Charles Evans' problems increased and they reached the South Summit with faulty gear and feeling very tired. The weather, too, had deteriorated with cloud and wind. The very stubborn Tom Bourdillon wanted to carry on, whatever the risks, but Charles Evans was sure that if they persisted they would never return. "If you do that, Tom," warned Charles Evans, "you will never see Jennifer again." So they came down.

That was a terrible night on the South Col! Charles and Tom had performed magnificently and, despite technical problems, had achieved their objective of reaching the South Summit. Now I had learned why

Tenzing had been so morose—he thought Charles and Tom were about to reach the top of Everest. He desperately wanted a Sherpa to be in the first summit team and he was always confident that he himself was the right Sherpa for this task. I, too, had a slight sense of guilt. I greatly admired what Charles and Tom had done but I had a regrettable feeling of satisfaction as well. They hadn't got to the top—there was still a job left for Tenzing and me to do. But the storm raged on and intensified, so it was already clear there was little chance of Tenzing and myself moving upward in the morning.

The day dawned in a fury of wind and drifting snow which after a few hours started to ease a little, although there was still streaming cloud over the upper mountain. Our main worry was the importance of getting Charles Evans and Tom Bourdillon down to safer levels. I talked to Charles about the final stretches of the mountain and, although he was never prone to exaggeration, he sadly told me that he didn't think we'd make it along the summit ridge. But I didn't take this too seriously—I had the confidence to believe I was a more experienced snow and ice climber than Charles or Tom and I felt I was probably fitter than either of them. We would see when the time came.

Around midday they emerged slowly from their tent and were joined by Sherpa Ang Temba who had come up with us to carry high on the mountain, but he had been nauseated all night so had to go down, too. To save oxygen for us they generously decided to do without it on the descent. I watched with great concern as they weaved their way up the slope toward the top of the Geneva Spur, the obstacle blocking access to descent of the Lhotse Face. To my horror, I saw Tom crumple and fall flat on the snow. Riveted with disbelief, I watched him drag himself to his feet, take a few more tottering steps, and then crash to the snow again. Clearly, he would need oxygen to have any hopes of getting down the mountain. Charles came back down with me and we quickly prepared an oxygen set which I carried up to Tom who was now on his hands and knees. With the oxygen turned on full volume, he was able to get slowly to his feet and very tentatively move up the slope again.

I returned to the tents and, when I told John Hunt and George Lowe of my considerable worry about the others getting down safely, John agreed that someone must go with them. Somewhat laboriously, he explained his conviction that he regarded it as his duty, as expedition leader, to supervise the action from the South Col. If something went wrong he might be needed higher on the mountain. George would have to go down as escort. I was greatly taken aback by this suggestion, as I was expecting considerable help from George, but I also realized how desperately keen John was to stay on the South Col, despite his exhaustion. It was difficult to know how to react to this decision. George had no such qualms. In strong and even bitter terms he pointed out how much fitter he was than John and how important he was to the success of the expedition. John had burned himself out, he said, on his great carry up the South-East Ridge and would be useless in an emergency. All very true, but unpalatable words to hear just the same. John remained adamant—George must go! I don't know why nobody mentioned Alf Gregory. He didn't seem to be around when these crises occurred. A disgruntled George started making his preparations for departure. However, it was only a few moments before John's sense of responsibility overruled his tired mind and he agreed that he himself was indeed the right person to take the party down.

I have never admired John more than I did at that moment. When we were alone, gray and drawn, but with his blue eyes frostier than ever, John gripped my arm and told me of his deep belief that we had a duty to climb the mountain. Many thousands of people had pinned their hope and faith on us and we couldn't let them down.

"The most important thing is for you chaps to come back safely. Remember that," he implored. "But get up if you can!"

I carried John's load for him to the top of the Geneva Spur and was distressed at how weak he was as he weaved from side to side. We arrived at the top of the slope only to see that Tom, despite breathing oxygen, had once again collapsed on the snow. It seemed that the whole expedition was falling to pieces. Noting my concern, Charles turned his warm and friendly smile on me and said consolingly, "Don't worry, Ed. I'll get them down."

John immediately decided he would take the back place on the rope and play the critical anchor role, but Charles merely did a middleman loop, handing it to his leader and said, "Get in there, John." Which he meekly did. With John in the middle position, they shuffled off. Watching them disappear from view down the steep and demanding Lhotse Face was a disheartening sight. George was with me and, to vent some of the guilt I felt at letting four exhausted men descend unaided, I turned on him and snapped unreasonably, "It will be all your fault, George, if they don't get down!"

George and I spent the rest of the day preparing the oxygen, food and equipment for the next day's assault, periodically ducking into our tents to warm ourselves. With the wind behind us, we crossed over the South Col and looked down the great East or Kangshung Face as no one had ever seen it from the top before, and a very awesome sight it proved to be. We turned back into the bitter wind and had a fearful struggle reaching our tents again, but were greatly encouraged at how fit we still felt and how freely we could work and move at 26,000 feet without oxygen. We were still worried about the descending party but we knew that with every hundred feet of height they lost, their strength would improve. As the day wore on, my thoughts turned increasingly to the next day ahead of us but I couldn't help dwelling at times on those rather awful moments with the departing team. Where were Tenzing and Alf Gregory, I asked myself, when we were making all our executive decisions, as I kindly described our rather ferocious arguments? Probably Tenzing was very wisely keeping his distance. And where was all the help when I was carrying loads and encouraging people up and down the demanding slope to the top of the Geneva Spur? I was pretty sure that Alf had been resting comfortably in his sleeping bag, conserving his strength for what he saw as the battles ahead. The altitude of 26,000 feet distorted everyone's judgment during this long and difficult day.

That night I moved with Tenzing into the relative comfort of a Meade tent. I had been wandering around all afternoon with a spanner in my hand (George claimed I looked more like a mechanic than a mountaineer) but it meant I knew precisely how much oxygen we had and decided we could spare a tiny bit for sleeping. It was still blowing hard, but at first I slept quite well, although periodically I'd waken stiff and cold to find my air mattress had deflated due to ice in the valve. It reminded me of an earlier time I had been sleeping with Tenzing at much lower altitude and woke to see him on his hands and knees bowing and murmuring in a strange fashion. I accepted that he was carrying out some sophisticated Buddhist ceremony until I realized that he was only inflating a faulty air mattress.

Early in the morning I was woken by a sudden quietness and realized the wind had stopped. Although it soon returned, it was much more spasmodic and a good sign for the day ahead. We started making our slow preparations and at 7:30 a.m. I crossed to George and Alf in the Pyramid tent. We agreed to start and accepted that we would have to carry heavy loads. Two high-altitude porters were supposed to go with us but, to our disappointment, we found that poor Pemba had been vomiting all night and would obviously have to go down. That meant we would only have the redoubtable Ang Nyima to help us, so all our individual loads would have to increase.

Thank goodness Tenzing was still so fit and strong. He was a remarkable man. He not only had the Sherpa's amazing ability to deal with altitude but was a skilled climber and had the unique motivation of wanting desperately to get to the top. Forty-five years ago carrying loads on a high mountain was just a well-paid job for the average Sherpa. Few of them had the drive to go any higher than they needed to. It is very different today, when many Sherpas are experienced guides with much mountaineering knowledge and considerable interest in pushing on to the summit. But in 1953 Tenzing and I were now reduced to one Sherpa instead of the planned three.

Our situation looked a little desperate, but George and I agreed there was no question of giving up. George, Alf and Ang Nyima would go ahead to establish the route and Tenzing and I would follow an hour later to conserve our strength for the next day. Our final preparations completed, George led his small group away across the South Col and slowly mounted the steep slope approaching the Great Couloir which shot up to the South-East Ridge more than a thousand feet above us. At 10 a.m. Tenzing and I made our move, heaving our cumbersome loads into place and turning on our open-circuit oxygen sets. As we breathed in the oxygen the loads seemed to lighten appreciably. Moving relatively easily, we crossed the South Col ice and cramponed up the firm snow above. High above us we could see the three tiny dots of our companions as they made their way into the couloir. The angle of the slope increased more than I had expected and we were forced to zigzag in order to gain comfortable height. A great crevasse stretched from side to side but we were able to cross it without too much trouble over a substantial ice bridge and continue upward. The slope was growing steeper when, to my pleasure, I came on a line of George Lowe's steps and we quickly moved up these, resting every forty feet or so for a breather. We were catching the others up and I could see the smooth swing of George's ice axe as he established a substantial route. Soon we were being peppered with chunks of ice traveling at great speed and we hastily moved to the side until George's team had hacked their way out of the couloir. While waiting, we turned off our oxygen to conserve it for higher up. Soon we were moving on again, reveling in George's steps and looking almost vertically downward to the tiny tents on the South Col. We climbed up to the right over mixed rock and snow and a few minutes later joined George, Alf and Ang Nyima on the crest of the South-East Ridge.

Despite all our efforts, we were a very happy and relaxed group. Our location was spectacular. Still rising above us was the craggy summit of Lhotse, but we could look over mighty Nuptse and see the superb peaks of Ama Dablam and Kangtega. Thousands of feet below us we could look down on Advanced Base Camp in the Western Cwm and it was even further down the other right-hand side to the Kangshung Glacier in Tibet. We were all going well but very much aware of the tremendous slopes sweeping down on both sides of us. Just in front was an incredibly lonely sight, the battered framework of the tent that Tenzing and Raymond Lambert of the 1952 Swiss expedition pitched over a year before and where they had spent an extremely uncomfortable night without food, without drink, and without sleeping bags. What a tough couple they had been, but perhaps not very well organized.

Feeling slightly embarrassed at our vigor, we carried on up the mixed rock and snow ridge. At 27,350 feet we reached the depot established with such effort by John Hunt and Da Namgyal. It was an ominously large pile and we needed all of it for higher on the mountain. But we didn't even know if we could carry such loads at this altitude, even using oxygen.

George and I discussed the problem. There were two particularly troublesome objects—a Meade tent weighing 14.5 lbs. and a large black oxygen bottle weighing 20 lbs. I've always been a good load carrier, so I told George that I'd take on the tent. George was a little doubtful as he knew it would give me a load of over 60 lbs., but we knew there was no alternative. Then we both looked at Alf Gregory. Alf was small, lean and very fit but had shown little enthusiasm for load-carrying in the past. This time we gave him no alternative. I handed him the black oxygen bottle and we removed most of his food and the cooker. George put a third bottle of oxygen on his frame, plus Gregory's excess gear, and Tenzing had another oxygen bottle. All of us now had over 50 lbs. each and I had more than 60 lbs.

We moved on and there was no doubt that our pace had dropped off considerably. Few, if any, people had carried these sorts of loads before at well over 27,000 feet. Instead of walking freely step for step, we were now battling for every foot in height. We came to a short but steep bluff and puffed our way up it with considerable effort. The ridge broadened onto a steep snow slope where the surface was very firm and George's ice axe started swinging freely again. We were getting very high now and the great summit of Lhotse was dropping away beneath us. We started looking rather desperately for a suitable campsite, but nothing appeared. We were just below the height Tenzing had reached with Lambert the year before and I didn't expect him to have much memory of the area. But I was wrong, he had recollections of seeing more suitable ground out to the left, above the Western Cwm. We plunged out in knee-deep snow, very much aware of the great drops beneath. Tenzing's site proved rather unsatisfactory but fifty feet up it looked more promising. We struggled up and, to our satisfaction, realized we had found a possible site for Camp IX, far from flat, but capable of producing a suitable area for our small tent. We were at an altitude of 27,900 feet.

We didn't waste any time. George, Alf and Da Namgyal had still to get safely back to the South Col. They removed their huge loads, gave us each a hearty handshake, and wished us every success before turning downward again on their return journey. We had every confidence they would safely reach the tents on the South Col.

Tenzing and I removed our oxygen sets and were pleased to notice no immediate discomfort. It was not an ideal campsite. There wasn't a large enough flat place to pitch a tent, so I decided we'd just have to dig out two ledges and spread the tent across them, which is what we did. Tying the tent down was a harder job. There was a small rock face above the tent, but we'd made the mistake of not having any rock pitons with us to make a strong belay. Instead, I hammered several frail tent pegs into a few cracks and hoped they would hold. We had a couple of empty oxygen bottles by then, so I dug holes in the snow, tied the guy ropes around the bottles, and stamped them well into the ground as deadmen anchors. Tenzing crawled inside to melt some snow while I checked our oxygen. It demanded quite a bit of mental arithmetic, as I had to work out the number of liters left in a bottle by the pressure shown on the dial. I estimated that during the night we could breathe oxygen at one liter a minute for four hours and this would help us get a little sleep.

The setting sun bathed the giant peaks of Makalu and Lhotse in warm red light. They seemed almost close enough to touch. Far below fleecy clouds floated above gloomy valleys. I joined Tenzing in the tent where he was cooking chicken noodle soup. Astonishingly for this height, we were really hungry. Out came all our delicacies, with the tinned apricots being a special treat. We also drank ample liquid. It was very cramped inside, particularly when we tried to crawl into our sleeping bags. I have such big feet that I decided to remove my boots for the night. Tenzing left his footwear on, while I used mine to prop the toe of my sleeping bag off the ice. Tenzing lay on the bottom ledge, almost overhanging the slope, while I stretched out on the top ledge with my legs across Tenzing in the bottom corner of the tent. We started getting the odd fierce gust of wind and I had some concern as to whether the tent would remain in place, but when I started our oxygen flowing we quickly warmed up and dropped off to sleep peacefully on and off for four hours and then wakened feeling cold and miserable.

At 4 a.m. I looked out the tent doors and could already see signs of the early morning light. Tenzing peered over my shoulder and then pointed and said, "Tengboche," and there, sure enough, was Tengboche Monastery, 15,000 feet below us. The temperature was -27°C, chilly enough in our flimsy tent. We made our slow preparations for departure, eating well and consuming plenty of vital fluid. My boots were frozen solid and I cooked them over the primus stove until they were soft enough for me to pull on. We were wearing every piece of clothing we possessed and I checked my camera for the last time, setting it at a standard aperture and then placing it carefully inside my clothes and zipping up my windproofs. At 6:30 a.m. we crawled out of our tent and were ready to go.

Above our camp was a great steep bulge of snow and, as my feet were still cold, I waved Tenzing on to take the lead. Surging on with impressive strength, he ploughed a knee-deep track upward and I was happy to follow behind. We reached the top of the bulge at 28,000 feet and, as my feet were now warmer, I took over the lead. Towering over our heads was the South Summit and running along from it to the right were the great menacing cornices overhanging the Kangshung Face. Ahead of me was a sharp narrow ridge, icy on the right and looking more manageable on the left. So it was to the left I went, at first making easy progress, but then experiencing one of the most unpleasant mountaineering conditions—breakable crust. The surface would hold my weight for a few seconds, shatter beneath me, then I lurched forward knee-deep in powder snow. For half an hour I persisted and was encouraged at how well I was moving in these difficult conditions. I crossed over a little bump and saw before me a small hollow on the ridge and in that hollow were the two oxygen bottles left by Evans and Bourdillon. I wiped the snow off the dials and saw that the bottles were less than a third full of oxygen, but this could give us another hour of endurance on our return. That could be very useful later.

We had made considerable height, but there was much more ahead. A 400-foot-long snow slope rose steeply up toward the South Summit. Alternating the lead, we made our way forward, but it was an extremely uncomfortable experience. A thin skin of ice covered deep soft snow. On one occasion there was a dull breaking noise and a six-foot-wide piece of ice around me shattered and slid away down the mountainside. I slipped backward three or four steps and fortunately stopped, but the ice carried on with increasing speed far out of sight. It was rather frightening, but we had no alternative, we must keep going. With a considerable feeling of tension, we forced our way upward, the snow condition improved and we emerged with great relief onto the South Summit. We were now as high as anyone had ever been before. It was impossible not to dwell for a moment on the remarkable support we had received from our colleagues—John Hunt and Da Namgyal's lift to the depot on the South-East Ridge; George Lowe, Alf Gregory and Ang Nyima with their superb support to Camp IX; and the pioneer effort by Charles Evans and Tom Bourdillon to the South Summit. Their contribution had enabled us to make such good progress. But now the next move was up to us.

I looked carefully along the final summit ridge. It was impressive all right, but not impossible, despite what Charles Evans had said. We'd certainly give it a good try. We had a drink out of Tenzing's water bottle and I checked our oxygen supplies. Each of us had a bottle that was almost empty so, to save weight, we removed these and I attached our other full bottles firmly into place. It meant we had a total endurance of just under four hours. If we kept moving quickly it should be enough.

With a growing feeling of excitement, I moved down from the South Summit to the small saddle at the start of the summit ridge, cutting steps on the left-hand side below the great cornices and keeping just above the rock face sweeping into the Western Cwm. We moved cautiously, one at a time. I hacked a line of steps for forty feet, thrust my ice axe into the firm snow as a sound belay, and then brought Tenzing along to join me. After I had covered several rope-lengths, I noticed to my surprise that Tenzing was moving rather slowly and seemed in some distress. When he came up to me I examined his oxygen equipment. The pressure seemed satisfactory but then I noticed that his face mask was choked up with ice. I squeezed the mask to dislodge the ice and was relieved to see Tenzing breathing freely again. I checked my own equipment—it, too, held some ice, but not enough to cause me concern, and I quickly cleared it away. I moved on again, cutting line after line of steps.

Ahead of me loomed the great rock step which we had observed from far below and which we knew might prove to be a major problem. I gazed up at the forty feet of rock with some concern. To climb it directly at nearly 29,000 feet would indeed be a considerable challenge. I looked to the right, there seemed a chance there. Clinging to the rock was a great ice cornice hanging over the mighty Kangshung Face. Under the effects of gravity, the ice had broken away from the rock and a narrow crack ran upward. Nervously, I wondered if the cornice might collapse under my pressure. There was only one way to find out!

Although it would be relatively useless, I got Tenzing to establish a belay; then I eased my way into the crack, facing the rock. I jammed my crampons into the ice behind me and then wriggled my way upward using every little handhold I could find. Puffing for breath, I made steady height—the ice was holding—and forty feet up I pulled myself out of the crack onto the top of the rock face. I had made it! For the first time on the whole expedition, I had a feeling of confidence that we were going to get to the top. I waved to Tenzing and brought in the rope as he, too, made his way laboriously up the crack and dragged himself out beside me, panting for breath.

We didn't waste any time. I started cutting steps again, seeking now rather anxiously for signs of the summit. We seemed to go on forever, tired now and moving rather slowly. In the distance I could see the barren plateau of Tibet. I looked up to the right and there was a rounded snowy dome. It must be the summit! We drew closer together as Tenzing brought in the slack on the rope. I continued cutting a line of steps upward. Next moment I had moved onto a flattish exposed area of snow with nothing but space in every direction. Tenzing quickly joined me and we looked around in wonder. To our immense satisfaction, we realized we had reached the top of the world!

It was 11:30 a.m. on 29th May 1953. In typical Anglo-Saxon fashion, I stretched out my arm for a handshake, but this was not enough for Tenzing who threw his arms around my shoulders in a mighty hug and I hugged him back in return. With a feeling of mild surprise I realized that Tenzing was perhaps more excited at our success than I was.

But time was short! I turned off my oxygen and removed my mask. Immediately my face was prickled sharply with ice splinters carried in the brisk wind. I removed my camera from the protection of my down jacket, stepped a little down the slope and photographed Tenzing on the summit with his ice axe upraised and the flags flapping in the breeze—the United Nations flag, the Indian flag, the Nepalese flag and the Union Jack. Tenzing didn't have a camera and, to tell the truth, the thought didn't enter my mind to try to organize a picture of myself on top of the mountain. I felt a more urgent need to have photographic evidence that we had reached the summit, so quickly took shots down every major ridge. The view was most spectacular to the east, for here the giants Makalu and Kangchenjunga dominated the horizon and gave some idea of the vast scale of the Himalayas. Only a few miles away, Makalu, with its soaring rock ridges, was a remarkable sight. I could see all the northern slopes of the mountain and was immediately struck by the possibility of a feasible route to its summit. With a growing feeling of excitement, I took another photograph to study on returning to civilization—I was under no delusions that reaching the top of Everest would destroy my enthusiasm for further adventures.

The view to the north was a complete contrast—hundreds of miles of the arid Tibetan plateau. One scene was of particular interest. Almost under our feet it seemed, was the famous North Col and the East

Rongbuk Glacier, where so many epic feats of courage and endurance were performed by the earlier British Everest expeditions. Part of the ridge up which they had established their high camps was visible, but the last thousand feet, which had proved such a formidable barrier, was concealed from our view as its rock slopes dropped away with frightening abruptness from the summit snow pyramid. It was a sobering thought to remember how often these men had reached 28,000 feet without the benefits of our modern equipment and reasonably efficient oxygen sets. Inevitably, my thoughts turned to Mallory and Irvine who had lost their lives on the mountain thirty years before. With little hope I looked around for some sign that they had reached the summit, but could see nothing.

I noticed Tenzing digging a little hole in the snow and watched him place in it some pieces of chocolate and other food, small gifts to the gods which he believed spent some time on the summit of Everest. This immediately brought to mind John Hunt's request that I had completely forgotten. Just before leaving the South Col, John had asked me into his tent and then with slight embarrassment had told me a brief story. When he was about to depart from his home at Henley, an old priest who lived nearby had come to him and offered him a small crucifix, asking him if he would mind leaving it on the summit of Everest. Now John's chance to go higher had evaporated, he wondered if I would take the crucifix up with me. I was happy to agree, as John seemed to take the request very seriously. So now, remembering my promise, I fumbled around in my pockets, located the cross, and pressed it into the snow on top of the mountain, feeling a sense of satisfaction at having kept my word. (Some months later, an overseas letter was delivered to my home in Auckland. It contained a small medallion sent to me by a representative of the Pope in appreciation of my gesture on Mount Everest.)

We had been warned by expedition doctor Griffith Pugh that dehydration was one of the greatest risks faced by climbers going high. To compensate for this, Tenzing and I had spent a good part of the previous night quaffing copious quantities of hot lemon drink and, as a consequence, we arrived on top with full bladders. Having just paid our respects to the highest mountain in the world, I then had no choice but to urinate on it.

We had now been fifteen minutes on top. Tenzing had removed the flags from his ice axe and, as there was nothing to tie them to, he thrust them down into the snow. It was time for us to leave. I replaced my mask and turned on the oxygen. Immediately I noticed a distinct brightening in my vision. I had proved that man could breathe without supplementary oxygen on the summit—a fact no one had been too sure of before. Oxygen certainly helped, but I had been going so well from our top camp I was able to approach the summit with growing confidence. Coming down off the summit I found it much easier following our established tracks, and was soon peering down the forty-foot rock step and, with a little concern, lowering myself into the crack between the rock and the ice. After much wriggling and jamming, I reached the bottom and waited for Tenzing to join me. Our previous track along the ridge made our return very much easier and soon we were back again on the South Summit. It had only taken us one hour from the top!

Our oxygen supplies were now running low, so it was important to move on quickly. The steep slope down from the South Summit was very firm and I got Tenzing to start off down cutting steps. Although a fine climber, he was not a particularly good step-cutter, so when he reached the end of the rope I started down after him and, in slightly peppery fashion, re-cut all the steps into more substantial form. Then I carried on ahead, producing a neat line of steps for several hundred feet. I moved out to the left onto the softer snow at the top of the great slope plunging down onto the Kangshung Glacier. It was quite a desperate place and we took turns stamping out firm footholds to ensure our security. One slip here could have been disastrous.

It seemed a long time before we headed back to the right onto the narrow ridge above our last camp and came to the depot of nearly empty oxygen bottles left by Charles Evans and Tom Bourdillon. We loaded these onto our backs and then carried on down and collapsed into our tent. It was 2 p.m. and we made a refreshing brew of lemon and sugar. Our main oxygen bottles were now empty and I removed them from our frames and replaced them with the bottles from Evans and Bourdillon which were almost one third full. It would be enough, I decided, to get us most of the way down to the South Col. We pushed our sleeping bags and personal gear into our packs, but left our tent and empty oxygen bottles behind. In those days we had no awareness of environmental matters. We moved slowly down the South-East Ridge in our tired condition, treating it with the greatest of respect, past the old Swiss campsite to emerge at the top of the great snow couloir leading down to the South Col.

I had hoped that the line of steps George had cut the day before would still remain, but, to my disgust, I saw that the brisk wind had wiped them all out. So once more I hacked zigzag after zigzag down the steep slope. Far below, I could see a tiny figure moving across the South Col and knew it must be George. Halfway down the snow softened and we took turns at plugging steps. I realized by now that our oxygen had run out, but we were still moving well. As we approached the bottom of the couloir, George came toward us and I felt a warm glow of affection for my old friend.

"Well, George," I said, "we knocked the bastard off!"

"Thought you must have," he replied calmly and poured us a drink of hot tomato soup from a thermos flask. Soon we were back at the flapping tents on the South Col where Wilf Noyce and Pasang Phutar greeted us and treated us with patience and kindness.

It was another cold and miserable night on the South Col. I slept a little, but was uncomfortable and restless. For some reason I didn't feel particularly excited about our success. I had no sense of ultimate achievement—I just felt I had done rather well on a big challenge. Our primitive walkie-talkies didn't operate from the South Col down to Advanced Base Camp, so we had no way of giving the news to John Hunt and the rest of the team. At first I was quite warm and comfortable in my sleeping bag and much of the time my mind churned over with a great mixture of thoughts—what a fine support Tenzing had been on the climb, and how glad I was that a Sherpa had been one of the first to reach the summit. I knew he had been even more excited than I was. And then there was George Lowe, now with me in the tent—what a good job he had done. He must have seen us coming down the South-East Ridge, gone to the considerable trouble of boiling up water to make soup, and then met us at the bottom of the couloir. Very agreeable of him, I thought. I tried to brush aside the feeling that if George had been with me we could have been equally successful. But having two New Zealanders on top wouldn't have appealed to our British teammates. Pity! George and I had been very good friends over the years. Earlier on the expedition George had spent a week or so working on the route up the Lhotse Face and the media had, in fact, called him "The Hero of the Lhotse Face." But I believed that George had done his greatest work on the South Col and above. I huddled down in my outer sleeping bag but I never really got warm until we had the primus going to melt snow for water. I was incredibly thirsty and seemed to need more and more liquid.

Finally morning came. I peeped out of the tent and the South Col looked as desperately unpleasant as ever. We made our preparation and packed all our personal gear to carry down with us. We had two bottles of oxygen left and, although we didn't really need oxygen, it was decided that Tenzing and I would each use one of the bottles. So I added one to my already cumbersome load. I was feeling rather weaker than on the previous day when we had come down from the summit, and the 200-foot climb up to the top of the Geneva Spur was quite hard work. Then, with relief, we plunged down the steep Lhotse Face, taking advantage of the steps that still remained visible from the descent of Charles Evans' party. We carefully crossed over the wide crevasse above Camp VII, expecting the camp to be deserted, but to our amazement and pleasure we were met by Charles Wylie and half a dozen Sherpas and were soon telling them our good news—much to their delight. Their presence in Camp VII was still another example of the constant back-up maintained by our expedition at all times—a somewhat different approach to that of many modern expeditions.

George, Tenzing and I, roped together again with George in the lead, set off down the steep icy sections of the Lhotse Face, going much more freely at this lower altitude. Although the terrain was more difficult and dangerous, it was familiar to us and we cramponed the icy stretches with confidence, slipping along the fixed ropes. We treated the great ice bulge below Camp VI with care and made good time along the 400 feet of fixed ropes. Soon we were at the bottom of the Lhotse Face and on easy ground. At Camp V we were greeted by happy Sherpas and our packs removed from our backs. Then we plunged on through soft snow down the Western Cwm.

We could see a few movements around Advanced Base Camp, but clearly they had no suspicion of what had happened higher on the mountain. There was so little action that I was convinced that everyone felt that we had been unsuccessful. Finally, George could stand it no longer and raised his ice axe in the air and pointed it vigorously toward the summit. Everyone at Advanced Base Camp went rigid with shock at first and then slowly came toward us. As the message finally penetrated, they broke into a shambling trot with a look of unbelievable hope on their faces. Next moment John Hunt had thrown his arms around my shoulders in a deeply emotional fashion and I realized, perhaps for the first time, just how important success on Everest was to him. There were even a few tears rolling down his cheeks. We received a mighty welcome from our other companions, too, although I sensed with a few of them an understandable feeling of envy. But there was no questioning the warmth of the welcome from our doughty Sherpas who had done so much for us and now clustered around grinning, with hugs and handshakes. They looked on Tenzing with awe and respect. All our efforts and planning and team spirit had been rewarded with great success and Mount Everest had been climbed for the first time!

Forty years later John Hunt and I stood at Tengboche Monastery and looked at the magnificent view of Everest and Lhotse. With a wry smile, John apologized to me for his emotional display on that remarkable occasion.

2

A NEW PAIR OF OVERALLS

W E RELAXED AT ADVANCED BASE CAMP AND SIPPED MUGS OF HOT tea. James Morris, our *Times* correspondent, interrogated us quickly about the climb. James had realized that if he could get quickly to the small army radio post at Namche Bazaar and send out the news of our success, it could reach London in time for the Queen's Coronation on 2nd June. By mid-afternoon he had his story and with two energetic Sherpas as his guides he descended the Icefall and rushed down the valley to Namche. His message was couched in a special code and when it reached the British Embassy in Kathmandu, Ambassador Summerhayes translated it and then, in great excitement, sent it out over the diplomatic wireless to London. It arrived on the evening of 1st June and was handed over to *The Times* newspaper who, instead of keeping it to themselves, very sensibly distributed it to all the media. So on the morning of the Coronation, as the excited millions gathered in the streets of London, all the newspapers had headlines proclaiming "All this and Everest too!" And a great roar of pleasure went up from the huge crowds.

I had asked John Hunt what he planned to do if Tenzing and I had been unsuccessful. I had estimated that we could have held out for one more day at Camp IX if the weather had been bad on 29th May, but it might have been risky without any spare oxygen. Nobody had spent an extra day and two nights at 27,900 feet before. I felt the attempt by Tenzing and myself would be the last opportunity the expedition would have.

But John was very positive. "I would have made another attempt myself personally," he told me. Remembering that it would require another lift of supplies to the South Col and above, and how weak John had been when leaving the South Col, I had considerable misgivings about this idea. But I have no doubt that he would have tried.

We descended to Base Camp and were still almost completely unaware of what was happening in the outside world. Then someone turned on a small radio and heard a BBC announcement telling the world that we had been successful. Strangely enough, hearing it stated over the BBC made me realize positively almost for the first time what an achievement it had been. I had innocently thought that it would be of interest to mountaineers, but not particularly to anyone else—but I was being proved very wrong.

John Hunt decided to walk quickly out to Kathmandu to make all necessary arrangements for the onward passage of the expedition members and he asked me to bring the major group and all the loads out rather more slowly. We descended down the Khumbu Glacier to a camp on the green grass and reveled in the flowers and the thick air. Then we came down the Dudh Kosi river to Ghat and crossed to the west over the "high route" to Junbesi. We were now on the main walking track to Kathmandu and started receiving daily mail runners from John Hunt with letters, telegrams and newspaper cuttings, all indicating that our success had caused quite a furor in the outside world.

We were halfway to Kathmandu when still another mail runner met us on a high track and handed over his bag to George Lowe. George quickly sorted through the mail and then, with a bit of a grin, handed me a letter addressed to "Sir Edmund Hillary, KBE." Very funny, I thought to myself, but then realized from George's hearty laughter that he believed there was some truth in it. With sinking heart, I opened the letter from John who briefly confirmed that the Queen had indeed made me a Knight of the British Empire. I was somewhat taken aback by this information—I did not regard myself as suitable knightly material. For one thing, I was far too impoverished to play the role. My mind flashed to a picture of myself walking around the little town of Papakura, south of Auckland, in a pair of well-stained overalls. My God, I told myself, I'll have to buy a new pair of overalls. George thought it was incredibly funny and couldn't stop laughing for the next half hour.

Two days' march from Banepa, which was on the rim of the Kathmandu valley, we were met by a scruffy bunch of Nepalis who ignored us but drew a rather nervous Tenzing aside and spoke to him at great length. They wanted him to sign a document and, although he was illiterate at the time, he finally signed it in desperation. The Nepalis gleefully departed.

Next night in our last camp before Banepa we were joined by John Hunt for the final day's march. John warned me that some Nepalis had arrived in Banepa waving a document signed by Tenzing claiming he had reached the summit first. A further problem had arisen. Some reporter had asked John to comment on Tenzing's skill as a mountaineer. In his rather correct fashion, John told them, "Tenzing is an excellent climber within the limits of his experience"—which is probably true of all of us, but hardly the answer to give to a somewhat overstimulated and nationalistic community. I would say that in the Himalayas, Tenzing was a skilled and formidable climber and it would probably have been more diplomatic for John to have said so.

Another incident was somewhat different, an intrusion from the western world. I was accosted by a well-dressed Indian reporter who said he represented a large English newspaper. They were offering to pay me £10,000 sterling for my story of the summit day. Rather angrily I pointed out to him that, as he already knew, I had signed an agreement with *The Times* in London. What would my companions think, I asked him, if I ignored the agreement and wrote for another newspaper? He was very frank. His newspaper believed the sum they were offering should overcome any hurt feelings I might experience, he told me. I was a little prone to violence in those days and when I clenched a fist, he made a rapid withdrawal.

Next morning we climbed up the hill to Banepa to be met by a huge crowd, including many more reporters and cameramen. There was absolute bedlam when they saw Tenzing. John Hunt had warned me that the region from Banepa to Kathmandu was rather left wing politically and he asked me to be patient with the crowd enthusiasm. Maybe he already knew something that I didn't? The official party manhandled Tenzing and John and myself into an open jeep. John and I were pressed down into the backseat with Tenzing standing upright holding on to the crash bar. Then all around arose the great cry, "Shri Tenzing. Zindabar! Shri Tenzing. Zindabar!" (Respected Tenzing. Great is he!) which actually pleased us all, as Tenzing was now being acknowledged as a world hero in his own country.

We seemed to drive on and on forever and the din was terrific. I suddenly noticed there were many banners stretched across the street, each printed with the same picture. Tenzing was standing on the summit of a mountain with a Nepalese flag in his hand and, from his other hand, a rope trailed down to a figure lying on its back with its feet and hands in the air—me! It was quite funny at first, but then got rather tedious and when a youth jumped on the back of our jeep and started shouting "Shri Tenzing. Zindabar" into my ear I turned around and gave him a hearty shove into the mud. No one else tried that little trick again.

As we approached Kathmandu, everything became more orderly and we received a very warm welcome from senior government officials. John Hunt, Tenzing and I had a little discussion about the actual reaching of the summit. I had certainly never regarded it as being important and we agreed that as a team, sharing the tasks on the mountain, we would say we had reached the summit together. Tenzing had the honor of a meeting with the King and then there was a great gathering in the main square, the central maidan. The King gave a short speech honoring us all, but I was a little annoyed when he went on to say that Tenzing had told him he had reached the summit first. But the crowd cheered heartily.

This question has been asked all over the world for many years and I expect people will keep on asking it forever. Fortunately, it is a matter of little consequence, as we can both take credit for our success. It is interesting in these days, when I have a warm relationship with all the people of Nepal, to look back on the Everest era when I was largely resented by the Nepalese and I wasn't particularly enthusiastic about them either.

When we went down to India the crowds were enormous and the credit was rather more evenly distributed. I remember landing in Delhi and there were literally tens of thousands of people lining the tarmac. When we walked down the aircraft steps, they all saw Tenzing and the crowd broke the barriers and rushed toward us screaming "Tenzing!" I have never seen a greater look of terror than in Tenzing's eyes and we were glad to slip through the crowd and leave him to his fate—which didn't, of course, prove terrible at all.

Prime Minister Nehru gave a very large reception and I enjoyed meeting him and found him an enormously impressive person. There were dozens of photographers present and they all wanted pictures of Tenzing and myself standing on either side of the Prime Minister. He told them, "You have ten minutes and no more!" I knew from experience that Indian pressmen took little notice of instructions, but after ten minutes of bedlam, the Prime Minister clapped his hands and said firmly, "Enough!" And to my astonishment, all the photographers disappeared. His charming and charismatic personality was awe-inspiring.

John Hunt had invited Tenzing to come to London with us but the formidable Mrs. Tenzing was insisting that she and their two young daughters, Pem Pem and Nima, should come too. The expedition members were perfectly happy but the Himalayan Committee in London was at first reluctant, only giving in when it was clear that, if Tenzing's family didn't travel, Tenzing wouldn't either. In fact we thoroughly enjoyed the company of his two delightful daughters and teased them unmercifully—much to their pleasure, I believe.

There was quite a political conflict over what passport Tenzing and his family should have—would it be Nepalese or Indian? Although

Tenzing spent his early life in Nepal, he had lived for the last seventeen years in Darjeeling, India. Prime Minister Pandit Nehru took personal control of the problem. Tenzing would have an Indian passport and Nehru even gave him a couple of his very handsome Nehru suits to wear on formal occasions. Nehru was very kind and generous to Tenzing but the senior officials in Kathmandu never forgave Tenzing for not accepting a Nepalese passport. However the peasant people of Nepal loved him.

We flew to London and another tumultuous welcome. Our good friend Eric Shipton, famous for his Himalayan explorations and Everest mountaineering, was at the airport to meet us and it was great to see him. Knowing my weakness for bananas, he handed me a bunch and I consumed most of them on the way into town. For a month, we went to a succession of receptions and cocktail parties and I found I was living on champagne and smoked Scottish salmon, neither of which I had tasted before. I started waking in the morning with a mild headache and realized it was my first experience of a hangover.

The famous runner, Roger Bannister, the first person to break the four-minute mile, was a physiologist at Oxford and he invited me up to his laboratory to try and find out how I had managed to be successful on Everest when so many others had failed. I panted and puffed on a treadmill while Dr. Bannister did a multitude of tests. When he had finished, he worked out the results and shook his head in disbelief. "I don't know how you did it!" he told me.

Eric Shipton invited us up to Eskdale where he was running an Outward Bound school. There was torrential rain and the Esk was in great flood. George and I decided it would be an entertaining idea to paddle down the foaming Esk in two-man canoes and the others all willingly agreed. It was a lively trip and in the end everyone tipped over, although George and I almost made it to our landing spot. As we swam to shore, George yelled, "I've lothed my teeth." His upper plate had popped out into the swirling waters. This was a considerable disaster for George, as he was delivering an important lecture in London in a few days' time. He would somehow have to get replacement false teeth on short notice. As we waited for dinner we roared with unkind laughter as George, on the telephone, tried to convey to our expedition friends in London his terrible problem. I hadn't realized how difficult it was to speak clearly without a plate.

Sweating and confused, George joined us for dinner, fielding a number of cheerful comments about confining himself to soup and mashed potatoes. Halfway through the meal, one of the staff came into the dining room with a message for Eric Shipton. There was a local farmer who wanted to see him urgently. He was brought in and triumphantly produced a top set of false teeth. "Found it washed up beside the Esk," he said. "Thought it might be useful." A relieved George hastily clapped it into place and hurried off to ring London and cancel all emergency procedures.

Another weekend the expedition was invited to a combined gathering in North Wales with senior members of the Alpine Club. We were based on the very pleasant Pen-y-Gwryd Hotel and I arrived a little late only to discover that everyone else had headed off up Snowdon. I had no boots or mountaineering equipment, but set off up the mountain after them in a pair of sand shoes and casual clothing. I was about halfway up and moving very easily when a properly booted middle-aged gentleman, sporting an Alpine Club badge, appeared out of the mist. He stopped abruptly, looked aghast at my lack of equipment, and proceeded to give me a thorough dressing down. It was inexperienced and ill-equipped people such as myself, he told me, who gave the mountains a bad name. Fuming, he disappeared down the hill and out of sight.

After a pleasant climb I returned to the Pen-y-Gwryd and entered the warm and comfortable bar where I was greeted by my expedition companions and introduced to our Alpine Club hosts. Soon I was shaking the rather limp hand of the gentleman who had berated me on the mountainside and I have rarely received a more distraught welcome.

We were interviewed by the BBC and the announcer asked George what my first comments had been on coming off the mountain and meeting him on the South Col. Somewhat to my regret George mentioned with a certain relish I had said, "Well, George, we knocked the bastard off." This utterance was quickly blasted around the world airwaves and later my mother told me she was horrified at my comment.

I had a number of astonishing invitations through the mail from women who invited me to marry them. One enthusiastic female actually included a photograph. At the bottom of the letter she said, "If you don't wish to marry me, please return the photograph." I hastily posted the photograph back to her. I believe George and I were lucky in being New Zealanders. I think many of the English members of the party found the constant dealing with lords and dukes and all the rest of it somewhat overwhelming but, although George and I were always respectful, we managed not to be overwhelmed. In fact we met it all with a great deal of laughter and enjoyment. We were meeting so many titled people that when we received still another invitation to still another grand event, George joked, "If there aren't any dukes there, I'm not going."

Our most important invitation was to a Buckingham Palace garden party. Dressed in unfamiliar morning suit with long tails and top hat, the expedition members mixed with hundreds of dignitaries as though to the manner born—well, almost! At the conclusion of the garden party we were conducted deep inside the palace to quite a small but very pleasantly decorated room. There we waited rather nervously until an official entered and announced in stentorian tones, "Her Majesty the Queen." The Queen came in, followed by most of the royal family, and we were all greeted individually in a very relaxed fashion. The Queen was tiny and charming and behaved just as we expected a Queen to do in those days. Then for me came the most important moment. A small stool was placed in front of the Queen, I knelt on it, a short bejeweled sword was put in her hand, she touched me lightly on each shoulder and said, "Arise, Sir Edmund." Whether I wanted it or not, I was now a knight and expected to behave as one. It was quite a change from my early days as a bee farmer in New Zealand.

There was only one thing on this great occasion that made me feel slightly uncomfortable. It would have been nice if Tenzing had received a knighthood too. He was given the George Medal, the highest civilian award for bravery in Britain, but in view of his great contribution to the expedition it would not have been unreasonable for him to have received the same decoration as I did. After all, I could hardly be regarded as knightly material in those days either. Some people claimed at the time that Indian and Nepalese citizens were not permitted to accept foreign titles, but I don't believe this is completely true. If Tenzing had received the KBE I consider it would have been universally applauded in India and Nepal.

After six weeks of entertainment and adulation in Britain, George Lowe and I flew back to New Zealand at the beginning of August. But first we made a brief two-day stop in Sydney for a very special purpose. For a number of years, I had been very friendly with lawyer Jim Rose, who was President of the New Zealand Alpine Club. I visited his house on many occasions and could not but notice his attractive young musician daughter who always seemed to be flitting around when I was there. Louise joined several groups I took for weekend trips to Mount Ruapehu and I soon discovered that, though not an outstanding alpinist, she had climbed a few mountains and was a most enthusiastic walker and mountain-lover. But she was eleven years younger than me and must have looked on me as being incredibly ancient. At the end of 1952 Louise was granted a scholarship to the Sydney Conservatorium of Music and when I watched her ship depart, it felt like the end of the world. I also had the feeling that Louise herself was sad about the parting and she certainly impressed on me that I must spend some time with her in Sydney on my way to Everest the following March.

Neither of us was particularly demonstrative, but we exchanged a lot of friendly letters. When I flew to Sydney, en route to India, I spent two days with Louise and they were possibly the two happiest days of my life. We sat on the grass in the Sydney domain and listened with great pleasure to outdoor musical concerts. We walked hand in hand across the Sydney Harbour Bridge and halfway across I kissed Louise for the first time. This was a major breakthrough for me. But by the end of those two days we had developed an understanding that we would see a good deal more of each other in future. I wrote to Louise from Singapore, but still found it impossible to say completely what I felt.

> Hello whizz Darling,
>
> I've had lots of ideas for some time now about you and my main job will be to try and persuade you to agree to some of them. I wonder what my chances are? Anyway I'll be frightfully disappointed if you turn me down and I'll probably rush off and become an irascible embittered hermit somewhere . . . Here I am on a trip that I suppose any New Zealand climber would be mad keen to go on and I spend all my time thinking of something quite different—in fact you! I'm determined to do well on this trip because one of my ambitions has always been to get really high and I know that if I can be really successful I will be able to do reasonably well with my book . . . I've decided that I am going to conduct a long range campaign on you that if I don't tell you how I feel no one else will. As long as I can keep you thinking of me now and then it will be a start.

So then I went off to Everest to a certain degree of fame, but, at that stage, certainly no fortune. After the climb I was back in Kathmandu and wrote a very frank letter to Louise about the aftermath of the expedition.

> Nepal (and India) have gone completely mad over Tenzing's success and he has become almost a God. Unfortunately the Communists have been trying to get Tenzing to say that he got to the top first and then dragged me up. They have been trying to discredit the expedition and make political capital out of it so things have really hummed! As you know it matters little who actually gets to the top first—it's so unimportant that we never think of it, but over here it has assumed great importance. Actually, as I think I may have told you, I did all the leading for the last two and a half hours and did in actual fact reach the summit a rope length ahead of Tenzing. At first I used to get

rather pipped at all this inaccurate and often unpleasant news-paper talk but now, after discussions with Tenzing, who is in a rather unpleasant position, we've agreed to a compromise story and say "we reached the summit almost together" and let it go at that.

So George and I arrived in Sydney and it was marvelous to see Louise again. The media suddenly realized that I possibly had a girlfriend in Sydney and tried desperately to find her. It was great fun for us playing hide-and-seek and they never did discover her name or address. We had sufficient time together to confirm to each other that we'd like to get married some time. But what about her music? And what about my forthcoming lecture trip around the world? We were a little too dazed to come to any sensible decisions on that.

Reluctantly, I boarded a Solent flying boat with George for the trip across to Auckland. We landed on the beautiful Waitemata Harbour and taxied in to Mechanics Bay where we had been warned there was a colossal crowd to welcome us. In those days, New Zealand didn't go in for large crowds unless it was for a rugby football match. And this had a distinct resemblance to one with as much waving and cheering as if George and I had just scored a couple of tries. The Mayor of Auckland was there to welcome us, as were our families, and it was quite a relief to escape to the peace and quiet of our homes.

That night the city held a welcome in the Town Hall and the crowd overflowed into the streets. George Lowe can be very funny when he's in the mood and he performed magnificently. People would have been dying of laughter in the aisles if there'd been room in the aisles for them to lie down. I was presented with a magnificent white easy chair designed to epitomize Mount Everest and for quite a while it was the only piece of furniture I possessed.

Next day I called on Phyl and Jim Rose and Phyl questioned me about my relationship with Louise. I pointed out my problems—how ancient I was, the question of her musical career, and my impending lecture trip around the world. Phyl disposed of these difficulties with ease. Plenty of people got married when they were ten years or more older than each other, she told me, and there was lots of time for Louise to carry on with her music in the future. Why didn't I get Louise across from Sydney, marry her, and then both of us go off on the world tour together? It sounded a great idea, but what if she said no? Phyl was more than equal to that problem. "Would you like me to ring her?" she asked. So my future mother-in-law proposed over the phone on my behalf and fortunately got an enthusiastic response. What a coward I was, but I was mighty pleased at the result.

Louise flew into Auckland and all preparations were made for the wedding. Meanwhile, George and I traveled through New Zealand giving lectures in crowded halls. Our marriage was held on 3rd September, Louise's twenty-third birthday, in the delightful little chapel at Louise's old school, Diocesan High School. All day rain had been threatening, but as we emerged from the chapel under an arch of ice axes, a watery sun broke through and bathed us in light. At the first sight of Louise, who looked radiant, the cheering crowd swept the police cordon aside, and brought the departing wedding cavalcade to a stand-still. All the way to the Rose home in Remuera, where the wedding breakfast was to be held, people stood on the pavement or leaned over their front fences and waved.

The Himalayan Committee had supplied George and me with Economy air tickets back to London, but now I had to obtain a ticket for Louise as well. I had virtually no money but I did have a signed contract for a considerable sum for a personal book on the ascent of Everest. I called on my local bank manager and tried to raise a loan for £400 sterling. The manager took great delight in cross-questioning me on my financial past, present and future and then, when he had sufficiently mortified me, he reluctantly agreed to make the advance. I had become a little used by then to being treated with respect, but he certainly brought me down to earth. I have never been an enthusiastic supporter of bank managers ever since.

Next day we flew to Sydney and the following day to Singapore where we were warmly welcomed and stayed as guests with the

Governor-General. George and I gave two lectures in Singapore to crowded houses, but I have to admit that the young and attractive Louise, with her warm and cheerful personality, was a much greater hit than George and I ever were. In London we hired a two-bedroom apartment so that there was accommodation for George, too. When I look back on it, I realize that the three of us had some very happy times together.

Before our main lecture program started, Louise and I were invited to Brussels to take part in a major presentation of new English films. Our group was led by a famous English actress and what a charming person she was. The organizers very much wanted me to say a few words in French, so I wrote out the following statement: *"Je suis très heureux d'être ici et de pouvoir vous remercier pour tous les félicitations que l'expédition Hunt a reçu du Belgique."* I had to learn it off by heart and practiced it going up and down in the elevator. The famous actress learned it first, Louise learned it second, and I was a poor third. But when I finally appeared on the stage I produced it without hesitation and to tumultuous applause.

Then our Everest lecture program began in earnest and we did dozens of talks in London and all over the United Kingdom. We had a team meeting and agreed that each lecture would have three of the expedition members performing and that for each lecture we'd earn £25 sterling each. This was to enable all the expedition members to share in the financial benefits, but also to emphasize John Hunt's determined approach that this was a team effort and no one person—namely me— would benefit more than anyone else. For some hundreds of lectures, I bent over backward to stress the team side of things until one day I suddenly said to myself, Hey, Ed, my boy, you did a pretty good job on the mountain, too. Don't play yourself down. And from then on I wasn't afraid to suggest that I was, in fact, a rather useful member of the team. None of the expedition members made much from our lectures, but what became the Mount Everest Committee accumulated a substantial amount. This money was allocated to assist other expeditions with their finances and proved very useful to them. Years later I myself approached the MEF to help financially with the building of a school requested by the Sherpas of a high-altitude village, only to be turned down flatly as the Committee advised me that such a contribution was not covered by their constitution. As the Sherpas had done so much for British Himalayan expeditions I considered this a miserable response and still have not forgiven them.

We were invited to Paris to speak in the Salle Playel before the French President. John Hunt had an interpreter's badge in French and Alf Gregory had a French wife so was fairly fluent. But Ed Hillary only had his Auckland Grammar School French. They wanted me to give a final twenty minutes on the ascent to the summit. I sorted out a suitable number of slides and wrote out a narration in English. I then had a French interpreter translate it into first-class French which I found almost incomprehensible. So I translated it myself into my schoolboy French and then had the interpreter make a few changes to make sure it was understandable. When my time came, I had more or less learned it off by heart and I rolled out my Auckland Grammar French with great enthusiasm. There were some bursts of unexpected laughter, so I obviously wasn't producing Parisian French, but there was substantial applause at the end and my French mountaineering friends said my accent was decidedly unusual, but certainly understandable.

Toward the end of the year Charles Evans, George Lowe and I did an extensive series of lectures in North America. In New York we were special guests at a meeting of the distinguished Explorers Club and John Hunt and I were made Honorary Members (for many years now I have been Honorary President). Then the National Geographic Society honored us with their highest distinction, the Hubbard Medal. It was arranged for this to be presented to us by President Eisenhower in the White House. John Hunt came over especially from London for this occasion and we drove through the front gates of the White House with a considerable sense of anticipation. After a brief conducted tour of the impressive building, we were led into the Oval Office and put in line with John at the head and me next to him. After a brief wait a door opened and President Eisenhower entered with an aide beside him. He looked at us in a startled fashion and it was clear that he didn't have the faintest idea who we were. He leaned down to his aide who whispered in his ear and he straightened up, smiled, came over and shook John's hand and went down the line saying a brief welcome. We then followed him out into a large room crammed with radio equipment, cameramen and press—it was to be a coast-to-coast hookup.

We lined up, with John on one side of the President and me on the other. The National Geographic Society President gave a long talk about the Society, obviously taking full advantage of the nationwide coverage to boost the National Geographic, then invited the President to present the Hubbard Medals. The President turned to John Hunt and, in a clear voice, said, "Sir Edmund Hunt." I knew how mortified John would be, so I leaned over and whispered in his ear, "Sir *John* Hunt." He quickly corrected himself and went on to make the presentation to John. Then he turned toward me and immediately all the lights went on and the cameras started turning—it was extremely noticeable. (I asked one of the pressmen later why they had waited until I came on and he said, "You were the guy who got to the top.") The President then said a few appropriate words and handed the Hubbard Medal to me. We stood there for a few moments with slightly strained grins on our faces. It had been an important occasion for me, but, after the anticipation, it became rather an anticlimax. Worse was to follow. A strong voice spoke up from the media: "Give it to him again!" Without a change in his pleasant smile, the President stepped forward, took the medal out of my hand, and presented it to me again. I suppose he handled a dozen oc-casions like this each week, but for some reason I had a great sense of disappointment.

Maybe our most memorable lecture was in Toronto. We had adopted the procedure of George Lowe speaking first and we could tell from the reaction to George's jokes what sort of audience it was. Then Charles Evans would speak and, finally, I'd give the summit story. In Toronto I was standing behind the curtain and listening to George going well and eliciting hearty laughter from the large audience, when I noticed a smell of smoke and I peeped out from the curtain up at the projector and I could see a ruddy glow developing. I crept out on the dark stage behind George and whispered in his ear, "The projector's catching fire, George. Finish your part quickly and we'll have the half-time break." Without missing a beat, George hurried through his presentation and then announced the time out. I then watched in horror as, just before the lights came on, a glowing projector was manhandled out of the upper tier seats.

The organizers assured me they were making arrangements to get a new projector. However, we couldn't allow the half-time break to go on forever, so we decided that Charles Evans would start his lecture without slides and that's what we did. When he was almost through his presentation he saw in the dim light a projector being put into place and requested, with relief, "Next slide, please."

A voice rang through the theater. "Sir Edmund says you can't have any slides until he comes on."

The audience roared with laughter, but that is precisely what happened. Charles Evans manfully completed his lecture without slides and I carried on my slide presentation as though nothing unusual had happened.

Our concentrated lecture tour of some months had been hard work but satisfying in many ways. Louise had been an enormous success with her friendliness and charm. I think she epitomized what every American would want his daughter to be. I had already become completely dependent on her calmness and common sense. But now we'd had more than enough. We were glad to board our aircraft for the long flight back to New Zealand and, for the first time, to enjoy a short period alone together.

3

From Bees to Flying Boats

At the turn of the century New Zealand was a distant corner of the British Empire, almost as far from Great Britain as you could go before you started heading back. Though it was a remote and raw colonial society, it yet had many liberal characteristics. It was the first country in the world to give women the vote. Life was certainly tough in those days—a constant battle for survival—but it produced pioneer people who were both hardworking and amazingly creative. My family came from the Northern Wairoa district of New Zealand which was quite an isolated area a hundred miles to the north of Auckland. My mother's family owned a farm and a large store at a place called Whakahara and were highly regarded and moderately affluent. My mother and her sisters were brought up in a very genteel fashion and all played the piano, as young ladies did in those days. She trained as a schoolteacher, which was a very respectable profession, and started her teaching in the important country town of Te Awamutu. She lived with the family of the local bank manager who was definitely one of the influential members of the community. Mixing with the right people was quite important to my mother.

My father, on the other hand, had to struggle a little more for his existence. His mother had emigrated from Ireland and was a remarkable lady with lots of energy and ideas. She had the misfortune to meet my grandfather who was born in Yorkshire and trained as a watchmaker. He traveled to India, made friends (and money) with a rich maharaja and then carried on to New Zealand as a well-heeled gentleman. Unfortunately, he lost most of his money betting on the horses and it was left to my grandmother to raise and educate her four children. Although she had no artistic training, she taught herself to paint and sold many of them. She was clever with handicrafts, too, and sold hand-sewn dresses to the community. She put her four children through school and gave them a solid background of character.

My father's personality was molded into a mixture of moral conservatism and fierce independence. He disliked the family poverty and became very interested in the social ideas that were gaining popular support in New Zealand at the time. He started work on the local newspaper and was soon promoted to reporter and became a competent press photographer. When the Great War erupted, my father was quick to volunteer. He went overseas as a sergeant, served with the ANZACs in the grim Gallipoli campaign, was shot through the nose, and laid low with severe dysentery. He was invalided home and soon after his return in 1916 he married my mother. They moved to the small country township of Tuakau, forty miles south of Auckland, where my father had accepted the job of establishing a newspaper, the *Tuakau District News*. My elder sister June was born in 1917 and I was born in a hospital in Auckland on 20th July 1919. Just over a year later my younger brother Rex arrived.

My father was a practical person, but did not always complete every job he started. He began building a house on our seven acres of land but it was still unfinished by the time we moved to Auckland some sixteen years later. It must have been very trying for my mother who was brought up in reasonable comfort. When we were young, my father was very strict, but every evening before bed he relaxed and told us some new fairy tale he created as he went along about a character called

Jimmy Job who lived in a hollow tree. They were great stories and we loved them. It was the happiest time of our day. But as we grew older and more strong-minded, we all started clashing ferociously with our father's rigid views. He believed that the only cure for ill health was having no food at all and we hated this and would never admit we were unwell until we were very sick indeed. As a child, I was never given any pocket money and used to feel envious of those who were. I knew my father hung his trousers over the end of the bed. Late one night I crept into the room of my sleeping parents, extracted a half crown from my father's pocket and slipped out again. Next Saturday, I went up to Tuakau village and bought a large comic book which I read with great enjoyment. Inevitably, my mother inquired how I had managed to obtain the book and I told her that I had picked it out of the hedgerow. I'm sure she didn't believe me, but fortunately she didn't report it to my father. I had enough sense never to steal from his pocket again.

Tuakau Primary School was only half a mile away and, wet, fine or frosty, I walked barefoot every day to school as most country children did in those days. My schoolteacher mother coached me energetically so I did well at primary school and didn't have to spend a year in either Standard 3 or Standard 6. But this meant I was always much younger than the other children in my class, so I had almost no friends at school. My mother's attitude didn't help. She was so kind in many ways, but had the philosophy that you can judge people by the company they keep, and she didn't feel that my classmates had too much to offer. So at school I was very quiet and subdued. This was aggravated in the geography class when I entered Standard 4 and the headmaster, who was quite an unpleasant sort of man, asked me to point out the continent of Asia on the map. I had no idea what Asia was, let alone where it was, and I just stood there with a sickly grin on my face. "Don't stand there like a laughing hyena," he bellowed at me, and the class roared with pleasure. I cringed inside myself and can still visualize the occasion as though it happened yesterday.

The big event in Tuakau was the cinema. On Saturdays they had Wild West films and on Tuesdays and Wednesdays they had a long picture for adults. When my father was away, my mother used to go to the cinema and she'd take June because a girl could never be left at home by herself. This didn't suit Rex and me at all and we'd follow her around the house crying furiously until she weakened and took us too. I enjoyed those films very much indeed. They were probably the only exciting things that happened to me during the course of the week. Even in those early days, I was a great dreamer. I used to go for long walks about the area, or cut across the paddocks, jumping over the fences with my mind far away, just thinking about adventures and exciting things to do. I'd have a stick in my hand and imagine it was a sword and that I was fighting great battles.

My father was very strong on justice and a firm believer in corporal punishment to achieve it. As a result, I had many uncomfortable confrontations with him in the woodshed. My problem was that I always refused to admit that I was wrong, whether it was true or not, and this used to aggravate my father considerably. In retrospect, I realize that I must have been a difficult child. Although I can often remember thinking that the punishment was unjust or too severe, I can't ever remember actually giving in.

I passed out of primary school at the age of eleven—two years younger than average. My mother was determined that I should have a good secondary education and managed to get me into Auckland Grammar School, one of the best academic schools in New Zealand. I'll always remember that first day at Auckland Grammar. I got up and rode my bicycle down to the Tuakau station, got onto the train, and duly traveled into the Newmarket station. By following a long line of grammar boys, I found my way to the school and into the huge hall which was quite overwhelming. Fortunately, they told everyone where to sit, but I didn't talk to a single one of my companions. The headmaster read out the forms that all the students had to go to, starting from the sixth form and going right down to the third form, which was when I listened very carefully for my name, but he read on and on and on and finally came to an end without having read my name at all. And then he instructed all the various classes to go to their rooms. So all this huge mass of young people rose up and departed and I was left alone in this enormous hall, not knowing what to do or where to go. Finally, a kindly teacher saw me sitting there alone, checked his list and directed me to the correct room.

I don't think in that first week, I talked to anyone. At lunchtime I'd go to a little scrubby area at the back of the school and eat my sandwiches. There were quite a lot of ants and I used to watch the ants moving steadily around, intent on their various purposes. So by the end of the first week I was much more friendly with the ants than I was with any of my fellow students. My confidence received another blow when in the first week the muscle-bound gymnastics instructor cast his jaundiced eye over my scrawny physique, rolled his eyes to the heavens, and muttered, "What will they send me next?" No believer in sparing his victim any discomfort, he told me my ribs flared out in a most unnatural fashion, my back needed straightening, and my shoulders were rounded. He placed me in the misfit class with the other physical "freaks." I never got over this sense of physical inferiority. I was never ashamed of what I could actually do, but only about the miserable way I looked. I started in one of the lowest classes, but at the end of the first term, I was raised to the second form, 3B, so I must have been doing rather better than I thought.

For three and a half years my train left Tuakau station at 7 a.m. and arrived back at 6:15 p.m. It was a long day for a very small boy, but then I started to grow—five inches one year, and four inches the next. I became tall and lean with increasing strength. The train became an important part of my life. Holding on to the handrails and running furiously alongside, then leaping aboard at the last desperate moment— this was living! My increased strength helped me to become a good fighter on the train. I learned skills which most of my companions didn't have. For instance, if there was a boy who I knew was good at boxing or wrestling, I could always beat him because I would grab him round the waist and throw him down into the corner of the seat and then just lie on top of him and he would be unable to move. Often during these scuffles, a window would accidentally be broken. The guard used to come along at the end of the line and put all the windows down and I knew that I'd be in trouble if he found the broken one. So I'd break all the glass out, lift the window up, lock it, and then lean out into the freezing winter air just as though I was looking at the scenery passing by. The guard would come along, close all the other windows, but would leave mine open. When I arrived at Tuakau station I would quickly leap off and nobody would blame me for the broken window.

I also did an enormous amount of reading and dreaming on board the train, at one stage getting a book a day out of the school library, and I even did moderately well academically. I actually enjoyed my last year in the sixth form at Auckland Grammar School. This was when I managed to persuade my father to give me the money to go with the school party down to Mount Ruapehu in the middle of the North Island. It was the winter of 1935 and, unknown to me, was a particularly good snow year. The train arrived at the National Park station at midnight and there was snow everywhere—on the railway lines, on the trees, and on the great mountains outlined in the bright moonlight. I had never seen snow before and for ten glorious days I skied and clambered around the snow-covered mountainside. It was the most exciting thing that had ever happened to me at that time and undoubtedly the start of my enthusiasm for snow and mountains.

For a long time, my father had been involved in keeping bees, initially as a hobby and then as a profitable sideline. My mother, my brother and I all worked hard in the business. Every weekend, all through the school holidays, and even on long summer evenings, I was fully involved with the bees. I received no pay or even pocket money, which wasn't all that unusual for farming families in those days, and I really enjoyed the challenge of it. Finally, my father had a disagreement on principle with the directors of his small newspaper and he resigned and took up commercial beekeeping full time. This meant my brother and I were even busier, carrying 80-lb. boxes of honey for extracting and even 120-lb. crates holding two four-gallon tins of honey. By the time I was sixteen years old I was as strong as a man and worked harder than most.

We had moved to Auckland and rented a house when I was fifteen years old. Then came the major surprise. My father decided to buy a very nice new home on Remuera Road, one of the best suburbs in Auckland. Where he obtained the money I had no idea. I always believed he had nothing to spare and he certainly displayed extreme reluctance to give any cash to us children. My mother was still determined that I should continue my education and go to university. When she pointed out to my father that the university holidays covered the major honey production period, he finally agreed. I was still only sixteen years old and I began two rather miserable years at university. I don't know why I was so unhappy, but I seemed unable to absorb the information and my memory was appalling. I was studying mathematics and science because I had done best at those subjects at grammar school, but it didn't seem to work. Maybe I was just mentally lazy at that period of my life. I was certainly very young and devoid of all social skills. By the end of my two years I hadn't passed a single examination and I didn't have a single friend. It seems a bit ironic that in later years I was to be given five honorary doctorates, wrote a number of books and proved to be rather good at organizing expeditions.

During my university years, my father only gave me the few pence needed to travel the five miles by bus to and from our home, so I jogged the distance instead and accumulated a little money. I used this to take lessons in jujitsu and, later on, boxing. On one memorable occasion at the boxing gymnasium, we were visited by the New Zealand champion welterweight, Vic Calteaux, who was training for another fight. He was a ferociously strong-looking man, but when the instructor asked for volunteers to spar with him, I thought why not? I was taller and bigger and felt I could look after myself. Vic Calteaux took it all very casually, ducking and diving and making no effort to hit me. I thought he was being just a little bit too careless, so, as I rather prided myself on my straight left, I reached out and whanged him firmly on the nose. The result was certainly all I could have asked for. Calteaux went quite berserk and pummeled me as though the world championship depended on it. Finally, he delivered an enormous blow to my solar plexus and put me completely out of action.

I have stayed well clear of professional boxers since that day.

So my brother, Rex, and I returned to beekeeping. My father had quite a big operation with 1,600 hives of bees and, apart from our food and lodging, it didn't cost him anything—it was certainly cheap labor. I was too big now to be taken to the woodshed anymore, but arguments we had in plenty. Although I enjoyed much of the work, particularly when the honey-gathering season was in full swing, I became rather tired of the relentless drive to work seven days a week for no financial return. But somehow the years passed and we stuck together.

We had never been a strong family in religious matters, although back in the Tuakau days we used to attend the local Anglican church regularly. We sang the hymns and listened to the sermons, but I don't think we were deep believers. However, my father always had plenty to say and he even represented our church at the Synod in Auckland as a lay member. Our minister was a pleasant young man and his wife was the daughter of the Bishop of Auckland. When the Bishop agreed to come to Tuakau and carry out a confirmation service, the young minister really swung into action. We youngsters went through an intensive period of training and the enthusiastic minister assured us that confirmation would absolutely transform our lives—we would become immediately noble and holy—and I certainly believed him. When the Bishop arrived on the Sunday evening, we looked on him with worshipful eyes (he was actually a rather pleasant gentleman) and the service began. I was expecting a flash of illumination but no such thing occurred. When I walked out of the church I realized that I was no holier than before. It was a great disappointment to me and certainly seriously affected my religious beliefs from then on.

Many years later, the family was struck by another form of religious activity. A Dr. Herbert Sutcliffe was in town and he was talking about a new philosophy—Radiant Living. My family and I went along to his first lecture and we were very impressed. It was a combination of Christianity, psychology and health and fitness and it just seemed to fit our needs at the time. We became members and when Dr. Sutcliffe introduced training classes I qualified first in the course and became a

Teacher of Radiant Living. I gained quite a lot from Radiant Living—
I learned to speak confidently from the platform and even started
thinking more freely on important topics. But finally my enthusiasm
faded, as it always seemed to do. I developed the conviction that I was
trying to escape from ordinary life, so I reluctantly withdrew from the
organization.

When war was declared in 1939 I immediately applied to join the air
force and become a pilot but was very frustrated when I was advised
that it would be a year or more before I would be called in for training.
This was a very unhappy period for me as I was suffering from a
religious conscience revival and a feeling of uncertainty about everything. In the summer of 1939–40 I was still not yet twenty, but so
weighed down with the worries of the world that I managed to persuade
my father to give me some time off and I spent my meager savings on
a short trip to the Southern Alps. I had a much older friend with me who
had a very strong personality and, as he was strongly opposed to war in
any form, I was constantly having to battle with my beliefs.

The weather was superb as we approached the mountains and my
heart sang as I looked up at the great peaks. How wonderful they were!
I checked in to the Hermitage Hotel and then eagerly strolled outside.
High up in a narrow gully above the hotel I saw a small patch of snow
and almost instinctively started up the loose rocks in my light shoes.
Finally, I reached the snow and stamped around in it with great excitement. As I sat in the lounge that evening, I felt a certain sense of elation.
I don't know where my older companion was, he seemed to have drifted
out of my consciousness. And then the sound of voices hushed and I
looked up to see two young men coming into the room. They were fit
and tanned and looked very competent. I could hear a whisper going
round the room: "They've just climbed Mount Cook." And soon they
were the center of an admiring group and the pretty girls fluttered around
them like moths drawn to a flame.

I retreated to a corner of the lounge, filled with an immense sense of
futility at the dull nature of my existence. These chaps were really

getting some excitement out of life. Tomorrow I must climb something! I managed to recruit an elderly and rather portly guide who agreed we would attempt the ascent of the modest Mount Oliver. On a crisp clear morning we climbed until we reached the last thousand feet of firm snow. The guide was much too slow for me and I kicked steps upward to the crest of the ridge. Not too far away was the rock summit and soon I was scrambling up with wild enthusiasm. Far above me was the great peak of Mount Cook. Someday I'll climb that, too, I resolved. I returned down to the Hermitage after the most exciting day I had ever spent.

When I was about twenty-two years old, I had my first notable relationship with a member of the opposite sex, and indeed the only one until my marriage twelve years later. How I met her and even what her full name was, I don't now remember. She was a couple of years younger than me, slim, pretty with beautiful auburn hair. I could never understand why she bothered with me. We had a warm relationship and it was certainly a new experience for me. I was still working hard for my father and receiving very little pay in return, but whatever I did obtain I hoarded carefully—it wasn't very much. Finally I bought her the cheapest of engagement rings which she seemed to prize greatly.

Then my chance came! It had been a poor honey season throughout New Zealand and the Beekeepers Association decided to purchase some honey from Australia to meet their commercial commitments on the local market. My father and mother were invited to go to Australia to make the necessary purchases and this meant they would be away for a month. We had completed the extracting of honey from our apiaries but I knew of a small group of hives that still had honey in place. On the departure of my parents, I removed the boxes of honey, extracted it, and filled a number of four-gallon tins. I then put an advertisement in the paper and, as sugar was short in those days, I had a rush of replies. For the first time in my life I had £25 in my pocket, a vast sum of money to me. I spent it carefully, but did take my girlfriend on a weekend holiday to Lake Taupo—we stayed in separate rooms, of course.

I was naive to think my actions would not be discovered by my father on his return from Australia. He made me give back all the money I had not spent and then paid me nothing for some months until he felt I had reimbursed him for the residue. I didn't really feel particularly guilty about the actual money—after all I was doing a great share of the work involved in the beekeeping business—but I did have a sense of shame about the sneaky way I had carried it all out. My romance faded, largely due to lack of money, I suspect, and although I make no great claims to being depressingly honest, I don't believe I have carried out such an energetic crime since that noteworthy occasion many years ago.

My father had never approved of my going into the air force. He thought I could be better employed in honey production which was a reserved occupation, like ordinary farming. Unknown to me, he applied to have me retained in this essential work and his application was immediately granted, so a beekeeper I remained. However, as time passed, my thoughts returned increasingly to the air force and I made such a nuisance of myself that my father finally agreed to institute action to get me released. It wasn't until the beginning of 1944 that I was called into the Royal New Zealand Air Force and I started a new life with appreciably less discipline and a great deal more relaxation. I really enjoyed my air force tour of duty.

Our initial training was carried out in a series of camps called Delta in the Wairau valley of Marlborough, now one of the best wine-growing areas in New Zealand. Our first camp was essentially basic training and we were divided up into platoons. A little to my surprise, they chose a beefy but rather unintelligent young man as platoon leader—he certainly wouldn't have been my choice. This was my first experience of living together with a group of young men and, as I was older than the average, I quite enjoyed it. On one occasion, we were returning by bus from some project and our team leader and another rather aggressive young man started shouting abuse at each other. When the bus stopped for a break, our team leader jumped off first and when his opponent started coming down the steps he grabbed him, pulled him off the bus, and proceeded to knock him into pulp. There was blood everywhere and no question about who won the contest. I thought this had gone on long enough so I thrust myself between the contestants, grabbed them each by their jackets and pushed them apart. They were so astonished that their enthusiasm for the fight rapidly faded. Then I felt a thump on my back and looked over my shoulder to find another young man prancing around and obviously looking for a punch-up. In disgust, I threw the two original contestants aside, returned to the bus and climbed aboard. The whole platoon followed me somewhat subdued. It was a lesson to me not to interfere in a mob situation. When our course finished, we moved on to our major camp. I was pleased that the two aggressive ones simply didn't make it.

Cheshire Camp was the main depot for aircrew training and, though they worked us very hard for five and a half days, we were fairly free from midday Saturday until Sunday night. Best of all the Wairau valley was surrounded with modest but interesting mountains. Winter was approaching, so the temperatures at night were very cold, while the days were sunny and fine. I couldn't keep my eyes off the great snowy peak towering up to the south. Mount Tapuaenuku was 9,465 feet, and I resolved to climb it when time permitted. In the interim I tackled lesser peaks almost every weekend. The trouble was getting companions to go with me. One good friend said to me after a particularly arduous trip, "It was great fun, Ed, but I'm not going to do it again!" So most of the time I had to do solo climbing. Then I met Jack McBurney, a gunnery instructor, who enjoyed the mountains as much as I did and we climbed a lot together.

We were given psychological tests to determine our suitability as aircrew. When the psychologist discovered I planned to attempt Mount Tapuaenuku he expressed interest in coming too. As he would be able to get a vehicle to drive the eighty miles to the mountain, it sounded perfect. I organized a three-day leave weekend, but then the doctor rang and said he couldn't make it, so that meant no vehicle. I was pretty sure that he had just changed his mind, but I decided to do the trip myself.

I had a crazy friend in Cheshire Camp who had an old motorbike and he had frequently offered to take me up to the hills. I approached him now and he agreed to drive me over the pass to Awatere valley. We left on the late Friday afternoon, but it wasn't a very propitious beginning. The entrance to the camp was covered in ice and we skidded violently and ended up in the ditch. No harm had been done, so we got on board once more and set off over the gravel bypass road. It was a terrifying ride—we didn't come off again but we were very close to it. By the time we had crossed the pass and descended to the valley I decided I had had enough. I thanked my friend and he turned back to camp, while I started walking. It was five miles before I reached the nearest sheep station where the owner's wife invited me inside, fed me generously and gave me a comfortable bed in the shearers' quarters. Early on Saturday morning I was away again, hoping to get a lift from a car or truck. But I only managed two short pickups and had to walk over fifteen miles, quite an effort with my cumbersome pack. The few people I met warned me against carrying on alone, but the snow-covered Tapuaenuku was growing more and more impressive and my excitement grew. I reached the Hodder river which drained off the mountain and walked up the gravel riverbed to make many fords of the ice-cold water before I finally reached the Shin Hut, used by local shepherds in the summer.

By 4 a.m. on Sunday morning I'd only had four hours' sleep but had a quick breakfast and at 5 a.m. crossed the river and started up the main ridge. I climbed to the snow line at 5,000 feet and it was hard going through the soft snow. I was startled to hear what sounded like a thin human voice calling for help, then realized it was the eerie wail of the native parrot, the kea, and I pushed on. I reached 7,000 feet, cloud came over the peak and it snowed heavily, but I kept moving. I was rewarded at 8,000 feet by clear skies. The climbing was more difficult here, a long sharp ridge and a steep icy slope. Then the clouds swept in again but I carried on until there was nowhere else to go—I was on the top. I immediately turned downward through the fog and was thankful that I had taken compass bearings on the way up. At 7 p.m., well after dark, I arrived back at the Shin Hut—I'd been going for fourteen hours. I just crawled into my sleeping bag and dropped immediately off to sleep.

I was away again at 4 a.m. on the Monday morning as I had to get back to camp that same day. I walked for at least twenty miles down valley and there wasn't a single vehicle going my way. Two going up valley stopped and their drivers said that everyone in the valley was quite sure I would be dead by now. Then my luck changed and I got a lift all the way to Blenheim city, where I could pick up the air force bus to camp and idly listen to the young airmen discussing their recent social conquests. But I didn't care as I had an enormous sense of satisfaction. I'd climbed a decent mountain at last!

I did quite well in the final examinations, coming fourteenth out of the 260 students, which I thought was rather good for an academic drop-out like me. Because of my age, twenty-five, and my reasonable marks I was posted to Navigation School in New Plymouth. I enjoyed navigating our twin-engined planes over the Tasman Sea and obtained much satisfaction out of climbing the nearby volcanic cone of Mount Egmont nearly every weekend. After qualifying second in our class and above average in the practical navigation, I did a gunnery course which involved firing a machine gun at a drogue towed by another plane. I'd done quite a lot of rifle shooting at fixed targets at Cheshire and had produced one of the best records, but up in the air I was hopeless. I not only rarely hit the trailing drogue, but on one occasion put a bullet through the tail of the leading plane, which produced a severe reprimand. Nobody was hurt, so I didn't feel too worried about it.

In February we flew to Lathala Bay in Fiji where we were formed into crews to operate the Catalina flying boats as search-and-rescue aircraft by the Royal New Zealand Air Force. The Catalina was a fine aircraft, rugged and dependable, but very slow, so accurate navigation was an important factor. I enjoyed the long night flights when I had to rely almost entirely on astronomical navigation. I particularly remember one eleven-hour flight when I guided our plane solely with a succession of star shots taken by my sextant. We flew over a tiny volcanic island called Tanna with a crater glowing red like a cigarette butt and a succession of red hot boulders being thrown up into the night sky.

On the whole my navigation training worked out very well, but I did make one serious error. We had a six-hour low-level exercise—a square search which would be useful for looking for a damaged aircraft or ship.

It was a very rough day and we bumped around like crazy, starting from the great cliffs of Kandavu Island and changing course very frequently. Most of the crew felt ill and lay down on the bunks, but the pilots and I had to keep going. It was almost time to head back to base and I was enormously relieved and looking forward to reaching stable ground again when the captain announced, "Kandavu ahead!!" I was really shocked—we should have been thirty miles from Kandavu. I hastily ignored my navigation plot and started it all again from Kandavu. An hour later there was still no sign of Lathala Bay and when the captain obtained a radio bearing we had to turn ninety degrees to starboard to get home. Next morning the senior navigation instructor and I went through my records and it immediately became clear what had happened. It hadn't been Kandavu at all but another island thirty miles away the captain had sighted. I'd been right on course. "Don't believe what the pilot tells you," said the instructor. "Believe your navigation plot." And from then on that's what I certainly did. One good thing about the Catalina was that, in an emergency, we could have landed in the water beside a village inside the reef and actually asked people where we were.

On completion of our operational training in Fiji we were posted to the Solomon Islands for routine search and rescue duties. Halavo Base was on Florida Island, opposite Guadalcanal, and our captain wished to make an impressive arrival. We landed very smoothly and were congratulating ourselves when we cut across a corner of the reef and ground to a halt. Water started coming in through a hole in the bow and our captain yelled for two men to jump overboard and push the aircraft off. Ron Ward, the senior radio operator, was of similar size and energy to myself and we leapt overboard in our clothes and easily released the aircraft from the reef. "All aboard," shouted the captain and, as Ron and I scrambled over the side, he opened the throttle to get the plane up on a step with the hole clear of the water and roared into the concrete pull-out ramp. In a moment we had been safely dragged ashore. It certainly wasn't the sort of arrival we had planned.

Life settled into a very comfortable routine. Halavo Base was small but well supplied. Every second day we had some sort of flying task—a patrol, a search, or mercy trips. But we had lots of spare time too. Ron Ward and I discovered we had kindred interests, mostly involving lively activity despite the warm temperatures. Ron had brought a mast and sails up from Fiji and when we discovered the framework of a 14-foot boat we sheathed it in canvas, had our engineers install a small engine and propeller and stepped the mast. It was a remarkably effective craft and we sailed into all the inlets and around the many small islands embracing Halavo Base.

When we heard there were crocodiles in the area, our hunter instincts were aroused and we started carrying a couple of rifles with us. We nosed into one shady inlet and noticed a log floating in the water, then immediately realized it must be a crocodile. Ron and I both raised our weapons and fired simultaneously. There was a great thrashing and splashing and when it had all subsided we cautiously poled our way into the inlet, well aware of the rather fragile sides of our boat. When we were over the spot I thrust around with a long harpoon we were carrying and finally struck a slowly writhing body. I brought it to the surface and it was indeed a crocodile, only eight feet long but with vicious teeth. We dragged it back to base and strung it up on a gantry. Virtually everyone in the camp had a photograph of themselves taken with a rifle in hand, casually leaning next to the crocodile. I can imagine the lurid tales that went back home with each photograph. Ron and I never did agree about whose shot actually killed the creature.

The end of the war with Japan signaled the rundown of air force activity in the Pacific and the Catalinas became very busy transporting men back to New Zealand. Our crew was chosen to stay in Halavo as standby for search and rescue, so we were unable to spend much time away from base and life became very boring. Someone discovered an abandoned motorboat with an apparently seized-up engine. Our flight engineers got it going again, while we caulked and painted the hull. When we relaunched the boat we were very happy with its speed. Its 180 horsepower marine engine pushed us along at more than thirty knots. To our great pleasure it was faster than the Base Commander's runabout. We renamed the boat the *Jolly Roger*. One Sunday morning Ron and I rose early to take one of the airmen across the bay to the American Naval Base at Tulagi to attend a Catholic church service. It was a pleasant sunny morning with a fresh breeze putting quite a chop on the sea. Ron and I pumped out the *Jolly Roger* and filled the two tanks with petrol. These tanks were suspended above the engine and I noticed that one of them was a bit loose but didn't bother too much about it. When the airman joined us we shot off across the bay at full speed and did the four-mile journey in eight minutes.

We deposited the young airman at Tulagi and turned for Halavo. We were now heading straight into the sea and it was quite bumpy, so I eased back on the throttle. After a mile or so we came into the lee of Palm Island where the seas were flat calm and I opened out to maximum speed again. When we emerged from the shelter of the island, the sea was quite rough and we hit waves with a succession of mighty thumps. The next moment we heard a loud crack behind us and a sheet of flame shot through the holes around the engine compartment—the petrol tank had broken loose! The fire was well beyond our control, although the engine was still roaring merrily on. Ron and I had both been scorched already and I knew we would have to bale out before the other tank exploded. I yelled to Ron to jump and then let go of the wheel and stood on the seat. Next moment the boat hit a big wave and veered sharply. I was thrown off balance and fell on my back on the engine covers through which flames were spurting. I wasn't wearing a shirt and could feel my flesh sizzling and the pain was quite considerable. I really had the feeling that now I knew what a piece of bacon felt like. I had just enough energy to roll off the engine hatch into the water. The *Jolly Roger* charged on for another hundred feet and then exploded in a great sheet of flame.

The salt water was extremely painful on my burns and we were a long way from shore, at least 500 yards. I just flopped around for a while, not worrying too much about going anywhere, until Ron yelled at me to get moving. Every now and then I'd feel myself giving out and I'd flop over onto my back and float and try to do backstroke, but I'd just go round in circles. Ron, who wasn't as badly burnt as I was, although badly enough, kept yelling at me and I'd flop over again and start paddling once more. I didn't have much clothing on anyway but to help my swimming I tore off pretty well everything. After what seemed like an eternity I felt my foot touch the bottom, though I was past caring by this stage. We staggered up the shore and collapsed on the sand. The sun was beating down now and its heat on our burns was too much to stand, so we got back to our feet and staggered the half mile over the reef and along a road to the nearest habitation on Tanenhoga island. The sun was so unpleasant on our backs that at times we had to walk along the road backward.

The only people in residence were two U.S. sailors who were still in bed and were clearly flabbergasted at our appearance. We tried to explain that we were burnt and needed some assistance, but they just sat there with their mouths open. So we asked if they had any tannic acid and they finally produced a big tube. I put some on Ron and he put some on me and it seemed to ease the pain quite a lot. By now they realized we were in trouble and said they'd run us across to the Tulagi Naval Base in their boat. The boat trip was only a mile but it seemed much longer, as I was feeling pretty hazy by this time. The Americans had called ahead by radio and there was an ambulance to meet us at the wharf and we were soon being taken into the naval hospital and people were fussing around. The doctor gave each of us three quarts of blood serum, as well as numerous shots of morphine, penicillin and glucose. He seemed pretty worried about me as he was having great difficulty in finding a vein to get a needle into.

Our New Zealand CO turned up and I could see by his face that he wasn't too happy about my condition. He didn't tell me but he sent a message back to my parents saying, "Sergeant Hillary received second-degree burns. He was admitted to the U.S. Navy Hospital at Tulagi where he was classified as dangerously ill." The medical staff at Tulagi decided that Ron and I should be shifted to the much better equipped U.S. hospital on Guadalcanal and, as an American destroyer was about to leave, we were carried aboard and placed on deck in the shade of a

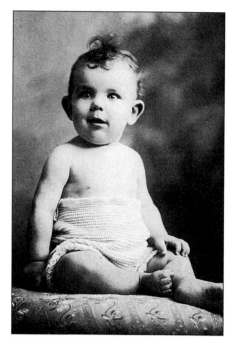

(*Above*) My parents before their marriage. In the Great War my father volunteered and served with the ANZACs at Gallipoli.

(*Below right*) With the 8-ft. crocodile Ron Ward and I shot in the Solomon Islands.

(*Above*) The infant Edmund.

(*Below left*) Mother with June, Rex and myself.

The New Zealand team of Hillary, Cotter, Lowe and Riddiford sets sail for the Garhwal Himalayas.

Eric Shipton, having just made the first crossing of the Ama Dablam Col with me and three Sherpas in 1951. Eric has always been my hero and he treated me like an energetic younger brother.

Leaving for the Himalayas with George Lowe to join the 1953 Everest expedition.

At first Tenzing and I could face the camera with grins of triumph, but by the time we reached Kathmandu it was another story. The expression on our faces, and on John Hunt's, tell it all.

Who else but George Lowe could be best man at my wedding to Louise
and read out the telegrams?

Checking our slides on the American
lecture tour with Louise, George and
Charles Evans.

The Hillary family, with Peter, Sarah
and the new baby, Belinda.

"IT'S THE I.G.Y. PEOPLE FOR YOU, ED, — NOW THEY WANT TO SHOOT YOU INTO SPACE!"
— N.Z. HERALD 71.58

The International Geophysical Year sponsored the Trans-Antarctic Expedition.
I had my own agenda.

The Old Firm that drove to the South Pole: Hillary, Murray Ellis, Jim Bates,
Peter Mulgrew, Derek Wright.

With Peter and June Mulgrew after Peter's accident on Makalu.

The first team at Kunde Hospital: Dr. John McKinnon, Nurse Yangjen Sherpa and Diane McKinnon.

Tenzing and Daku came to visit New Zealand and Louise and I took them off into the hill country.

Ang Rita Sherpa, my right-hand man, with my daughter Sarah and son Peter,
who climbed Everest himself in 1990 and phoned me from the top.

A typical group of villagers present a petition for improvements.

A collar and tie for my first nine-to-five job, with Prime Minister David Lange, who appointed me High Commissioner *(above)* and Rajiv Gandhi *(left)*.

June and I on our wedding day.

four-inch gun. I can remember the succession of faces coming along to look us over and then I went off to sleep.

I woke up in the hospital at Guadalcanal as I was being taken into the operating theater, and seemed to spend a long time there. The doctor was a very pleasant person and seemed to know what he was doing. He told me I had forty percent of my skin burnt off and I was lucky to be alive, but if they could prevent infection I'd be OK. I was confident right from the start that I would survive. Even so, the first week was rather miserable with the extreme discomfort of heavy bandages in the hot sticky conditions and being woken day and night for penicillin injections. I had 140 of them and at night they were trying. The male nurse was a somewhat moronic character and he'd bare my bottom and then throw the hypodermic syringe from what seemed like ten feet away. I cringed every time but he, in fact, never missed. I was greatly relieved when he was transferred elsewhere, no doubt to punish some other poor patient.

The doctor told me I would be in hospital for many months and the way I felt the first week I suspected this might be true. But by the second week my burns were healing well and I was staggering out of bed for short walks. By the third week I was bored to tears and making a thorough nuisance of myself. Then Ron Ward was classified as being well enough to leave hospital and return to New Zealand, and I didn't see him again for many years (by then he was a school principal and a senior inspector). I couldn't understand the attitude of most of the patients who seemed perfectly happy to relax in the comfort and attention of the hospital. I must have been an appalling patient to have around.

My importuning of the doctor finally bore results. He expressed his astonishment at the rapidity of my healing and agreed he would be pleased to see me go. After three weeks I emerged from the hospital still swathed in bandages, a bit shaky and a lot thinner, but with few signs of infection. I knew I could largely thank my fitness for that, plus my luck at striking on an excellent surgeon who later became very distinguished in his profession in the United States. All I wanted now was to return home. I found it infuriating to be kept waiting several weeks for "observation and treatment." Finally, some intelligent person decided I could just as well have my "observation and treatment" at home. To my joy I was flown back to Auckland and given my discharge with sick leave. In the cooler temperatures and with good fresh food I soon made a rapid recovery. I also had £100 in cash in my pocket from my air force pay, quite a lot of money in those days.

I returned to New Zealand with two major ambitions—one was to get back into beekeeping and the second was to do all the climbing I could. I was more than a little surprised when my father advised me he had enough staff at present and he didn't need my services. I hadn't realized how trying I must have been to my father and how bitter he felt about it. Fortunately, I had matured somewhat during my time in the air force, so I was able to shrug this off. As I had ample funds I went off mountaineering in the Southern Alps with my good friend Jack McBurney. We were strong and energetic but had not yet developed any great skill in technical climbing. With the Alpine Club route guide in one hand and an ice axe in the other we climbed a number of excellent peaks. It had been a most enjoyable holiday.

I came back home to Auckland to find that it had been a very poor honey crop and my father was happy to pay off his staff and employ me on a work-now-pay-later basis. This was the beginning of my increasing influence in our honey business and I became more and more responsible for its administration, despite the lack of remuneration. However, I used my carefully hoarded air force money to do mountaineering trips over the next few years. In the first winter I returned to Tapuaenuku with my younger brother Rex and another friend, Allan Robb. Despite cold weather and much snow we did a traverse of the mountain and bivouacked on the south side in heavily falling snow. Next morning we struggled down the long rocky ridge, seeking a way down to the Dee river. Late in the day we reached the end of the spur and found it dropped abruptly 600 feet to the water. Darkness had fallen and we had to get down somehow. We commenced a rather hazardous procedure. Rex had no mountaineering experience but a lot of confidence in me. I lowered him on the end of the rope until he found a suitable ledge, always hoping that it would never be further than half the length of the rope. Then I lowered Allan down and finally double roped down myself. After half a dozen of these procedures in pitch darkness the slope eased off a little and we were able to climb down to the river and camp. Under the conditions it had been quite a demanding week, but one of many adventures experienced in the years to come which built up my expertise on snow and ice and paved my way to the Himalayas.

4

SOUTH OF EVEREST WITH SHIPTON

MY BROTHER, REX, WAS A YEAR YOUNGER THAN ME AND HE, TOO, was part of our family beekeeping business. Rex and I worked well together as a team. He was smaller than me but very strong and vigorous. In the friendliest fashion we competed energetically with each other, often running side by side with heavy loads of honey to pile them on our truck. Why did we persist in working with a father who paid us so little and whose views varied so often from our own? The main reason I believe was because we actually enjoyed the beekeeping. Our thirty-five apiaries were spread out on fertile dairy farms up to forty miles away, so we were always on the move. The spring and summer, when the bees were gathering nectar, was a time of great excitement. The weather made beekeeping a tremendous gamble, of course. Each apiary we visited could have a substantial crop of honey in its hives or almost nothing. Rex and I reveled in the hard work and increasingly the field activity fell into our hands. Our father was a hard and somewhat ruthless man but I never lost my well-concealed respect for his tremendous work ethic. But finally even he had reluctantly to concede that he would need to pay us just enough to live on—but no more!

When Rex married and started producing a family I was still warmly welcomed into his home. He was incredibly agreeable about the time I took off to go to the mountains and, in retrospect, I am all too aware that I abused his generosity and hospitality. Rex became an excellent carpenter and plumber which stood him in good stead in later years when he sold his bees and became a successful builder, which also opened up a whole new area of collaboration for us in the Himalayas. But that is looking ahead.

By 1946 my life started to assume a more regular pattern. We worked long and hard on the bees and received a modest salary. In return for the long hours we worked in the Christmas and New Year period my father agreed I should take an unpaid holiday at the end of January for summer mountaineering. The wintertime was not so busy so I had little difficulty in getting to the mountains over that period. Despite my very modest income my needs were few, as I didn't smoke or drink and had a very limited social life.

Probably the most important turning point in my climbing career occurred when I met Harry Ayres, New Zealand's outstanding mountain guide. My climbing companion was Allan Odell and Harry's client was Susie Sanders, one of New Zealand's best known women climbers. We followed along behind Harry and Susie on Aiguille Rouge and Mount Haidinger and I was enormously impressed with his skill, in particular his ability to wield an ice axe on icy slopes. Later a client canceled and Harry had a spare week so I joined up with him and we climbed Mount Cook, at 12,349 feet New Zealand's highest peak. I climbed a good deal with Harry after that and although I never achieved his degree of skill I learned a great deal from him and became a rather useful step-cutter.

I started to do more and more climbing in the winter and became an experienced ski-mountaineer, traveling with a variety of companions. One winter Jack McBurney and I spent a month or so together. First we had two weeks shooting deer which were regarded as pests in New Zealand. We shot a score of them, skinned them and backpacked out huge loads of skins to be sold for quite a useful sum. Then we went gold panning up the Cook river in freezing conditions. We certainly didn't get much gold, so our enthusiasm for this faded rather quickly. In heavy snow and poor visibility we crossed over the Copeland Pass and fumbled our way down toward the Hooker valley. I was leading down in terrible conditions when I stepped on a corniced crevasse which broke off and precipitated me into its depths—which only happened to be about twelve feet down. It was very peaceful out of the storm, so I yelled to Jack to come on down which he thankfully did. We had a leisurely lunch and then we noticed that we were nodding off to sleep. We realized hypothermia was setting in, so we quickly packed our gear and scrambled out into the storm. If we had really gone to sleep we would never have woken up.

To save a little extra money for skiing I worked for six weeks on a hydroelectric project at Lake Pukaki. My job was surveyors' lineman for one of the younger engineers, Norman Hardie (who later climbed the world's third highest peak, Kangchenjunga). The workers on our site were a motley lot. They seemed more like jailbirds to me. The local police force were regular visitors! The pay for linemen was good but not good enough, I decided, so I took a second job at night and became a tally clerk with a pile-driving gang. The first night I joined the four-man gang after dinner and we walked through the frosty air to a large muddy pond on the downriver side of the dam. There was a dinghy on the shore and we used it to row out to a floating platform supporting a tall tower. The task was a simple one; to test the depth and consistency of the clay in the pond by driving a succession of steel pipes into it. The hammer was a great iron contraption suspended from the tower and pulled up by hand. My job was to take a tally of the number of blows required to drive a foot of pipe into the clay.

The four-man team was not an impressive group; they ranged from a small, wizened character with a bitter, debauched face to an enormous Maori who seemed to lack the customary good nature. Work commenced—if you could call it work—and the four men pulled the weight to the top of the tower with the greatest of ease and duly let it fall with an almighty clunk—and I made a notation in my book. At the end of an hour nobody had achieved a sweat and they had driven a pipe down a total of twelve feet.

"OK, that's the lot for tonight," said the little man and the four of them got back in the dinghy. "Coming, mate?"

Somewhat dazed I asked for an explanation, and got it. They were working on contract, so much a foot of pipe, and someone had made a mistake. Twelve feet of pipe in a night was enough to give them all a substantial pay packet. It was really none of my business, so I rowed ashore with them and went to a small hut already crammed with a dozen other men. A stove was red-hot in the corner and a game of cards was going strong. For six hours I listened to crude stories and idle chatter and I have rarely been more bored. At the end of the eight-hour shift I was more than happy to escape back to bed.

The second night was as cold and frosty as the first. Out we went to the platform and this time it took us nearly two hours to knock a pipe down twelve feet. We rowed ashore and the gang headed for the hut, but I stayed behind, I couldn't stand another six hours of dirty jokes, so I jumped back into the dinghy and rowed out to the platform again. In the next six hours I operated the hammer by myself and drove in another thirty feet of pipe, recording it all in my notebook. At the end of the shift I went off to bed feeling a lot happier.

I was back on the survey job next morning and felt none the worse for the night's work. During the afternoon I felt a jab in my ribs, and there was the little man.

"The fellas aren't too happy about last night," he hissed out of the side of his mouth in best Mafia fashion. "If you do it again they say they are going to throw you into the lake."

I grabbed his jacket and pulled him close, until we were eyeball to eyeball. "You plan to throw me in the lake?" I queried genially.

"Not me, mate!" he hastened to assure me. "It's the other fellas."

I released him and he slunk off back to his hut. Nobody said anything that night as we rowed out to the raft but there was tension in the air. It took two and a half hours to drive the pipe down twelve feet—the clay was getting much tougher—but finally the job was done.

"Let's go ashore," said someone, but nobody moved.

"Coming, mate?" one of them asked me.

This was it, I knew, and I braced myself.

"Not me, friend!"

For a few seconds nothing was said and the atmosphere quivered with violence. It was the big Maori who made the first move.

"Let's knock the bloody thing down a bit further," he suggested. "I've had a gutsful of sitting in that hut . . ."

And knock it down we did—eighty feet that night. I can't say I ever became bosom friends with this quartet, but over the next few weeks we didn't spend another hour in the hut. Finally the "bosses" caught up with the contract and had it modified, but the men had made a lot of money before the change came.

In February 1948 I carried out the most demanding climb I ever did with Harry Ayres. The South Ridge of Mount Cook is one of the most prominent features visible on the approach to the National Park and, although a number of people had tried, no one had been successful in climbing it. Harry and I decided to have a go. We waited around in the hotel for a few days for the weather to clear and then moved up the Hooker Glacier to the small Gardiner Hut. We had another climbing pair with us, Guide Mick Sullivan and Ruth Adams, a very fit and energetic young lady. We had decided that the greatest chance of success was to bivouac high on the flanks of the mountain, so one afternoon we climbed up the Noeline Glacier in pleasant weather conditions and finally reached the summit of Nazomi at just over 9,000 feet. A ridge from Nazomi joined up to the South Ridge itself.

We established a very rough camp and spent a cold and miserable night on the hard rocks. Early in the morning the weather was still fine, so we loosened up our frozen limbs, had a light meal, packed all our gear in our rucksacks and headed down to the Endeavour Col at the start of the South Ridge. The ridge rose in three great rock steps in increasing degrees of difficulty. The first step was fairly loose rock but not too difficult, the second step was much more demanding and we had to dodge one vertical section by cutting a long line of steps on very steep ice. But we were going well. The crux of the climb came on the steep third rock step. We battled our way halfway up and reached a narrow ledge. I eased to the right around a corner and saw a deep crack at chest height. I thrust my ice axe into it and it made a secure belay. However, it was an extremely exposed position—if I looked straight down I could see the Ball Glacier thousands of feet below me.

Harry moved around into position and then with superb athleticism jumped up on the belay crack and spreadeagled on the face. He reached up but the next major crack was eighteen inches beyond his outstretched fingers. We were perched in a most dangerous situation. Getting down wouldn't be at all easy, we somehow had to reach the next horizontal crack. With my left arm firmly around the belay I thrust my right arm straight up in the air and suggested to Harry that he stand on the palm of my hand. Understandably Harry hesitated, not at all sure about how safe it would be. Then like a great cat he put a foot on my palm and threw himself upward with such speed I hardly felt his weight. His fingers were firmly in the horizontal crack and, with much wriggling and grunting, he forced his way up and disappeared out of sight. Finally his distant voice floated down. "I've got a good belay, Ed, but you'll have to climb up the rope."

I've never been all that great at climbing thin Alpine ropes hand over hand and this was no exception. Slowly I grappled my way upward, arms quivering with the strain, I had more than 20 lbs. of gear in my pack and this didn't help. Finally, to my enormous relief, I reached Harry's crack and was able to struggle over the top and reach Harry himself sitting with a good body belay. It took a few moments to get my breath back while I looked down the fantastic east face of Mount Cook. Then we carried on cautiously over a hundred feet of steepish rock until we came to the final summit cone of mixed ice and rock bands. Here we put on our crampons again and, hacking steps where necessary, made our way up the last snow face, aware of flashing reflector lights from far below at the Hermitage Hotel where everyone was watching our last energetic efforts. Then we were on the top—the South Ridge had been climbed at last.

*   *   *

1949 was an important year for the Hillary family. My sister had gone to England to complete a master's degree at London University and was about to marry an English doctor. There had been a bumper honey harvest so we were more affluent than we had ever been. It seemed a good opportunity for my father to retire and let my brother and myself start buying the business with a long-term loan. Mother was in favor of this move—she was anxious to be at her daughter's wedding and see something of Europe—also she had quite a lot of confidence in her sons. After protracted discussions my father reluctantly agreed on the basis that he retained some of the bees and all of the buildings, vehicles and property. So Rex and I began operating the business on our own account and with the minimum of equipment.

My parents duly went to England and were present at my sister's wedding. They bought a new car and we waited to hear that they were setting out on their tour of Europe, but nothing happened. By the end of the New Zealand summer, in April 1950, my brother and I had completed the honey crop and had a little money in hand. I then received a letter from my mother saying that Dad had lost all interest in going anywhere or doing anything. Would it be possible, she asked, for me to come to England and drive them round the Continent? At short notice I decided to go, and booked myself the cheapest berth available on a ship from Sydney to London. Two of my friends were leaving for Cambridge University at a similar time and we agreed to join up somewhere and do a bit of mountaineering together. I packed my climbing boots and ice axe and set off to see the world.

I crossed the Tasman Sea to Sydney in one of the TEAL flying boats and then loaded my gear on a taxi and drove from the Rose Bay Terminal to the P & O *Otranto* at the main wharves. I'd never seen an ocean liner before and just stood beside my baggage and looked aghast at the milling throng. I hadn't been there long when a large powerful man with an air of authority came up to me and brusquely enquired if I was a boarding passenger. On confirming that I was, he said, "Leave your baggage here. Go over there, fill out a form and present your tickets." I was mighty thankful for his generous help—obviously he was in charge of the wharf—although I was vaguely puzzled by the fact that he wasn't wearing a tie and he could have done with a shave. I duly returned with my documents completed.

"That's the lot," he told me. "Go aboard now and your baggage will be taken to your cabin."

What service, I thought, and with effusive utterances of thanks I turned toward the gangway.

"Hey!" shouted my impressive friend, "how about paying the porter!"

I had never paid a porter or tipped anyone before and I was horrified at having made such a simple mistake. I looked anxiously around. "Where's the porter?" I enquired.

He jabbed a huge thumb in his chest and roared, "I'm the porter, mate!"

At the end of May I drove my parents through France, Italy, Switzerland, Austria, Germany and Holland. I was resigned to being bored—who would choose to see Europe with elderly parents?—but to my astonishment I enjoyed every moment of it. Mother was completely in her element and even Dad gained a new lease on life. Restrictions on taking funds out of Britain made our finances rather tight but never desperately so. Each morning Mother purchased food in the village market—she had only a few words of the local languages but this never seemed a problem. At lunchtime we'd choose a beautiful corner off the main roads and cook a simple but adequate meal on our camp stove. We usually ate and slept in cheap pensions but sometimes we'd treat ourselves to a meal at a good restaurant. Everything was made easier by the glorious spring weather, I cannot remember a single day of rain. Back in London I made the usual pilgrimage to Westminster Abbey. The royal tombs made history come alive for me and so did a hundred other relics of a mighty past. As a citizen of a new country with little history I felt I was being accepted back into the ancestral fold—it gave me an astonishingly warm feeling. In those days, like most of my fellow New Zealanders, I was British first and a New Zealander second. But it wasn't long before we thrust ourselves firmly out of the family nest.

It was soon time to leave on my last project—a climbing trip to Austria and Switzerland with two fellow New Zealanders, Cecil Segedin and Bruce Morton. Cool beers on hand at the end of a climb were one advantage the Stubai Alps offered over their more rugged New Zealand counterparts, but we could not claim to have been physically or technically extended to any great extent in Austria. We hoped for better things in Switzerland. We started at Grindelwald under the great North Face of the Eiger. Cecil Segedin had to return to London but was very keen to climb the Jungfrau before his departure. Access to the Jungfrau is made a great deal easier by the tunnel and train that go straight through the center of the mountain and emerge at the Jungfraujoch station. We climbed the Jungfrau with considerable ease and then deposited Cecil in the railway station for his journey back to Cambridge. Bruce and I plunged down the five miles of the Aletsch Glacier to the Concordia Hut which was occupied by a number of Swiss climbers. One handsome Swiss girl asked what I thought of Switzerland and I was appropriately enthusiastic, although I'd only been there three days.

"Yes," she agreed, "Switzerland is the most beautiful country in the world."

"You must have been to many other countries?" I questioned.

"No," she said. "Not any! But Switzerland is the most beautiful."

Ho hum! I thought.

In two successive days we climbed the Finsteraarhorn and the Mönch and then had a day off in bad weather. As a final climb in this area we planned to traverse over to the Dreieckhorn (12,500 feet) and then climb the higher Aletschhorn (13,784 feet). We left the hut at 3 a.m. and reached the summit of the Dreieckhorn at 8 a.m. after some pleasant climbing but no great difficulty. Ahead of us stretched two miles of ridge toward the Aletschhorn and we cramponed along this with considerable speed. Ahead of us on the summit was a friendly middle-aged Englishman and his Swiss guide who had come up the much faster direct route. The rather grumpy guide asked us which route we planned to use on the way down and we said the direct route. At which he grimaced and said, "You must go down first." When we reached the long rib dropping to the glacier we understood why he was so anxious for us to lead down. Showers of rocks came belting down behind us and we only reached the glacier unharmed by sheer good luck. We were on the glacier by two o'clock and, after a certain amount of dodging amongst the crevasses, we came to easier going and were soon back at the Concordia Hut. To our astonishment we were cheered resoundingly by the hut staff who said they had been able to watch us every foot of our climb.

Despite our big day we decided to return to the valley, a short walk of a couple of hours. We had just finished packing and paying our bill when I noticed the grumpy guide coming in the door. I looked around for the Englishman but there was no sign of him.

"Where is your client?" I asked the guide.

"Down a crevasse!" he told me, then reluctantly went on to explain. While crossing an ice bridge it had collapsed and the guide who was on safe ground literally lowered the Englishman into the depths until he was lodged on a snow ledge. The guide hadn't been able to pull him out so had left him there while he hurried off for assistance. A party of carpenters, bricklayers and guides was quickly assembled and, laden with ropes, blankets and a sledge, they set off up the glacier. I had offered our services only to have them gruffly declined.

After the rescue party had departed Bruce and I decided we couldn't go down the valley and leave a compatriot in a crevasse—maybe the chap would appreciate talking to another English-speaking person? So, despite our rebuff, we set off after the team and soon caught up to them. We were approaching a group of big crevasses at the foot of the ridge and, as the trail was now fairly obvious, Bruce and I raced ahead. The unfortunate victim had been down the crevasse for several hours and I didn't know what to expect as I crawled carefully up to the shattered ice bridge—blood and injuries, possibly even death from exposure? I poked my head over the edge and looked down. A small neatly dressed figure with a hat on his head was stamping around on a snow bridge fifty feet below and swinging his arms across his body to keep warm. I shouted a welcome and in formal fashion he expressed his pleasure at seeing me.

He was perfectly all right he said, but rather chilly. The rescue team was very expert! One of the men was lowered and the Englishman was soon hoisted out on three ropes, dragged down the glacier on the sledge and assisted into the hut. Next morning, although stiff and sore, he was not much the worse for his adventure. When we departed, his grumpy guide actually waved us good-bye.

Time was running out, but we had an enjoyable few days in the Zermatt area. We climbed the formidable Lyskamm and the beautiful Weisshorn, but our plans to climb the Matterhorn were frustrated by two days of heavy snow. At first we had found the Swiss guides we met rather non-cooperative and arrogant toward amateur climbers and most of them had never heard of New Zealand. But when we got to know them, and they realized we were not completely hopeless technically, they became much more friendly. It was a great experience for us in Switzerland and Austria, although the climbing we did bore little relationship to the problems we regarded as normal in our native New Zealand.

By chance I sailed for New Zealand on the *Otranto* and in virtually the same six-berth cabin. I was back just in time for the beginning of the honey season.

George Lowe was a schoolteacher who spent the summer holidays as a junior guide in the Southern Alps. Even though we didn't climb together for some time, we became good friends and this was encour-aged by the fact that George's father was an orchardist, but also had a thriving beekeeping business. In 1950, George set off the spark that finally got us both to the Himalayas. We were walking down the Tasman Glacier together when George suddenly said, "Have you ever thought of going to the Himalayas, Ed?" I admitted that the thought had certainly entered my mind, so we decided we would try and see what we could do about it.

Later George told me that another formidable group of New Zealand climbers had plans to go to the Himalayas and they had invited him too. On his suggestion, they invited me along as well. The plans were very ambitious with an attempt either on Everest or on Kangchenjunga and a team of ten or more climbers. But one by one the members dropped out due to lack of finance and in the end there were only four of us left— Earle Riddiford, Ed Cotter, George Lowe and myself and we were operating on the minimum of finance. As our major objective we chose the peak Mukut Parbat at 23,760 feet in the Garhwal Himalaya.

We decided to seek advice from an expert. Dr. Noel Odell had been on Everest in 1924, 1933 and 1936 and was the last man to see Mallory and Irvine alive in 1924. He was spending his retirement years in Otago University, so we wrote to him and he was quite dogmatic. We didn't need special equipment but should just take exactly what we used in New Zealand, an ordinary Alpine tent and the clothing we wore in the Southern Alps. We were used to wild weather and we wouldn't need any expensive equipment at all and, of course, we'd be completely at home in the snow and ice. Much of his advice was sound but a lot of it wasn't. It seemed much colder at 20,000 feet than at home and our boots in particular were quite inadequate.

Earle Riddiford regarded himself as the expedition leader and he certainly organized permission from the Indian government. But George and I didn't accept him as such in the field. We were the lead pair, we felt, and confident of our ability. We were very democratic in our decision-making and we had many arguments about plans and policy. A few other New Zealanders had been to the Himalayas before and done quite well, but we were the first all–New Zealand team and keen to make our mark. In January 1951 we had a test run on home ground, an attempt on the formidable unclimbed Maximilian Ridge of Mount Elie de Beaumont, regarded as perhaps the most difficult and remote unclimbed ridge in the Southern Alps. Our four-man Himalayan team was joined by an experienced climber friend, Bill Beaven, and, carrying loads of 70 lbs. or more (I always seemed to have a good deal more), we back-packed up the Tasman Glacier, planning to spend the night at the Malte Brun Hut. As I approached the foot of the gully running several hundred feet up to the hut I was met by a young man who came bounding down to meet me and offered to carry my load up to the hut. No one had ever offered to carry my load before, but it was too good an offer to refuse. I handed my pack over and saw his legs buckle slightly at the knees. Although I didn't know it at the time, he was Fred Hollows who became a famous eye specialist, helping the blind in many third world countries—obviously he started his helpful attitude early in life.

Next morning we climbed up the head of the Tasman Glacier, crossed the Tasman Saddle, sidled over the head of the Murchison Glacier and reached the Whymper Saddle which few if any climbers had crossed before. We rested on the saddle and looked with considerable concern down the steep 3,000 feet to the floor of the Whymper Glacier. How we managed to climb down with our 70-lb. loads I don't quite know but ultimately we did reach the glacier and moved down to a pleasant campsite behind the moraine wall. It had been an extremely arduous day, one of the toughest I could remember. Our objective was the Burton Glacier which meant crossing the Maximilian Ridge which no one had ever done before. We made a number of reconnaissance climbs without success and retreated down to a flat shingle bed when the rain set in. For two days it poured and for the five of us in a 7-foot-by-7-foot tent it was the height of discomfort. When it cleared, George Lowe, Earle Riddiford and I, without much optimism, did another stiff climb up steep slopes toward the Maximilian Ridge and across a broad snow basin. To our delight a pass at 6,400 feet did exist, although not a particularly easy one. We descended cautiously back to our camp and then carried half loads up to the pass to ease our burden for the next day. In the morning we climbed up the difficult smooth rock, picked up the rest of our loads and grunted our way down into the next valley. We moved up valley and finally came to the large bivouac rock that had been discovered by a party exploring from another direction. It was a great campsite and, although we had two wet days, we kept warm and dry. When the weather permitted we did a reconnaissance up the ragged Burton Glacier and made the first ascent of a modest virgin peak.

It was a clear night and we made our preparations for our big climb. We knew it would be a long day so we left at 1 a.m. George Lowe and I climbed together and Earle Riddiford and Ed Cotter followed along behind. (Bill Beaven had developed chicken pox so was out of action.) By 7 a.m. we had ascended the long glacier again, climbed along the crest of the subsidiary ridge and reached the summit of the virgin peak. Cramponing along steep slopes off the peak we were soon down on an extensive snowfield. We turned one large crevasse on the right under the great precipices of Elie de Beaumont and then carried on up the steepening snowfield. By 9 a.m. we reached the extremely impressive Maximilian Ridge. Above us was a prominent rock step and we were at 9,000 feet but still a long way from the summit.

The rock step proved a considerable problem. Two-thirds of the way up it became smooth and overhanging in places. We made several unsuccessful attempts to climb this direct; then George Lowe moved out to the left onto the Whymper Face and cut a long line of steps up the top hundred feet of this great steep slope to regain the ridge above the step. From here on George mostly led along the spectacular ridge. Our nylon rope was a hundred feet long and this proved a blessing. Both on the face and the rocks above we were able to run out the full length and, largely by good luck, get excellent belay positions at approximately this interval.

From the top of the step we looked along a level narrow corniced ice ridge to the foot of a rock ridge, rising abruptly for 600 to 700 feet to the Anna Plateau. The latter section looked grim, but having gone so far I think the feeling was that we would get up somehow. George Lowe cut steps along the level ridge, and eventually both ropes moved on to the rocks. From now on it was an exhilarating climb on rock that was steep and exposed but beautiful stuff to climb. The weather was perfect and the rocks warm. The ridge rose in a series of six big steps, with various smaller towers. Each step hid what lay ahead. The crests of the second, third and fourth steps were ice-covered and gave George plenty of work with the axe. The rather airy-fairy work along these crests took us back to the days before crampons. It was slow going and we were moving one at a time. The fifth step was something of a problem and was turned on the Burton Face, with mixed climbing up snow and rock to regain the crest above. George surmounted the last tower and let out a glad shout. The way was clear up an ice ridge to the plateau. Both left and right we were face-to-face with great ice cliffs and the ridge sneaked up through them to the Anna Plateau with spectacular views down on the ice slopes below the Lendenfeld Saddle. We were on the ice plateau at 2 p.m. after the most completely enjoyable climb any of us had experienced. Another hour up the standard route took us to the summit and we had been climbing hard for fourteen hours.

George Lowe had performed magnificently on this climb, as indeed had everyone. Earle Riddiford and Ed Cotter traversed the mountain in difficult conditions to rejoin Bill Beaven at the rock bivouac. I was now showing signs of chicken pox that I had picked up from Bill, so George and I descended the abrupt slopes to the Tasman Glacier and finally spent the night in the Malte Brun Hut. Certainly we felt that after this magnificent climb we were ready for our Himalayan journey.

With thirty-four packing cases of food and equipment we left New Zealand at the beginning of May 1951 by flying boat to Sydney, ship to Colombo, and train for day after day through Madras and Calcutta and up the valley of the Ganges. Then we followed a windy road up to Ranikhet in the foothills of the Himalayas. Here we met our four Sherpa porters. Pasang Dawa Lama, Thondup, Nima and Tenzing were just as we expected Sherpas to be—small, cheerful and incredibly tough. We also employed thirty local porters to help with the loads lower down and then walked for ten days over rivers and 10,000-foot passes. The view from the Kuari Pass at 12,400 feet was stupendous. We could see mighty giants like Nanda Devi, Dhaulagiri, Gauri Parbat and Nilkanta—all well known to us from our reading. We arrived at the sacred shrine of Badrinath and were surrounded by a multitude of pilgrims, mostly devout older people who were making this important journey toward the end of their lives. Here we paid off our porters and recruited some of the hardier mountain men and headed up toward the border.

We established our Base Camp at 17,000 feet on the Shamro Glacier on a carpet of mountain flowers, a pleasant grassy place with a small stream of fresh water. Then George Lowe, Ed Cotter and I started establishing a route toward Mukut Parbat which loomed formidably above us. I don't know where Earle Riddiford was at this time—he often seemed to disappear on his own agenda. Blocking the Shamro valley was a large icefall and on the first fine day we made our way up between crevasses and seracs to reach the top of it. Ahead of us we could see a suitable site for our next camp at 19,000 feet. Before returning we climbed a nearby peak of 20,330 feet and felt a sense of excitement on reaching the summit of our first 20,000 footer.

Two days later we set off to establish Camp II on Mukut Parbat. Heavily laden with gear, we found the heat very trying as we climbed the icefall and noted where an ice avalanche had swept over our previous tracks. Plugging slowly along we reached the head of the glacier and then cut steps up a steep slope onto a rock and snow saddle between the Shamro and West Kamet Glaciers. Here there was an excellent campsite, well protected from the wind, with a good flat position for our tents. Our altitude was now 19,000 feet and we had wonderful views of mountains and valley on all sides. We sent the Sherpas back down to Camp I for the night and we were soon driven into our tents by the cold.

The morning sun hit our camp at 8 a.m. and made life pleasant again. Above us was a great icefall split by enormous crevasses and ugly ice cliffs. Somehow we had to get through this icefall to reach the summit ridge of Mukut Parbat. Ed Cotter and I set off on a reconnaissance and were able to make a safe route through the lower portion before the heat of the sun and tiredness from our previous day of heavy backpacking sent us scampering back to camp. We returned to the attack two hours earlier next morning. It was particularly cold and we pulled on all the clothing we had. Our bodies kept reasonably warm but our feet gave us a lot of trouble. None of us had particularly effective boots and the higher we went the more we suffered. On the steep upper slopes George and I took turns at chipping a safe stairway in the hard frozen snow. Winding in and out among the giant crevasses and great pinnacles of ice, we were always seeking a safe route while suffering agonies with our feet. Just before eight o'clock we managed to cross out to the left to an ice shelf shining in the rays of the early morning sun. With cries of thankfulness we sat down, took off our boots and massaged our feet. It was at least an hour before we could continue with safety and comfort.

We next crossed several snow bridges over wide crevasses, and entered a large snow basin before swinging to the right through a particularly broken area. A very shaky snow bridge was crossed with careful belaying of the rope around a well-sunk ice axe shaft. We cut up a steep ice slope and emerged on a snowy saddle at over 21,000 feet, from which we could look straight out onto the high plateau and the barren mountains of Tibet, while above us towered the great ridge of Mukut Parbat. Our reconnaissance had been successful and the problem of the icefall had been solved.

We established Camp III on an ice shelf just under the Tibetan Col. The 11th July dawned fine but very cold, but with our inadequate footwear we were afraid of frostbite and didn't dare leave our tents until the sun reached us at 8 a.m. Then we roped up—Earle, Ed and Pasang on one rope, George and myself on another. We climbed our ice steps onto the col and were once again greeted by a freezing wind. George forced a fine route through deep cold powder snow up a steep face and finally onto the main ridge of Mukut Parbat. The snow on the ridge was frozen hard and gave an excellent grip to our crampons but the strong wind made conditions very unpleasant. At 22,500 feet George and I reached a rocky outcrop where we could shelter from the wind. George was having a lot of trouble with his feet again and mine didn't feel too comfortable, so we cut a couple of seats in the icy slope, tied ourselves securely to a belay, and removed our boots to massage our feet back to life. The others were quite a long way behind but they climbed up to us and then, a little to our surprise, carried on through.

When our feet had recovered George and I moved on again, all set to get to grips with the upper part of the mountain. We crossed an icy bump and saw the ridge narrowed appreciably and dropped away in a shallow dip before sweeping up again toward the summit. Perched in the dip, cutting steps in hard ice, was Earle and his progress was very slow indeed. George and I waited, getting colder and colder. We were so accustomed to being the leading pair that we felt quite frustrated. Earle was climbing very slowly but we knew there was no way he would allow us to pass him, he had that sort of aggressive determination. George and I had a brief discussion. The other team was not as fit as we were and we frankly doubted if they would have time to lead the apparent difficulties of the ice ridge and reach the summit before dark—and meanwhile we would get mighty cold waiting behind them. Shouting across the wind, the two parties debated the matter. It was now after midday. The question was whether we should retreat now while still fresh and return to the attack tomorrow? In the end, George and I decided to return, while the others went on. That was our mistake.

Earle was far from physically robust but he displayed his remarkable determination and willpower. He carried on relentlessly and, when he weakened, Pasang took the lead. They reached the summit at a quarter to six in the dim evening light. We were greatly worried when darkness fell and there was no sign of the team. Finally, at 9 p.m. it was pitch dark and we heard their voices and welcomed them into our camp, massaging their cold hands and feet and warming them up with hot drinks. They had certainly achieved a remarkable effort.

In deteriorating weather, we retreated off the mountain and back to Badrinath for a period of rest. There was mail waiting for us and some interesting news. Our financial problems were eased when Earle received a substantial draft from one of his relations and generously offered to put it toward our meager expedition funds. And someone had sent a cutting from a London newspaper saying that the famous British explorer Eric Shipton was to lead a reconnaissance party through Nepal to the south side of Everest in a few months' time. What a trip to be on, we all thought.

After a few days in Badrinath I became very restless. I wrote in my diary: "Boredom setting in! I can't sit around writing and resting with the same ease as George and Earle. My main desire is to get back up and climb a few peaks and then hurry home to the bees." Earle said he was not feeling well, so we left him there and the rest of us headed back to the Shamro Glacier. That first night we weren't in the best of moods as we cleared a site for our tents. A huge rock was blocking the way and I braced myself to move it. "Don't bother," said George grumpily, "I've tried to move it and can't. I don't imagine you can!" I looked at him in surprise, then grabbed the rock and heaved it out of the way. I was prepared to concede that George was better than me at many things, but brute strength wasn't one of them.

We had a delightful time up the Shamro Glacier. Not having Earle there seemed to make everything so much more relaxed. We made five more new ascents, the highest being 22,180 feet, before returning to Badrinath very pleased with our total of seven new peaks, as we headed back in pouring rain over flooded rivers and slippery tracks to the hill station of Ranikhet.

When I read the newspaper article in Badrinath saying that Eric Shipton was taking an expedition to the south side of Mount Everest I cheekily wrote a letter to him suggesting that a couple of the members of our expedition would be very well acclimatized and, being excellent snow and ice climbers, we could make a substantial contribution to his team. Unbeknownst to me Harry Stevenson, the President of the New Zealand Alpine Club, also wrote to London recommending that one or more members of our team should join Shipton's party. All the same we were totally amazed when we arrived at our small hotel in Ranikhet to find among a sizable batch of letters waiting for us a flimsy envelope formally addressed to the New Zealand Garhwal Expedition—from Eric Shipton himself. It was his approval "for any two of you to join my party if you can get permission to enter Nepal, bringing own food and supplies." This was the chance of a lifetime. But which two would it be?

I don't think there was much doubt that George Lowe and I were the strongest climbers in the team. I had a little money remaining, but George had nothing left. Earle Riddiford, on the other hand, had been sent some funds by a relative, supposedly for expedition use. As the expedition was now over, he claimed this for himself. Also Earle had persisted with the climb of our highest summit, Mukut Parbat (23,760 feet), and finally got to the top. So there was some justification for his arguments that he should go to join Shipton. But there was a great deal of acrimonious discussion before it was reluctantly agreed that Earle and I should accept the invitation. I can still see George's accusing glare as we drove away in the bus. As seems often the case nowadays, the final decision as to who ultimately goes to Mount Everest is purely a question of money.

I respected Earle's dogged determination but I can't say that I actually liked him—none of us did. On no occasion did I share a climbing rope with Earle and I had no wish to do so. But when it came to organizing things we got on reasonably well together. He had his particular skills and I had mine. Before he died Earle was successful in achieving his greatest ambition, purchasing back the huge Riddiford sheep station established by his forebears but later sold by the family. Earle had firm objectives and didn't give up easily.

I had always regarded Eric Shipton as a heroic figure. He was a master of all the skills that any New Zealand mountaineer had to develop: he had explored remote areas; carried heavy loads over difficult and often untouched passes; and battled turbulent rivers and fierce ridges in magnificent wilderness areas. The chance not only to meet him, but actually be part of his team on a reconnaissance of the south side of Everest was an unbelievable opportunity. The Everest massif straddles the border of Tibet and Nepal. It is possible to stand on the summit with one foot in Nepal and the other in Tibet. Traditionally Everest had been attempted from the north, the Tibetan side. This was because the high mountain kingdom of Nepal was closed to westerners and, from what little was known about the unexplored south side of Everest, it seemed to be a tangled mass of impossibly steep peaks shielding the world's highest mountain. Then in September 1949, Communist China invaded Tibet, the Red Army pouring in waves across the border to occupy vast tracts in the east, this Chinese "liberation" putting the old route to Everest out of bounds to all western climbers for three decades.

In May 1951, a young British climber, Michael Ward, wrote to the Himalayan Committee (a joint committee of the Royal Geographical Society and the Alpine Club which handled all seven British expeditions to Everest between the world wars) suggesting a reconnaissance that autumn to the southwestern flank of Everest. Aerial pictures revealed little of Everest's unique topography. The Committee agreed and Shipton, a veteran of the 1933, 1935, 1936, 1938 expeditions, was asked to be leader. Shipton was of two minds. He was just ten days back from a diplomatic posting in China and looking forward to enjoying an English summer with his family, free from the suspicion, hatred and fear that long characterized life in Kunming under Communist rule. But his Sherpa friends on previous trips to Everest had always waxed lyrical about the beauty of their Solu Khumbu homeland on the other side of the mountain and Shipton couldn't resist the challenge of seeking a route from the southwest.

Not that he held out much hope for success. He deemed it "highly improbable" that an alternative accessible approach to the roof of the world existed. "No experienced mountaineer," he wrote at the time, "can be optimistic about the chances of finding a way up any great Himalayan peak. The vast scale on which these giants are built greatly increases the likelihood of the climber being faced by sheer impossibility—an unclimbable wall, slopes dominated by hanging glaciers, or avalanche-swept couloirs." He was particularly gloomy about the Western Cwm. This spectacular hidden valley, a freak of mountain architecture, was first glimpsed by the great English climber, George Leigh Mallory, while climbing up to the Lho La in 1922 and Shipton put their chances of finding a practicable route up it to the summit at about thirty to one.

Shipton had told us to bring our own food, so Earle Riddiford and I, plus two of our Sherpas, Pasang Dawa Lama and Nima, traveled in extremely uncomfortable buses and trains down to Lucknow to stock up. Unfortunately, no food suitable for the high mountains was available, so we bought a variety of canned goods at considerable cost and we made up many loads of these. It was extremely hot in Lucknow— 37°C in the shade—and we found it very trying after our months in the Himalayas. In the evening Earle and I were invited to visit a gentleman's club, once the sole preserve of the British Raj, but now occupied by upper-class Indian army officers and senior officials. It was a sadly run-down building, although there were still signs of its original grandeur.

But our hosts were friendly and generous beyond belief to a couple of rough New Zealand climbers who were heading off to Mount Everest. Standing in the center of the bar was a lonely bottle of Scotch whisky waiting to be opened on our arrival. With thirty or forty members present we only had a sip each, but as I was rather abstemious in those days, it was sufficient for me and I greatly appreciated the honor they were doing us. Forty years later we visited many such clubs in India, but they were now impressively decorated and there was food and spirits in abundance.

Then it was back on board a train across the Gangetic valley and a fearful struggle with our vast quantities of luggage which Earle and I and our two Sherpas ruthlessly manhandled into crowded second-class carriages. For two days we rattled our way to the east and the further we went the more vigorous the monsoon rains became. We finally reached the railhead at Jogbani in the evening darkness and relayed our loads across to the empty verandah of a dakh bungalow which at least gave us protection from the rain. Huge mosquitoes harassed us all night and we had little sleep and masses of bumps on our arms and faces.

In the morning we contacted Mr. Law, a genial Scottish engineer who was supervising a large jute mill, and he was able to tell us that Shipton and his party were five days' ahead. He gave us his frank opinion that the renewal of the monsoon would make traveling very difficult for us. There was quite a clearance in the weather during the day and we saw a snowy summit far to the north. Our friend assured us it was Mount Everest itself, although we found this a little hard to believe. Mr. Law recommended we charter a large ex–Second World War four-wheel-drive American truck to cover the forty miles to the village of Dharan, so we loaded everything aboard and struggled for mile after mile along an extremely soggy track. After about twenty miles we came to a bridge across a small stream with boggy sections of road on either side. Despite successive charges, the driver was unable to get through and he advised us that we would have to unload the truck and carry all our supplies to the other side before it would have any chance of crossing.

The four of us started relaying the loads with mud halfway up our calves. A group of young men drifted up to watch and I tried to employ them to help us with the carrying, but they refused to undertake such arduous work. One particularly objectionable youth perched on the bridge railing and cracked many jokes at our efforts which brought roars of laughter from his companions. He chose to do this once too often. As I was trudging over with a particularly heavy load, I contrived to give him a hearty push off the railing and sent him floundering into the stream below. From then on a deathly silence prevailed as we completed our ferrying. A mighty charge from the empty truck got it safely through, we reloaded and carried on to Dharan.

Here we paid off our driver and managed to employ twenty porters, appointing Pasang our sirdar. Over the next two days we crossed two high ridges and descended into the valley of the Arun river. Determined to catch up to Shipton's party we pushed our way up the river, having to cross a number of flooded side streams en route. Earle and I had much experience of crossing mountain rivers in New Zealand and we ushered our laden porters over without too much trouble. But then we came to a mighty stream, 200 yards across and sweeping down with great vigor. Thirty local porters with their own extremely heavy loads on the way to market were squatting together beside the bank obviously too afraid to cross. But we were not prepared to wait for the river to go down, so some New Zealand expertise was called for.

Earle and I removed our packs and left them with our two Sherpas. Then we each grasped both our ice axes firmly and moved into the water with the lighter Earle upriver and me behind with my feet firmly on the bottom. Wave after wave swept past us, the water was up to our waists as we shuffled slowly across. I was protected from the current by Earle's body who was sometimes swept off his feet, only to be supported by my shoulder. It was an exhilarating experience and we were laughing with pleasure as we emerged on the far bank. Nearby was a cluster of young trees and with my ice axe I hacked out a bough about eight feet long. We held the long pole in the line of the speeding water and helped by its extra weight and support we made an easier return trip to our Sherpas and porters. Then with five or six laden porters clinging to the tree trunk we crossed the wide stream with ease. Backward and forward we went and when we made our final crossing we realized there were no local porters remaining on the lower bank. Unbeknownst to us they had joined our ferry service to get themselves safely over. So we had brought fifty porters over rather than twenty but as we had hardly noticed the extra numbers we just laughed and wished them well.

Several hours further up the river our sirdar Pasang obtained the information that Shipton's party were probably in the village of Dingla high up the great hillside on the other bank of the river. The Arun was a mighty river swollen with monsoon rains, out of our fording league. It could only be crossed by boat. We were directed to the riverbank where half a dozen long dugout canoes were parked with a dozen tough-looking Nepalis sheltering under a woven bamboo matting. After some negotiation they agreed to take us across, so with considerable trepidation we knelt inside their unstable craft and were swept out into the violent current. Our two boatmen paddled like crazy and soon we were out in the middle of the river but we were fast approaching a mighty rapid which would have quickly swamped us. To my astonishment the front paddler suddenly jumped over the side of the boat and stood in water less than a foot deep. He was clearly on a shingle bar and he steadily dragged the dugout upriver for 400 or 500 yards. Then he leaped in again and some furious paddling carried us across the second great current safely to the far shore. Our paddlers were brave men indeed and certainly earned their modest pay.

Our Sherpas and porters arrived rather shaken by the experience and needed a rest on the bank before they could carry on. Earle and I decided to head off up the hill as quickly as possible in order, we hoped, to meet up with Shipton's party at Dingla. Carrying only our sleeping bags and personal gear, we raced up the hill for several thousand feet until we were high above the river and at the outskirts of Dingla were delighted to hear that some sahibs were still there. We were directed to one of the larger houses and I led the way up the dark stairs to emerge into a dimly lit upper floor. A strongly built man with a short grizzled beard turned toward me with a welcoming smile and I knew I was meeting Eric Shipton for the first time.

I believe that Eric and I had an instant empathy with one another. Certainly he treated me as an energetic younger brother and was happy to use my vigor and energy to the full. I in turn respected his great experience and knowledge and was pleased to respond when he had anything he wanted me to do. Eric's companions were an interesting combination. There was the veteran Bill Murray who was widely experienced in climbing ice gullies in Scotland and who had been the leader of the first Scottish expedition to the Himalayas the previous year; there was Dr. Michael Ward with an easy manner and a good record of rock climbs; and there was the fifteen-stone Tom Bourdillon, a formidable climber on British rock and in the European Alps. And finally there was their sirdar, Angtharkay Sherpa, probably the most renowned Sherpa sirdar and climber in his day. Small and compact with a fiery enthusiasm Angtharkay had great vitality and I warmed to him immediately.

Earle Riddiford on the other hand was rather cool to both Shipton and Angtharkay. Earle, of course, was a champion of our sirdar, Pasang Dawa Lama, who had played an important role in getting Earle to the top of Mukut Parbat. Earle was constantly singing Pasang's praises and even suggested he should be co-sirdar with Angtharkay, a suggestion that Eric ignored. Earle's praise for Pasang knew no end and he even suggested his technical climbing standard equaled that of my climbing mentor in New Zealand, the great Harry Ayres. This was too much for me and I told Earle so. In rage he warned me that if I made another criticism of Pasang he would knock me down. I looked at the rather weedy Earle in astonishment and in true schoolboy fashion said, "You and what army?" And that pretty much finished the discussion and the topic.

Shipton was having great difficulty in getting porters, due to the reluctance of local people to travel in the miserable monsoon conditions. But finally all was ready. With overladen porters we slowly battled our way across rain-sodden ridges and down to wild rivers with unstable bridges. The blood-sucking leeches were terrible and we became covered with bleeding and sometimes infected sores. We reached the large remote village of Bung and had many curious stares from the tough Rai people who had never seen foreigners before. Many years later we built a clinic and a school in Bung. Then it was up and up over a jagged ridge past Sherpa houses and monasteries with icy snow on the narrow passes, to plunge down the other side into the immense cleft of the Inukhu valley and, in some trepidation, cross the shaky bridge spanning the narrow rocky gorge over the tumbling river. Thirty years later we financed a steel suspension bridge over this river in the same location.

As always in Nepal it was up again forever, over a 10,000-foot mountain pass, to camp in the very small village of Pangkongma. Now we were entering the great Dudh Kosi valley, the entrance to the Mount Everest region and, almost as if a light had been switched off, on 21st September the monsoon rain stopped and we had superb views of Everest, Lhotse, and Cho Oyu. Our hearts thumped in our chests as we approached the home of the Sherpas and the highest mountains on earth.

Shipton was renowned for his abstemious habits as far as food and drink were concerned, so the party had appreciated the canned food Earle and I had purchased in Lucknow. The very large Tom Bourdillon suffered particularly from our short rations and, when interviewed by the BBC back in England about expedition food, he made the significant comment: "The main thing about expedition food is that there should be some!" It wasn't all bad. As we moved up the spectacular Dudh Kosi valley, following the narrow track through the forests high above the river, we were able to supplement Eric's regime in the villages through which we passed. At Phakding we tucked into new potatoes, green peas, pumpkin and lamb chops, crawling into our sleeping bags that night contented and physically replete.

As we moved on through Sherpa village after Sherpa village we were warmly welcomed by the local people to whom Shipton and Angtharkay were famous characters. We climbed slowly up the formidable hill to the main Khumbu village of Namche Bazaar. Over several days we paid off our low-altitude porters and recruited some tough and well-clad local Sherpas to carry our supplies to the higher altitudes. Our journey up to the foot of Mount Everest was spectacular in the extreme. Lining the valley were the great spires of Ama Dablam, Kangtega and Tamserku and always in front of us the great triangle of Everest with its long plume of snow, peeping above the mighty Nuptse wall. I had never seen anything like it before.

We moved up the Khumbu Glacier in frequent snow showers and finally established our Base Camp in a lateral trough at 17,500 feet where Everest and Nuptse seemed to lean over our heads. On our right was a great icefall grinding down from the Western Cwm on the south side of Everest. It looked an impossible approach from this direction.

Eric Shipton had earlier confided his doubts that we would find a satisfactory route up the south side of Everest. But he was very philosophical about this and suggested that, if his suspicions proved correct, then the main purpose of the reconnaissance would have been completed and we could head off and explore the untouched mountains to both the east and west of Everest—something that really appealed to him and also to me.

Shipton invited me to join him on a reconnaissance of a prominent ridge on the peak Pumori. Maybe from there, he suggested, we would be able to see if any practical route existed up Everest. The two of us crossed over the moraine to the bottom of the ridge and climbed slowly upward, first to 19,000 feet and then up steeper rock and ice to nearly 20,000 feet. Puffing a little from the altitude we turned and looked toward the Khumbu Icefall and the Western Cwm. Our eyes swept up the tumbled icefall into the cwm, and up the steep slopes to the South Col. Overcome with amazement, we realized that Eric's presuppositions were no longer credible—a formidable but potential route did indeed exist up the mountain from this side.

Bubbling with excitement, we returned to our Base Camp on the near side of the Khumbu Glacier to convey this news to our companions. We were ill-equipped to go very high on Everest but at least we could try to solve the immediate challenging problem of the icefall. With determination we attacked the tumbled and shifting ruin of crevasses and great ice blocks still covered deeply in monsoon snow. We made considerable height in very dangerous conditions until Earle was caught in an avalanche and almost swept to his death, at which point we decided to retreat until the snow conditions improved.

On 23rd October Eric Shipton and I, with two Sherpas, tackled the icefall again. The snow conditions were very much safer but other problems had developed. The icefall had become shattered and unstable and a very shaky "atom bomb" area had developed. We picked our way carefully across and made considerable height until time ran out and we had to turn back to camp. The other members of the team had now joined us so next morning we climbed rapidly up our established route. Not without trepidation we crossed the ice blocks and crevasses of the slowly subsiding area and hacked our way in and out amongst great ice pinnacles. Tom Bourdillon did a fine lead up the corniced upper lip of a large crevasse and we followed after him to emerge on a long snowy shelf. Ahead we could see a deep and narrow valley sweeping up away from us. At the head of it was the great peak of Lhotse. With great excitement we realized we were on the threshold of the Western Cwm—the icefall was below us. It was time for us to retreat back to civilization and we split into various groups and all crossed tough and unexplored country to make our way back to Kathmandu. We were confident that we had solved the problem of Everest from the south and that next year we would return well equipped to tackle the upper part of the mountain.

Earle Riddiford and I were the first to arrive back in Kathmandu and were greatly impressed by this ancient city with its beautiful temples and friendly people. We were warmly welcomed by the British Ambassador, Sir Christopher Summerhayes, who first congratulated us on having found a new route up Everest and then carried on, to our horror, to say that it had been reported that the Swiss had obtained permission for two attempts on the mountain the following year, 1952. Our dreams were shattered. Now all we could do was wait to see what the Swiss achieved.

5

WAITING FOR EVEREST

THE JOINT HIMALAYAN COMMITTEE OF THE ROYAL GEOGRAPHICAL Society and the Alpine Club reacted to the setback to their plans with remarkable courage. They had permission for a British attempt on Everest in 1953 and they decided that they must go ahead with their preparations as though the Swiss expeditions, competent though they would be, would not in fact be successful. The Committee decided, therefore, to send an expedition in 1952 to Cho Oyu, a massive peak to the west of Everest and use it for experiments with oxygen equipment and investigations of high-altitude physiology. Eric Shipton was invited to lead the expedition and it was a thrill for me when he asked me to join the team. At my suggestion he had invited George Lowe, which gave me much pleasure.

Using Shipton's typical and slightly erratic approach, we followed a route into Khumbu that none of us had been on before. From the railhead at Jogbani, we walked across the sandy plains to Chisapani at the foot of the hills. Then our way led upward to Okhaldunga, along high wooded ridges and finally up the Dudh Kosi river to Namche Bazaar. The weather was excellent and we had superb views of Everest and Cho Oyu. We reconnoitered Cho Oyu from the Thami valley and decided that the southern side of the mountain was rather difficult. But the previous year Murray and Bourdillon had crossed the 19,050-foot Nangpa La into Tibet and reported that the approach to Cho Oyu from the Kyetrak Glacier seemed to offer a potential route and this clearly needed a reconnaissance. We established our Base Camp in the grazing ground of Lunak at 17,000 feet and a cold and desolate place it proved to be. Our physiologist Dr. Griffith Pugh took blood samples from us all and tested our percentage of hemoglobin. A high rate of hemoglobin was believed to indicate that the individual was well acclimatized. It was no surprise to George and myself when our reading came out appreciably the highest. We were clearly the fittest couple, so Eric asked us to take six days' food and cross the Nangpa La to reconnoiter the southern approaches to Cho Oyu.

On 24th April we headed up valley with three Sherpas. There was deep soft snow and frequent storms as we crossed over the Nangpa La and made to the right up the Kyetrak Glacier. We turned a corner and saw a subsidiary rock spur which joined onto the main snow-covered ridge leading up on to the face of the mountain. It certainly had all the signs of a potential route. George and I were feeling particularly strong so, before returning to the others, we decided to climb one of the fine snow peaks to the west of the Nangpa La, leaving our Sherpas to pack up and return to Lunak. We vigorously crossed over the Nangpa La, climbed up a long steep slope to 20,500 feet and then, taking turns with flashing ice axes, forced a way up a steep narrow ridge to reach the summit at 21,100 feet. The views of Cho Oyu were superb. We raced down the mountain, crossed the Nangpa La again, joined up with our Sherpas and, flushed with success, raced into Lunak.

Griff Pugh invited us into his tent. He had just carried out another test for hemoglobin on the rest of the party and wanted to do the same on us. We were full of confidence! While the rest of the party had done very little, George and I had reconnoitered the approaches, climbed an excellent peak, and had run virtually all the way down the glacier to camp. Griff could not understand his new readings and neither could we. We now had almost the lowest level of hemoglobin in the whole party.

At this point my confidence in this aspect of high-altitude science disappeared never to return.

I went to the large mess tent to find a violent discussion in progress. A message had come in that the Chinese troops invading Tibet had reached the Tibetan village just down below the Nangpa La. Eric Shipton was sorely distressed. A brave man himself, he hated the thought of any of his party getting into the grips of the Chinese. It was his responsibility, he felt, to protect all his friends from unnecessary dangers by not permitting camps on the north side of the Nangpa La. To my astonishment the formidable Tom Bourdillon was supporting Eric. Tom's wife was also in the Khumbu area and he felt that any danger to him could also spell danger to Jennifer. Earle Riddiford and Campbell Secord, another member of our team, bitterly opposed Eric's approach, not because of any urgent desire to climb Cho Oyu, but mainly due to their intense reluctance to accept any of Eric's ideas on principle. George and I had a great affection for Eric but with the arrogance of fitness we were confident that if any Chinese soldiers appeared we could run fast enough to escape them—of course we didn't think about escaping from their bullets. All afternoon the argument raged and our morale faded. By evening Shipton reluctantly agreed to a compromise—that we would attempt Cho Oyu from the northwest but we'd only use a small mobile party and establish no other camps between, one down on the Nepalese side of the Nangpa La and one up on the mountain itself. I think we all understood that any chance of success in reaching the summit of Cho Oyu had evaporated.

Fond though I was of Eric I did not think he handled the situation very well. By arguing all afternoon in his very competent fashion he demoralized all of us. It is easy to comment after the event but I believe he should have expressed his concern briefly, listened to all other viewpoints, and then made a firm decision, even if this did mean permitting a small, competent, well-equipped group to attempt the peak with some confidence of success. Campbell Secord on his return to London did his best to destroy Eric's reputation over this episode and this played a part in the London Committee's decision to replace Eric with John Hunt on the 1953 expedition.

We established a camp at Jasamba, below the Nangpa La, and then, constantly looking over our shoulders for any sign of the Chinese, we hastily ascended the Kyetrak Glacier to the foot of the spur leading to the main west ridge of the mountain. I went on alone up the spur and established a route until a long stretch of ice stopped me in my tracks. Next morning our whole team followed up my path and, roped to George, I cut a hundred-foot line of bucket steps to a rock outcrop. Then George moved through and plugged steps up the combination of snow and rock to reach the main ridge at 21,000 feet. Here there was an icy hollow and we duly pitched camp. We conducted our extra Sherpas back over the icy section and saw them hasten over the Kyetrak Glacier and the Nangpa La back to safety. It felt very lonely indeed on our ridge camp.

Over the next two days the weather was appalling. We pushed a little way up the ridge until nil visibility made us return. Charles Evans had developed severe laryngitis and when the weather improved a little later on the second day Charles was conducted down the spur by Secord and a Sherpa and safely over the Nangpa La.

Short on food and demoralized, Alf Gregory, Tom Bourdillon, George and I decided to make our last attempt. George and I led up the ridge and Tom and Alf followed slowly behind. Tom frankly admitted that he was greatly concerned about the snow conditions. We reached the point where the ridge abutted against the great ice face of Cho Oyu. I hacked a line of steps up a very steep firm snow slope and realized I was close to 22,500 feet but not really getting anywhere. When someone down below shouted, "Come down you silly bugger," I knew it was time to turn back. We had been a miserable failure and no one said a word as we retreated back to the ridge camp and finally over the Kyetrak Glacier. There to our astonishment we met Eric Shipton and Earle Riddiford and even forty-five years later I have no idea why they were there. Was it that they had come to help us with the assault on the mountain or to rescue us from our undoubtedly perilous situation?

Somehow I never thought of asking Eric and now I'll never know.

George Lowe and I were mortified by our poor showing and persuaded Shipton to let us return to the Kyetrak Glacier to attempt two fine summits we had noticed on the north side. Climbing in true alpine-style, we reached the summit of one peak of 21,500 feet and another of 22,600 feet. By the time we had returned to our Base Camp at Lunak some of our confidence had returned. But nothing could wipe away our sense of complete failure on Cho Oyu. In retrospect it would have been better to have abandoned Cho Oyu before dissension divided the group and gone off to attempt one of the many other great virgin peaks in the area.

So our main objective had been unsuccessfully concluded but there was plenty still left to do. A disgusted Earle Riddiford headed back to civilization with a twisted back—he never returned to the Himalayas but concentrated on his legal practice and his family sheep station. Tom Bourdillon led a group in testing oxygen equipment and Griffith Pugh did much research on high-altitude physiology. The results from both of these lines of scientific study were to play an important part in our approach to Mount Everest in 1953. On the other hand, George and I just went on climbing!

It was Eric's idea that George and I should try crossing a never before climbed pass to the east of Cho Oyu called the Nup La. In 1951 Earle Riddiford and his group had tried to get up the great icefall leading to the pass but had been defeated after making little progress. There was no doubt it was a considerable challenge.

We left the village of Khumjung accompanied by three of our permanent Sherpas—Angputa, Tashi Puta and Angje. None of them were great mountaineers but they were hardworking and loyal. Our loads were carried by half a dozen young Sherpas and one Sherpani. We made our way up the beautiful Gokyo valley, past the sparkling Dudh Pokari lake (as we then called it), when a heavy snowfall and low cloud slowed us down and we camped early. Next morning we continued in soft snow and heavy mist and dropped down a great moraine wall onto the smooth lower stretches of the Ngojumba Glacier. We followed the glacier to where it swung sharply to the left and the ice was broken and contorted. It took us some time to penetrate through this area and we finally climbed up onto a smooth crest. The view ahead of us was unbelievable. Towering over us on the immediate left was the enormous face of Cho Oyu and to the east of it in one great sweep stretched peak after peak, culminating in the summit pyramid of Everest nearly twenty miles away. The valley ahead was crammed full of an enormous icefall tumbling thousands of feet down in a rain of shattered ice. The icefall was split in the middle by a great rock buttress and high up in the far distance we could see a dip in the ridge—the Nup La.

The right-hand icefall had row after row of tottering ice pinnacles and even as we watched there was a mighty rumble and a wide section of ice cliff leaned over and tumbled down with frightening force. "Bohut kharab, sahib," said Angje and I had to agree that it was very bad indeed.

We pitched our tent on the smooth ice at the foot of the icefall where a good look at the central buttress indicated there was a possible route at least halfway up. The six hours we spent on the buttress next day was an experience to remember. Boulders were constantly tumbling down the face; with great effort we ascended a very steep chockstone, a huge overhanging boulder blocking the way, and barely made 500 feet before we realized we were unable to get any further. Even the descent was a breathtaking affair. Getting back over the chockstone was extremely hazardous and we literally ran down the lower gully with rocks bouncing all around us. It was with great relief that we reached the bottom safely and walked across to our camp. Our Sherpas had watched our climb with tentative admiration and once again Angje announced with some enthusiasm, "Bohut kharab." Once again we wholeheartedly agreed.

Later the same afternoon I went for a stroll with Angputa to the left side of the glacier looking for a possible route. For most of the way we passed a towering icewall a thousand feet high that we knew was impossible for us to climb. Then as we approached the left side of the valley I saw with quickening excitement a rounded sweep of moraine sneaking up above the icefall. It was easy going and seemed very safe.

We carried on a little further and my excitement grew. Despite the rows of crevasses and icewalls above us it looked hard but not impossible. As darkness fell we hurried back to camp and told George our good news. If we hadn't discovered this route we would have had to abandon the climb.

We left at 6:30 a.m. and George and I moved with considerable speed and reached the furthest point of the previous day in excellent time. George was a little reluctant to call the way ahead an easy route but agreed it had possibilities. We roped up, put on our crampons and made our way upward. This was the work we really loved—hacking our way up icewalls, crossing shaky snow bridges and descending down into crevasses and out the other side. In one place I chipped an airy highway on the thin crust of a blade of ice to get us across a seemingly bottomless crevasse. At first we were being forced to the left toward broken and impassable ice, then a lucky snow bridge led us back to the center again and rather easier ground. At 10:30 a.m. we cramponed on to a snowy knoll and saw in the far distance the Nup La, a 19,400-foot dip between two great 24,000-foot buttresses. The way ahead looked promising and we immediately decided to return and prepare a camp to be carried in the next day.

In the morning George and I agreed there was no need for both of us to lead the Sherpas up to establish the camp, so George stayed behind. I don't quite know why I seemed to be doing the majority of the work at this stage but, although George was perfectly capable of handling any mountaineering problems, he was also at times quite happy to sit around and relax. So I led off three rather reluctant Sherpas. We put on the rope and crampons at the usual place and then used our trail to cross the crevasses and icewalls. On the whole the Sherpas climbed very well, although Tashi Puta was rather nervous and crawled on his hands and knees over the exposed blade of ice. I was able to help him over with a hearty tug on the rope. We reached the crest of the icefall after three and a half hours of traveling.

My hopes of easy grounds ahead were quickly dispelled when we came to two huge crevasses and I had to hack my way down into them and out the other side again. It needed much work on the rope to get the Sherpas to follow me. We continued on over some dangerously crevassed country and the further we went, the more I realized there was still a lot of difficult ground between us and the Nup La.

Next morning it was unusually mild and now nature seemed to be ganging up on us. First we discovered that part of our track had been wiped out by an avalanche and second that all the snow bridges were softened by the warm conditions. Crossing the two wide crevasses was very hard work although having George along made everything much safer. We reached my furthest point and George led off across the murky expanse of the snow plateau. In the soft snow conditions we were breaking through into crevasse after crevasse. When there was a shriek from Tashi Puta and I turned to see only his head peeping above the snow, we decided we could go no further for that day. While George set up camp I took the Sherpas back over our route to collect supplies on the far side of the closest of the big crevasses. We climbed down into it and then out again and duly collected our loads. Once more I descended into the crevasse and started over the much softened bridge. Suddenly there was a whoomph and the bridge and I dropped into the crevasse. Instinctively I threw my cramponed feet against the far icewall and thrust my pack against the other. And there I hung suspended. It was thirty seconds before the Sherpas pulled the rope tight, long enough for me to have been crushed at the bottom of the crevasse if I had fallen. We duly extricated ourselves and returned to a somewhat demoralized camp.

Despite our fears, we were determined to carry on and we were greatly encouraged next morning when it was much colder. Maybe the snow would be more supportive? We weaved our way through a series of open crevasses, then came over a crest and saw a smooth gully running in the direction we wanted to go and above it was a long slope sweeping up toward the Nup La itself. Nothing could stop us now. We raced up the hill and to our immense joy reached the rocky crest of the pass. I had never felt a greater sense of achievement and of course in those days we had no climbing harness, front point crampons, curvers, pitons, carabiners or jumars. But we swung our long-handled ice axes with mighty enthusiasm.

In the late afternoon the clouds lifted and we were able to look down the Rongbuk Glacier and see the mighty summit of Everest. Supremely fit now, we spent a marvelous five days in Tibet. We raced down the West Rongbuk Glacier, hacked our way through the giant ice spires of the main Rongbuk Glacier and looked with trepidation at the Rongbuk Monastery ten miles away down a valley which we knew was now controlled by Chinese soldiers. We reached the Base Campsite of the prewar British expeditions, with its debris of batteries and rusty tins, and rushed up the East Rongbuk Glacier to the foot of the North Col. It was wonderful to look up these long slopes where so many famous British climbers had struggled toward the summit. We camped at 21,000 feet, a little way down the East Rongbuk Glacier, and next morning started the long and arduous day to reach well up the West Rongbuk Glacier before dark and camp again.

I crawled out of our tent at 5:30 a.m. and was horrified to see that the sky over Nepal was black as night and ugly clouds were surging up and writhing about the summits. We literally ran up the rest of the glacier and in just over an hour we were back on the Nup La. Great clouds were sweeping over the icefall below us which was already covered by thick fresh snow and we could hear avalanches of new snow thundering down the cliffs. We quickly worked out our technique. We would use 200 feet of rope. I would go down first to test out the ground, George would follow next with a tight hand on my rope, and the three Sherpas would follow behind as the final check. So in that order we headed off across the treacherous plateau. When I sank into a crevasse George pulled me out, and this happened time and again. Somehow, despite the blanketing snow, I was able to steer a reasonable course, although we had to find our way over dozens of crevasses before, to our great relief, we reached the two large crevasses and somehow scrambled our way in and out of them again. There was six inches of fresh snow on the lower icefall and at times we completely lost our route. By experience, good luck, or plain determination we battled our way down. It was an emotional moment when through the blizzard I caught a glimpse of the strip of moraine and I knew that we were safe at last. We struggled down a little further to a flat area and camped there. The Nup La was behind us and we had completed one of the most exciting challenges I had ever attempted. It had been close—one false move or a moment of inattention and our bodies would have remained down a crevasse forever. But at least the failure on Cho Oyu had now faded well into the past.

For two days we rested at a calm and peaceful lake beside the Ngojumba Glacier but our thoughts kept turning to the progress of the Swiss on Everest. It was now 5th June and they should be off the mountain by now. George and I decided to go over and find out. We ascended a long valley to the east, crossed over a high pass and descended down to the Khumbu Glacier. We carried on up the glacier to the Swiss Base Camp but there was no sign of them. Next morning we headed briskly down valley and met an old Sherpa at the first village. "Ask him about the Swiss," I said to Angputa and, after some exchange of conversation, Angputa told us the man wasn't too sure but thought that seven Swiss had got to the top. Lugubriously we carried on down valley to Pangboche where we were pleased to meet up with Shipton again but even more pleased to hear his news—Raymond Lambert and Sherpa Tenzing Norgay had established a route up the South-East Ridge to around 28,000 feet, as several climbers had done on the north side before them. Then they were forced to retreat. Everest was still unclimbed!

I was feeling very fit so decided to carry on down to Namche Bazaar to meet the Swiss and I literally ran all the way down the Tengboche hill and up and around the track to Namche and the Swiss camp. Several of them spoke excellent English and I was able to talk to them and find out the story of their very formidable attempt. Tenzing Norgay and Lambert were the strike team who had pioneered the route up the Lhotse Face. They had been the ones who had gone up the South-East Ridge and they were the ones who reached the highest point on the mountain. The Swiss were disappointed but still generous. When they asked where I had come from and I told them we had been all the way up to Base Camp and all the way down again they said to me, "You must be very fit. That is a long way to go in one day." I've never had the Swiss say anything like that to me before or since.

They had experienced some problems high on the mountain. The Sherpas who were supposed to carry gear from the South Col to the proposed site of Camp VII higher on the mountain, refused to go further. The three Swiss climbers, along with Tenzing, had no choice but to set off up the South-East Ridge with a tent, oxygen, enough food for one day, but no sleeping bags, and no stove to cook a meal or melt snow for water. Their crude breathing gear only worked when they were resting or standing still, so the going was tough. Tenzing and Lambert stopped at about 27,500 feet at what they thought would make a good campsite. Flory and Aubert joined them. The summit pair had yet to be determined. In tears, Aubert, himself a fanatical mountaineer, insisted that Tenzing and Lambert should have the honor. Deeply appreciative of their comrades' sacrifice, a sobbing Tenzing and Lambert embraced them before they departed back down.

It was a freezing night. With no sleeping bags, Tenzing and Lambert dared not close their eyes, so they shook each other to remain awake, pressed close together for scant warmth. Stricken by thirst, the best they could manage was a fragment of ice melted in an empty tin over a candle flame. The next morning, having had nothing to eat or drink for hours, they struggled manfully to a height of 28,210 feet, only 800 feet from the summit, until utter exhaustion forced them back. As it was, Tenzing barely made it back to the South Col. He kept collapsing and had to be dragged across the col to the tents. When Tenzing and Lambert had recovered, their companions, lacking flowers, draped garlands of sausages round their necks in salute. It had been a mighty effort and, although I later questioned the heights of their camp and the final point they reached, they had proved to be brave and strong men.

At the beginning of the 1950s none of the glaciers and passes to the east of Everest had been challenged by explorers or mountaineers. Eric

Shipton was very much aware of this and I was fortunate enough to make two forays with him in this direction. He could not resist one last excursion before returning home from our abortive 1952 Cho Oyu expedition, but he and I had already made one small exploration the year before, while waiting for the snow conditions to improve between our two assaults on the Khumbu Icefall. Our earlier 1951 foray deserves brief mention at this point.

With three Sherpa porters we moved up the Imja valley between the great Nuptse-Lhotse wall and the north side of Ama Dablam. To the south there was a 19,000-foot dip in the ridge and we made this our immediate objective. There were several sections of difficult climbing where Eric generously gave me the lead and with considerable enthusiasm I surged to the top of the pass. I looked down on a tattered glaciated valley, the Hongu, and there was a relatively easy snow slope leading to the floor. We camped in this lonely valley and, as we lay in our tent, Shipton, reading a book by candlelight and puffing on his smelly pipe, was a contented man.

We had noted a higher pass to the east and early in the morning we made our way across the moraine-covered glacier and started upward. There were several stretches requiring technical climbing and once again Shipton was happy to let me take the lead. I reached the crest of the 20,000-foot West Col to see a wide snowfield we later called the Barun Plateau. Dominating the scene to the east was the mighty bulk of Makalu (27,790 feet) and, closer at hand, Baruntse (23,570 feet). We were seeing a whole new area that no explorer had laid eyes on before. We returned to our camp, determined to examine this new region some time in the future.

We decided to descend a little way down the Hongu Glacier, thus circling around Ama Dablam and then trying to cross over a pass to the west that ultimately would take us back to Tengboche or Pangboche. We were unroped as we climbed up the easy side glacier and I rushed on in the lead, keeping a sharp eye out for any crevasses. This is a really easy way home, I said to myself as I came up to the crest of the Ama Dablam pass, which I estimated to be at about 19,600 feet. Then I looked down the other side and my heart sank. Six hundred feet of fluted ice dropped abruptly to the shattered Mingbo Glacier. Shipton soon joined me and a great discussion took place. The Sherpas preferred to return the easier way we had come, but I was insistent that we could get down this slope and Shipton agreed, so our decision prevailed. I roped up to Angputa and Eric tied on with the other two Sherpas.

Eric started cutting steps down the rather gradual slope toward the big drop and I noted that he wasn't particularly professional at the job, despite his great experience. I think he must have felt the same as he waved me through and I commenced cutting a zigzag of steps down the face. Angputa belayed me down each fifty feet and then I'd bring him down to join me. Halfway down the face there was a stretch of solid ice and it took me quite a time to cut through this extremely slippery section. I reached a place where there was a deep crack in the ice just large enough to take the shaft of my ice axe, and called to Angputa to come down with great care—he moved very cautiously! He was twenty feet above me when he slipped, fell and shot past me at great speed. I held grimly on to my belay and, fortunately, it stopped Angputa with a great jerk and he went sliding backward and forward across the face. I was very concerned that this accident might immobilize Shipton's two Sherpas, but this was far from being the case. Seeing one of their companions in a worse predicament than they were, they burst into uproarious laughter. And even Angputa laughed, too, when he realized he would fall no further. The Sherpas can be marvelous in moments of stress.

With surprising confidence Angputa managed to steady himself and I cut steps down to join him and got him safely back on his feet. From then on the slope eased a little, the surface became firm snow and we descended with relative ease. It took us all quite a while to find a way down through the broken glacier and, as darkness fell, we reached the snow grass at 17,000 feet. We were very tired and, without bothering to pitch a tent, we got into our sleeping bags amongst the clumps of grass. I can still remember lying there in great relief and looking upward at a brilliantly full moon.

*   *   *

With so much tantalizing unfinished business it was no surprise we seized our next chance to go to the east of Everest at the end of our Cho Oyu expedition in 1952. Eric decided he wanted to return to Kathmandu by a new route so, typically, started to the east before ultimately heading west. Charles Evans and two Sherpas crossed first into the Hongu and Shipton, George Lowe and I, with sirdar Angtharkay and a group of porters, crossed a few days later. We had rather heavy loads when we camped down in the Hongu and this irritated Eric a great deal. He burst out of his tent and told everyone to remove the cardboard cartons from all the food and just bundle everything together in kit bags. It made an appalling mess of our food and perhaps saved 10 lbs. overall in weight, but at least Eric was happy, although George and I didn't regard it as a very smart move.

We carried our heavy loads up the steep face of the West Col at 20,000 feet and emerged onto the high Barun Plateau, where we met Charles Evans who had looked over the East Col down into the Barun and had tried to climb an impressive peak on its south side. Charles had reached within 200 feet of the summit until he was stopped by a wide bridged crevasse that cut right across the ridge. Not having much confidence in the ability of his Sherpa companion to belay him safely, he had retreated. We had plenty of time so we decided to try the peak again, cramponing up the ridge, hacking a few steps here and there, until we came to the bridged crevasse. It was about twenty feet wide and well plugged up according to my judgment, so I walked across it confidently—much to Charles Evans' mortification. Charles then carried through on to the final summit pyramid and led us to the top. It was a marvelous view-point and we looked eagerly down into the great Barun valley and up the immensely impressive face of Makalu.

Once back on the Barun Plateau, George and I decided to do a quick rush up a pleasant peak on the north side and we reached the summit of this while Eric and Charles and the Sherpas waited patiently below. Then it was over the East Col and down a boulder-filled side valley toward the Barun Glacier. The easiest way to descend the valley was simply to jump from boulder to boulder and I naturally followed this procedure. I had always regarded Charles Evans as a very calm and non-competitive person, but I suddenly realized he was rapidly overtaking me and it was turning into a race. It was too good an opportunity to miss. As we flew down, one false step would have been disastrous for us both, but when I managed to pull away from Charles we both dropped down to a safer and more sensible pace.

After some hours we reached the moraine-covered Barun Glacier and Eric suggested we make our way up to the head with the hope that we might look over a pass into Tibet. For some hours we struggled upward, crossing dozens of open crevasses, few of them more than three feet wide. We camped at the head of the glacier just as a snowstorm swept up the valley. During the night the tents sagged under the heavy snow and by morning there was a foot of fresh snow everywhere. Reluctantly we agreed there was no chance of us going high on the ridge dividing the Barun Glacier from Tibet.

We packed up and turned downward but now conditions were much more difficult. The heavy fall of snow had bridged all the crevasses and it was almost impossible to locate them. George and I used our old technique. I roped up and went down in the lead, George followed me on a very tight belay, and all the others trailed along behind on a long rope acting as a substantial brake. I put a leg into a dozen hidden crevasses and even went up to my waist a few times, but George's reaction was lightning fast and I came to no harm. The snow thinned out as we got lower and soon we were stumbling over the glacial moraine and finally right down to the terminal face of the glacier. We walked out onto a high-altitude grazing area and looked around in astonishment. The valley floor was covered by some square miles of flowering crimson azaleas—a truly magnificent sight.

The monsoon rain had transformed the landscape, and myriads of tiny blossoms of every color were bursting through the arid soil. The air was thick and strong and we breathed it deeply into our starved lungs. But we were now in a world of rain, hundreds of waterfalls drifted gracefully down the mighty rock bluffs and the heavy clouds would split for a moment to reveal some startling summit before closing in again with torrential rain. I felt it was the most beautiful valley I had ever seen and I felt sure I would return to enjoy its flowers and sparkling streams and soaring peaks.

As we sheltered under an overhanging rock one of our senior and highly respected Sherpas told us a story. Dawa Tenzing had never been in the Barun valley before, but Sherpa mythology told of its existence. The valley contained an invisible village—a Shangri-La—where the gods lived and holy men came to die. It was a place of great beauty, as we had seen, and people lived there forever. I asked Dawa Tenzing if he hoped someday to end up in the invisible village, but he said he had been too great a sinner.

We were now rather short on food and hoping to meet summer graziers further down the valley and maybe buy a sheep from them. But Eric warned us that no one would have ever come down this valley before, so they might find us rather frightening or even suspect us of being yetis. He was right. We came over a hump in the valley and saw two men with loads walking slowly up toward us. They stopped, rigid with fear, dropped their loads and started rushing down valley. "Stop them, stop them!" shouted Eric. George and I quickly dumped our loads and set off at full speed. However when the locals looked around and saw two tall hairy beings bearing down on them, their speed increased markedly and they shot up a side valley and disappeared amongst the rocks. It was Angtharkay who thought of a sensible solution. "I will go down on the other side of the valley," he said, "and come up behind the villagers. I'll tell them some rather strange, but harmless people are coming down valley and not to be afraid." And that's what he did. We approached the nervous group of shepherds and after extensive nego-tiation were able to buy a young sheep. That night we dined in luxury.

Over the next two days we entered the dense forest of the lower Barun valley, which was equally beautiful, then climbed up over a 14,000-foot pass and dropped down into the heat and rain and leeches of the Arun valley, to spend a night in the village of Sedua where the houses were built up on bamboo stilts. We were offered the open basement of a large house for the night and, as it was well protected from the rain, it seemed very adequate. When I woke in the morning after a good night's sleep my scalp felt strangely stiff and on investigation I found my hair was full of dried blood. I shook my head and a leech the size of a small sausage fell to the ground—swollen with my blood! I felt reasonably philosophical about this as leeches had never worried me too much.

Through mud and slush and rain we made our way down to the swollen Arun river and crossed a shaky suspension bridge of twisted lianas over the raging torrent at Num. The hot muggy conditions were an unpleasant experience after the cool clean air of the mountains and we found walking in this heat barely tolerable. The Arun river was however now broad, fast-flowing and cool and there didn't seem to be any more rapids. So George and I manufactured a raft out of our two air mattresses and tied two bamboo poles across them with a nylon rope so that there was a gap of almost two feet. We did a trial run, each straddling an air mattress with water up to our waists. It worked magnificently and we decided to give up walking the next day and just float peacefully down the river.

Eric departed at 4:30 a.m. with the porters and in the early morning light we launched our craft and started moving rapidly downriver. It was superb and we were traveling twice as fast as we could have walked. We covered a couple of miles and then we heard a dull powerful roar drifting up valley. We paddled frantically toward the side but we couldn't control our ungainly craft in the increasing current. Then we noted a great series of bluffs thrusting out into the stream and high up on the bluffs Eric was waving furiously.

We could now see what we were approaching. The river was smashing headlong against an enormous bluff. The majority of the water was swept violently into a little smooth-walled bay where it formed an enormous whirlpool from which it flushed periodically into the foaming channel below. It was certainly a nasty sight. We held on grimly as our raft was picked up and hurled on the crest of a wave at the smooth rock wall. We thought we would be smashed to pieces, but our buoyant raft lifted us up and slid sideways down into the racing waters of the great whirlpool. We were completely out of control and one swirl threw us right into the gaping center so that the rushing water on the rim of the whirlpool towered over our heads. Our dangling legs were sucked greedily down, but our plucky little craft saved us once again and we shot out to the very edges. Around we went again and again!

Eric meanwhile was climbing down the steep cliffs on a rope held by the Sherpas. On the sixth revolution I saw him out of the side of my eye step down onto the little ledge above the whirlpool. A particularly violent fluctuation in the river threw us at the bluff on an enormous wave. We rode up for ten feet against the bluff and then slid off and were thrown against the rock on the innermost edge of the whirlpool. I reached out desperately and grasped a small hold on the rock and then George did the same. Somehow we managed to drag ourselves along against the current and then something struck me in the face—it was a rope thrown by Eric—and he pulled us powerfully along to his little ledge. We crawled out of the boiling water, pulled our raft to pieces, and then all of us were towed up the cliff by the Sherpas, mightily glad to be on solid ground again. It gave us the chance to repair and reassemble our raft and have another go. Eric couldn't bear to watch and went ahead along the bank. When we saw him semaphoring furiously, we pulled into the side to discover he had been indicating a very serious rapid ahead. We didn't put our boat into the water anymore and were happy to walk over ridges and valleys to the railhead in India.

In the post-monsoon season of autumn 1952 the Swiss were to try again to climb Everest. They found the Khumbu Icefall a little easier and used a better route up the Lhotse Face to establish a camp on the South Col, but then they were struck by the cold temperatures and strong winds of early winter. Lambert and Tenzing were once again in the lead but in the appalling conditions they only reached 500 feet above the South Col. Everest still remained a formidable challenge. It would need a very good expedition indeed to reach the summit.

6

GETTING TO CAMP VII

I ARRIVED BACK IN NEW ZEALAND TO FIND A LETTER WAITING FOR ME from Eric Shipton. He had, with some misgiving, accepted the leadership of the 1953 British Everest expedition and he wanted George Lowe and myself to join him. George and I had made strong recommendations that New Zealand's outstanding guide, Harry Ayres, should be included and Eric had readily agreed. It wasn't really surprising that three New Zealanders should be invited to join a British expedition. In those days we were classified as British subjects and New Zealand citizens, although we regarded ourselves as being nationally independent.

When the second Swiss expedition failed, I presumed that organizational activity in London would be reaching fever pitch. But rumors kept creeping through that progress was rather slow. Finally the news came that Eric Shipton had been arbitrarily replaced as leader by a climber, Colonel John Hunt, whose name was unknown to me. Eric Shipton's reluctance to lead the British 1953 expedition to Everest was not lost on the Himalayan Committee. George Lowe says Shipton was a very complex man. "Primarily," said George, "he was a philosopher. He had a poetic side to him. He liked the idea of loneliness. He liked the idea of the wildness of the world and he wanted to be there with as small a number about him as possible." I had to agree completely with George's view.

This attitude may not have endeared Eric to the Himalayan Committee, who were contemplating a wholesale assault on the world's highest mountain. As early as July 1952 there were rumblings in London that the legendary climber lacked the organizational ability and commitment to run a big expedition and that his exploratory spirit was in decline. Some members of the Committee, mindful of the Cho Oyu expedition's failure to reach the summit, and mindful, too, that the French had been given permission to attempt Everest in 1954, approached another English climber, John Hunt, who was serving with the British Army Corps in Germany, to see if he was interested in becoming organizing secretary of the expedition. Hunt, in his autobiography, says he nearly jumped over the moon with delight. There were also suggestions that he might become deputy leader to Shipton. Hunt heard nothing more until he was invited to London in mid-August to meet Shipton for the first time and discuss the job of organizing secretary. Hunt later described the meeting as a disillusioning encounter. Hunt himself says he was too keen, the chemistry all wrong, and he returned to Germany in low spirits, determined to put Everest out of his mind.

Shipton then offered the job of organizing secretary to another army officer, Major Charles Wylie, an able climber, familiar with the Himalayas, who had commanded a Gurkha regiment during the war and spoke fluent Nepali. In September Wylie joined Shipton at the Royal Geographical Society where a special office had been given to the expedition. Barely a week later the Himalayan Committee summoned them to the boardroom for a meeting. To their surprise they saw that the first on the agenda was "Leadership of the Expedition." Wylie was then asked to leave while this was discussed. He waited in the foyer for nearly an hour for an ashen-faced Shipton to come out.

"They have offered me dual leadership of the expedition," said Shipton quietly. "What do you think of that?"

"Not much," replied Wylie. "You can't have two leaders on a show like the Everest expedition."

"I quite agree," said Shipton. He went back into the boardroom and resigned.

Everest had been Eric Shipton's life and he got into a cab afterward an absolutely shattered man. After eight failed attempts on Everest, the Himalayan Committee decided that they needed a more forceful man in charge, somebody who was going to make sure they got to the top. Though he had not been on Everest, Hunt had a couple of prewar Himalayan forays under his belt and, as a military man, would have the necessary powers of organization. So that same day, 11th September 1952, a telegram was sent to Hunt offering him the leadership of the British expedition to Everest in the spring of 1953. Tied up with army exercises in the Rhineland, he couldn't take up the post until a month later. At his farewell dinner his colleagues presented him with a Corps flag and instructions to place it on the top of Everest.

George Lowe later told me that John Hunt wanted a completely new team made up of people he knew personally and was thinking of disposing of George and myself. I was so disappointed at Eric being dropped for someone unknown to me personally, and a senior army officer to boot, that I doubted whether I cared if I went at all. Apparently, Charles Evans, Tom Bourdillon and Alf Gregory told John Hunt that if George and I didn't go, they wouldn't go either. John accepted this ultimatum which was probably a wise move, as this group of five of us were the ones who were to go highest on the mountain. I received a very nice letter from Eric saying how sad he was to be replaced in such an abrupt fashion, but asking me to transfer my loyalty to John Hunt for the sake of the team effort. I decided to give it a go, but I had considerable reservations about having an expedition leader who might well issue orders in military style. (On the whole, mountaineers are an independent lot and like to be asked rather than ordered.) Which shows how little I knew about many military men.

Eric Shipton never did return to the Himalayas, but it was certainly not the end of his mountaineering adventures. He started a series of exploratory journeys onto the Patagonian Icecap in South America. It was just the sort of terrain for Eric. Access was up wild fjords and glaciers with strong winds and appalling weather. The icecap was a constant challenge and Eric pioneered many new routes, often using inexperienced companions who were foolish enough to express a desire to see life in the raw. Eric would snap them up and before they could think again, they would find themselves adventuring in earnest.

Would we have been successful if Eric had remained leader? I am inclined to say yes! Charles Evans and Charles Wylie, and even I, had sufficient administrative ability to strengthen Eric's reluctance in this field. Our affection for him would have inspired us to perform with great energy. Great leaders are meant to have a ruthless streak in them and Eric didn't have that, but neither did Ernest Shackleton as far as I can tell. Maybe the ability to inspire sheer affection can serve the same purpose. In any case, I could never forgive the Himalayan Committee for the boorish way they handled the removal of Eric Shipton, a great explorer and a remarkably good friend.

I arrived in Kathmandu in the early days of March 1953 and traveled to the British Embassy. Striding across the ambassadorial lawn to meet me was a fit, upright, sandy-haired figure—it must be John Hunt. With outstretched hand and friendly smile, he greeted a somewhat reluctant me with, "Hello, Ed, I have been wanting to meet you for a long time!" My reservations melted even further when John said he was expecting to call on me for sound advice. Obviously, I decided, John couldn't be all bad. It was clear at least that he knew how to handle potentially difficult members. Throughout the expedition he proved an outstanding organizer and I cannot remember him issuing a single direct order to anyone.

According to the standards of those days we were a huge expedition, not in numbers of climbers, as we only had eleven, but in the 800 porter-loads that had to be carried into Tengboche Monastery. It took seventeen days to walk from Banepa to Tengboche and for this long carry each porter received a total of 93 rupees, compared to the pay of 250 rupees per day demanded by porters these days. Of course inflation has contributed toward massive changes over the forty-five intervening years. The long march in was highly beneficial to our fitness and acclimatization. Tenzing Norgay, as sirdar, was in charge of all the Sherpas and porters and had a very responsible job. I came to know him rather better during the march and it was impossible not to be warmed by his flashing smile and charming manner, though I didn't really become a very close friend of Tenzing until the last few years of his life, when I was based in India.

We established our temporary Base Camp at Tengboche Monastery, a wonderful location with superb views of Everest and the spectacular Ama Dablam, and the Head Lama gave us blessings for the success of the expedition. We had several quite heavy falls of snow but it soon melted in the early spring weather. On Dr. Griffith Pugh's advice, we were undertaking acclimatization periods—climbing to 20,000 feet but sleeping much lower to enable us to adjust to the thinner air. I led a group to the first ascent of a 20,000-foot peak which thrust out over the Gokyo valley. It was of modest difficulty, but I was pleased how well everyone handled it. On 6th April we all regrouped at Tengboche and everyone had clearly benefited from the training.

I was gratified when, in the light of my 1951 experience, John Hunt asked me to take an advance party up the Khumbu Glacier to pick a suitable Base Camp and then reconnoiter a route up the icefall. My group consisted initially of Michael Westmacott and George Band, but, knowing what a good man George Lowe was on snow and ice, I asked if he could join us. John was a bit reluctant. I always felt that he was nervous of us New Zealanders hijacking his expedition with our energy and our snow and ice skills, but in the end he conceded that George's contribution would be valuable. Then Tom Stobart, our cameraman, and Griff Pugh, our physiologist, decided to come too, so we were quite a large group. We had a heavy fall of snow on the way up the Khumbu Glacier and several of our porters suffered from snow blindness, but in the end we reached the bottom of the icefall and came on the Swiss campsite of the previous year. It was a most uncomfortable place with rocks spread all over the hard ice, but there were some flat places suitable for tents, so it seemed the best available. George uncovered a huge pile of juniper wood and we regarded this as a great bonus. We had little concern for environmental matters in those days and systematically stripped all the juniper shrubs in the upper valley for our cooking fires.

I felt a great sense of responsibility about finding a good route up the icefall and regarded it as a challenge to complete the ascent within the six days before John Hunt joined us. Late in the afternoon of that first day I went off by myself and established a track through ice pinnacles and winding hollows to reach the foot of the icefall an hour later. I noted then that the lower part of it looked rather more difficult than it had in 1951.

On day one, George Lowe was suffering from dysentery so Mike Westmacott, George Band and I tackled the bottom of the icefall with considerable energy, crossing shaky ice bridges, cutting a line of steps up abrupt icewalls, and wriggling our way through narrow cracks in the ice. Westmacott did a fine lead up a steep icy corner which we called Mike's Horror and I crossed a great crevasse by a slender ice bridge with a vertical icewall above it and this was predictably called Hillary's Horror. We never liked this dangerous section and later found a better route to the left. Wriggling and jamming our way through a shattered area we later called Hellfire Alley, we knew we had come about halfway. Above it looked extremely difficult and we returned to Base Camp in a very subdued mood indeed.

Next day, Westmacott, Ang Namgyal and I returned to the attack. We climbed back up our established track with surprising ease, but in Hellfire Alley we had an unpleasant surprise—twenty feet of our track had been wiped out by blocks of ice tumbling from above. With a creepy feeling down the back of my neck, I hurried on up to the top of the alley. Without much difficulty we reached the furthermost point of the previous day, but how to get a little further? We tried a big sweep to the right until we were stopped by an enormous crevasse fringed with teetering seracs. No way there, so we returned to our starting place. It seemed that the only way was straight ahead, through the crumbled slabs of ice. To the right were two great blocks and I hacked a line of steps between them, climbed the last few feet, and emerged on top.

I immediately recognized the terrain ahead as the shaky part that Eric Shipton and I had called the Atom Bomb area. It was as though there had been an enormous subsidence and a wide shallow gully ran through the middle up to a broad ledge. But the gully was crisscrossed with horizontal and vertical crevasses. I started across the area on a tight rope from Westmacott. Each time I dislodged a chunk of ice there would be an intense subterranean rumble, but we finally crossed it and emerged on the flat area of the shelf to establish as reasonable a campsite as one can in an icefall. Well satisfied, we descended, devoting some time to improving the route, and arrived back at Base Camp in a somewhat happier frame of mind.

We had a long discussion that evening. We had reached high on the icefall but we were under no illusions that it was a safe route. Perhaps we should try a new line up the middle? During the night Westmacott became ill, but George Lowe had now recovered and George Band had acclimatized rather better, so on the third morning I set off with the two Georges up the center of the icefall. After two hard days I was happy to take it easy and the others did most of the work. At first the way was easier than our previous route, but soon we were amongst tall ice pinnacles and great ice blocks. When, with amazing suddenness, a great serac, only fifty feet to our right, split in half and avalanched close by us, we realized the middle way was highly unstable and retreated back to camp.

I was warm and comfortable in my sleeping bag when the door flap was pushed aside and a cheerful Sherpa thrust a note from John Hunt into my hand. John was well ahead of schedule and already camped just half a day down the valley. I didn't know whether this was indicating a lack of confidence in our ability or a keen desire to be personally involved in the "fun" of making a route on the icefall. But I decided to push immediately ahead with establishing Camp II the next day.

On the fourth morning, the two Georges and I departed with three laden Sherpas and made our way up the now well-established and flagged track. Despite striking some difficult changes and having to vary our route, we ultimately reached our ledge and pitched our tents on the appointed site. Tom Stobart and Griff Pugh had accompanied us up to do some filming, so they conducted the Sherpas down again, while George Lowe, George Band and I settled ourselves comfortably into our tents. There was the usual late afternoon snowfall and after dark we crawled outside to find four inches of fresh snow and sparkling stars above. It was an amazing experience to stand quietly in the middle of the icefall and hear the slow creaking and cracking deep within the ice.

Day five was a bitterly cold morning and, for fear of frostbite, we were reluctant to move until the sun hit our tents. Rotating the lead, George Lowe and I moved over thin icy bridges, and hacked hundreds of steps up steep icy slopes. We cut a stairway between two great slivers of ice and once again over and around shattered ice areas. Then ahead of us was a great icewall. We'd have to get up it somehow. I moved around a corner and saw, with a lightening of my heart, a great ice buttress leaning against the wall and above it the end of a small crevasse splitting the wall. With renewed energy I hacked a great line of steps up the buttress until I was pressed against the upper icewall. I managed to find a belay for my ice axe, whipped the rope around it, and George Band climbed up to join me. Then I eased my way to the right around an ice bulge and into the entrance to the crack. Cutting steps on both ice walls, I climbed slowly upward in the gloom until my head emerged into the sunlight. A quick wriggle and I was on top and ahead of me was the long sweep of the Western Cwm. With an enormous feeling of excitement I realized we had done it—the icefall was behind us. The two Georges struggled up to join me and we quickly crossed a solid snow bridge, climbed a small slope and stood looking down into a pleasant snowy hollow. It was an ideal spot for Camp III, safe and with plenty of space.

Delighted at our success, we hurried back down the icefall to Camp II, seeming to fly over all the problems that had harassed us on the way up. To my surprise, there were two figures standing outside the tents— John Hunt and Da Namgyal. John seemed elated at our news, although he was somewhat concerned at the dangers of the route. I took him halfway back up the last stretch to give him some idea of the way ahead, then all retreated to Base Camp. In my tent that night I couldn't help feeling a considerable sense of satisfaction. The icefall had been in worse condition than when we first climbed it in 1951 but we had forced a way up. We had also completed the job before John Hunt had arrived and this certainly warmed my competitive instincts. The first major step on the mountain had been overcome.

Following John Hunt's very sensible policy, we had a few days' break at lower levels and then returned to improving the route on the icefall. Westmacott and I established Camp III and overcame that demanding buttress and crack above it by suspending a rope ladder straight down the face. The great crevasse that cut us off from the Western Cwm was still a problem. We descended into it and crossed on an ice bridge to the far wall where there was a narrow slot running up to the top. I thought I could get up the slot but it would be an impossible task for laden Sherpas. The same afternoon a big party arrived with the first major lift up the icefall and everything seemed to have gone well. It was Tenzing's first trip above Base Camp for the year and I didn't think he seemed very happy. With the Swiss he had been one of the lead climbers but John Hunt had felt that at this stage his influence and experience would be more valuable organizing the other Sherpas and their loads up the icefall. I had considerable respect for Tenzing's reputation but it never entered my mind that we needed his help in tackling the difficult ice problems which I accepted we were quite capable of dealing with ourselves. No wonder Tenzing always had a warmer affection for the Swiss than he ever did for us.

The porters had brought three six-foot lengths of aluminium ladder and late in the afternoon we bolted them together and then lowered the ladder across the great crevasse. I enjoyed making sure I was the first to crawl over it which was indicative of the competitive attitude I had in those days. We had a discussion about who would go on from there to establish Advanced Base Camp in the Western Cwm. Perhaps rather arrogantly, I suggested to John Hunt that, seeing George and I were probably the most experienced snow and ice climbers, we should do it. John Hunt definitely got slightly offended and said, "I'm a good ice climber too!" We decided to keep off that topic. Someone had to go back to camp for a radio schedule and it is indicative of John's feeling at the time that a very reluctant Tenzing was sent back with Charles Wylie. Our team, with John Hunt, George Lowe and myself, pushed our way further up the Western Cwm, winding in and out through a multitude of crevasses and thankful for the snow bridges we always seemed able to find. We returned in the light of a magnificent sunset, washing the great peaks in glorious pink.

The next morning was fine and clear. We planned to establish the route to Advanced Base Camp and carry some loads into place. For the first time I roped up with Tenzing and it was immediately clear that we were a well-balanced couple. We arrived at the Swiss Camp IV well in the lead and commenced digging out the Swiss rations. These proved to be quite luxurious, which would improve our mundane food considerably.

After a couple of hours, Tenzing and I headed back in a hurry as we were going all the way to Base Camp. We moved quickly and were soon crossing the Atom Bomb area. On the far side was another of the innumerable crevasses and, instead of crossing the normal bridge, I just leaped in the air and landed on the overhanging bottom edge. It immediately broke off and plunged into the crevasse with me on top of it. Even though I was falling clear into the crevasse, I seemed to have plenty of time to think. And then the chunk of ice started to roll over and I realized that if I wasn't careful I was going to be crushed between it and the wall of the crevasse. So I can remember sort of flexing my knees and jumping in the air, and then we both carried on falling, but I was two or three feet clear of the chunk of ice. Then I had time to start realizing if the rope didn't come tight pretty soon I was going to come to a very sticky end at the bottom of the crevasse. It was at that moment, up top, Tenzing thrust his ice axe into the snow, whipped the rope around it in a good belay. The rope came tight with a twang, and I came to a sudden halt and swung in against the icewall, my cramponed feet against one wall and my backpack against the other. The chunk of ice carried on and smashed to smithereens at the bottom of the crevasse. The rope had come tight very quickly and I had little difficulty in cutting steps and climbing out of the crevasse. I had been impressed with Tenzing's skill and rope work and his happiness to keep going hard and fast. For the first time an idea entered my mind—it seemed very unlikely that John Hunt would let George Lowe and me climb together—you couldn't have *two* New Zealanders getting to the top—but what about Tenzing and me? It seemed a good idea and I decided to encourage it.

For the next few days many loads were carried to Advanced Base Camp and Evans and Bourdillon with their powerful closed-circuit oxygen reached 23,500 feet on the Lhotse Face. I persuaded John Hunt to let Tenzing and me do a one-day trip from Base Camp to Advanced Base and back, something that had previously taken two days. We used open-circuit oxygen on the way up and nothing on the way down. It was highly successful for, despite appalling weather on the descent, we completed this challenging task in very good time. It probably served only one purpose—to show how fit a team Tenzing and I were, but I was sufficiently calculating to regard it as important for Hunt to keep us in the front of his mind.

For most of the night of 6th May John Hunt's light was shining and his typewriter tapping away, but when he called Evans and myself for a conference next morning he was his usual drawn-faced but positive self as he told us the tasks he had allocated to all the expedition members for the next couple of days and asked for our reactions. He was proposing that Charles and Tom Bourdillon should use the powerful closed-circuit oxygen equipment to make a thrust for the South Summit at 28,700 feet. The final push to the top would be made by Tenzing and myself, using the more reliable open-circuit oxygen. The terms "first assault" and "second assault" which became attached to these two endeavors were completely misleading. Charles and I agreed with John's recommendations and I was left in no doubt that the final summit assault would be the responsibility of Tenzing and myself.

Then we crossed over to the large tent where the whole expedition was gathered and as we went inside it was impossible not to feel the air of suppressed excitement and anticipation. As Hunt started talking there was a sudden hush, everyone concentrating on his words. John repeated the plans he had discussed with us: George Lowe, Mike Westmacott and

George Band were allotted the difficult task of opening the Lhotse Face; the important job of getting the Sherpa porters and their loads to the South Col went to Wilf Noyce and Charles Wylie; while John Hunt and Alf Gregory were to be the support party to help establish the highest camp at 28,000 feet.

As expedition doctor, Mike Ward was asked to be a reserve, but he went predictably berserk, lashing out at John Hunt, saying he was quite unfit to go really high, that he should run things from Advanced Base, and that Mike himself should take over John's tasks higher up. From comments made many years later, it also appeared that the cheerful George Band felt the two New Zealanders had been a little pushy—as they may well have been. Otherwise people mostly accepted John's decisions, though in the end things didn't work out as he had planned anyway. In fact everyone did a useful job on the mountain. Dr. Griffith Pugh, for instance, strongly emphasized the need for us to improve our liquid intake and his advice played an important part in our success.

The Lhotse Face party had problems right from the start. George Band developed a cold and had to return to Base and Mike Westmacott, despite his good efforts on the icefall, seemed unable to get above 22,000 feet. He was transferred to the responsible task of keeping the constantly changing icefall route open. Which he did with great success. So it was pretty much over to George Lowe and Sherpa Ang Nyima to carve a route over the Lhotse Face, but unpleasant weather made their progress very slow. Wilf Noyce and I, with three Sherpas, carried loads up to George's camp at 23,000 feet where we discovered him recovering still from a sleeping pill taken the night before. Even as we had lunch together George went to sleep with a sardine sticking incongruously out of the side of his mouth. I took the Sherpas on with loads to 24,000 feet and dumped the gear there at the site for Camp VII. This was the highest I had been before and I was very pleased at how strong I felt at this altitude without oxygen. On the way up with Wilf I noticed he was following faster than I was leading and the rope was trailing on the ground between us. Almost instinctively I increased my pace and made sure from then on that the rope remained tight between us. In retrospect

I realize this was an unnecessarily competitive act, probably motivated by my conviction that Wilf Noyce was very fit and a potential summiter himself.

But still George Lowe wasn't making the hoped-for progress. Even when Mike Ward and Dawa Tenzing joined him on 17th May, they didn't get much above 24,000 feet and reported that the weather conditions remained very unpleasant. Time was passing and the upper Lhotse Face was defeating us. Strong winds and cold temperatures made every extra hundred feet a challenge. John Hunt decided that a desperate and courageous push was needed, so on 20th May Wilf Noyce and nine Sherpas made their way up to Camp VII at 24,000 feet and George Lowe came down. Next morning, we waited anxiously for the whole group to move upward but only two men emerged. Noyce and Sherpa Annullu slowly climbed the 2,000 feet of the upper face and disappeared onto the South Col. It was a great moment for us! On the lower slopes, Charles Wylie and another group of Sherpas were making their way up to Camp VII. This meant our entire group of high-altitude Sherpas would be at Camp VII that night. If they didn't all carry on to the South Col the next day, our whole assault would have failed.

I'm not very good at begging, but I went over to John Hunt's tent and literally pleaded with him to let me and Tenzing go up to Camp VII and spur on the major lift the next day. I was absolutely sure that Tenzing and I could go to the South Col and return and still be fit for our assault on the summit. A little to my surprise, John agreed and I told Tenzing the good news while Tom Bourdillon prepared two open-circuit oxygen sets. Then we were quickly away and made great time up the ice steps and fixed ropes of the Lhotse Face and arrived at Camp VII in four and a half hours, just before Noyce and Annullu returned from the South Col.

Tenzing's presence was a great morale booster for the Sherpa porters and made all the difference to their attitude. In a quite amazing fashion, our fourteen porters settled down to a peaceful night. Early in the morning it was windy and very cold and at 8:30 a.m. we crossed the deep crevasse above camp and started up the top half of the Lhotse Face.

Tenzing and Charles Wylie and I were using oxygen, but not the porters. Our two-man team led off across the great traverse, kicking and cutting steps and doing a lot of preparation. Charles Wylie stayed with the Sherpas to encourage them on, but already they were going more and more slowly and some lay down on the slope for a rest. Two in particular were in considerable distress, so Tenzing and I each took an oxygen bottle from their loads. One Sherpa gave up completely and Charles Wylie added his 20-lb. oxygen bottle to his own load. Pressing on, Tenzing and I crossed over the top of the Geneva Spur and dropped down to the wide and desolate expanse of the 26,000-foot South Col to dump our loads, including our half-used oxygen bottles. Moving easily without oxygen, we climbed back up the slope to meet Charles Wylie and his gallant band of thirteen porters coming over the top. That day fourteen loads were put in place on the South Col and we had achieved some success at last.

Tenzing and I picked up the exhausted Sherpa and then descended all the way down the Lhotse Face. John Hunt wasn't wasting any time— at the bottom of the face we met the closed-circuit team of Evans and Bourdillon on their way up. With them was an elated John Hunt himself. Clearly the assault was under way. In two days' time it would be the turn of Tenzing and myself to start the long trip toward the summit, after which neither of our lives would ever be the same again. For me there would be the joy of marrying Louise, but also the need to come to terms with being a public face and a focus of attention in the year of traveling that followed the ascent of Everest.

7

THE CHALLENGE OF MAKALU

LOUISE AND I RETURNED TO NEW ZEALAND FROM OUR LECTURE TOUR in the United States at the beginning of 1954 and it was great to be home. But we only had a meager six weeks together, for I had agreed to lead a New Zealand Alpine Club expedition back to my favorite valley, the Barun. We had a marvelous six weeks, as it was the first time that Louise and I had really been alone together and I quickly learned how fortunate I was to have such a wife. Louise was warm and loving, yet very independent, with a great love of the outdoors and a multitude of good friends. She had made it very clear to me that she accepted me as a climber and was happy for me to leave her and go to the end of the world, if I so wished. But for the first time in my life I had a strong reluctance to leave home. However, leave home I finally did.

This was the first time I had been overall leader of a Himalayan expedition but I felt little concern about my ability. At various times I had run parts of the Everest climb—on the icefall and the push to the summit—and George Lowe and I had shared the leadership of many smaller adventures. I planned and organized the New Zealand Alpine Club expedition and had a clear idea of what we wanted to undertake. Included in my party were my good friends from the 1953 Everest

Hillary and Tenzing, names to be forever linked. I believe we were a good team.

The Khumbu Icefall was the first major hurdle to cross. Vast and unstable, it has claimed more lives than any other part of the South-East Ridge approach.

An avalanche sweeps down the
Khumbu Icefall.

© Royal Geographical Society, London, 1953.

Advance Base Camp at 21,200 ft.
in the Western Cwm.

© Royal Geographical Society, London, 1953.

Looking up the Western Cwm
and the Lhotse Face, our route toward the South Col.

© Royal Geographical Society, London, 1953.

Evans and Bourdillon (*above*) return
exhausted from the South Summit
(28,700 ft.). Then it was our turn (*above
right*). Note the flags for the summit
already wound round Tenzing's ice axe.

© Royal Geographical Society, London, 1953.

(*Middle right*) Tenzing and I rest on the
South-East Ridge.

© Royal Geographical Society, London, 1953.

(*Lower right*) John Hunt after his
heroic carry to 27,350 ft. Now he
could only wait and hope.

© Royal Geographical Society, London, 1953.

The South-East Ridge from the South Col. © Royal Geographical Society, London, 1953.

The summit ridge had a sting in its tail which became known as the Hillary Step.

© Royal Geographical Society, London, 1953.

The picture that went round the world.

© Royal Geographical Society, London, 1953.

The view east from the summit of Everest. Makalu is in the right foreground and Kangchenjunga, the world's third highest mountain, can be seen on the horizon.

The calm before the media and political storm at Advance Base. Neither Tenzing nor I could begin to comprehend how our lives were about to change.

Assembling the first hut at Scott Base, McMurdo Sound (*above*),
and Scott Base after the winter storms (*below*).

The Weasel and the Caboose crossing the névé of the Skelton Glacier with Mount Huggins behind.

Traveling through a crevasse area south of Depot 700.

(*Below*) One we missed—two tractors pull a third out of a crevasse.

Bunny Fuchs covered with drift snow after digging out the tunnel entrance, 3rd August 1957; -53°C; wind speed 55 knots. © George Lowe.

Bunny in his lead Sno-Cat approaches the South Pole.

expedition, George Lowe and Dr. Charles Evans, and a number of very experienced New Zealand mountaineers.

Once again we walked up the Arun river, crossed the swing bridge at Num and climbed up to the village of Sedua. There was heavy snow on the mountains and it was quite a struggle crossing the snow-covered Barun Pass and descending down to the Barun river. The valley seemed as beautiful as ever and for two days we made our way upward to 15,500 feet and pitched our Base Camp tents on a mossy ledge beside the river. It was one of the most dramatic campsites I had ever used, for towering 12,000 feet above our heads was the great peak of Makalu with its fantastic rock ridges and ice-clad faces.

I split our party up into several groups and some carried out wide exploration of the Choyang and Iswa valleys, previously unvisited by foreign explorers, at the conclusion crossing high passes to rejoin the main expedition in the Barun valley. Meanwhile Brian Wilkins, Jim McFarlane and I, with five Sherpas, set off up the Barun Glacier on a reconnaissance. It proved to be a somewhat disastrous journey. We climbed two rather easy mountains of more than 20,000 feet. Then Wilkins and McFarlane broke through the lid of a deep crevasse when descending a glacier. Wilkins managed to climb his way out again, but, in helping to extricate McFarlane, I suffered three broken ribs and McFarlane himself experienced severe frostbite to his hands and feet. In considerable discomfort, plus shortage of breath, from the pain of my ribs, I struggled down valley with a Sherpa helper and organized an expedition rescue team to get McFarlane back to Base. It took four days of hard work to carry him over the ten miles down the glacier and we were greatly relieved when he was finally comfortable back in Base Camp.

Our main objective had always been the ascent of Baruntse (23,570 feet) and we had no plans to attempt the much higher Makalu. But our frequent views of Makalu had indicated that there was a potential route high on the mountain up the small Makalu Glacier, so we decided to investigate. Early in May the majority of the party moved up valley and established Camp I at 17,000 feet on the Barun Glacier. My broken ribs were still troubling me and I was forced to stay behind, but I was kept well informed of our excellent progress by runner. The first day on the glacier was an easy scramble up loose shifting moraine until Camp II was established at 19,200 feet. Next day they reached a large snowfield and established Camp III at 20,800 feet.

By 12th May I was thoroughly bored with inactivity and started off from Base Camp with Wilkins and some Sherpas to join the others. I seemed to go reasonably well, although excessive breathing gave me considerable pain in the chest, but, as a supreme optimist, I felt sure the pain was only temporary and would soon pass away. I was actually well ahead of the others and started looking for Camp II but simply couldn't find it. Even when Wilkins and the Sherpas arrived, we were still unsuccessful. We had no tents and little food and in the end just crawled into our sleeping bags on a flat stretch of shingle. Our dinner was a tin of salmon and a bar of chocolate which was reasonably satisfying. It was bitterly cold in the morning and we didn't move until the sun reached us. Just as we were about to carry on we heard some cheerful voices and half a dozen Sherpas appeared out of the broken ground ahead. They laughed heartily when they saw us, as Camp II was only another quarter mile on, hidden amongst the pinnacles. A message from Charles Evans was very encouraging. From Camp III at 20,800 feet, they had crossed one ice terrace, climbed some steep ice pitches and then found another broad and safe snow terrace at 22,000 feet. Here Camp IV was established on a little snowy platform under a great ice bulge.

This was excellent news and, despite a constant pain in my chest, Wilkins and I were anxious to join our companions. We climbed up to Camp II, well concealed amongst the seracs, had a cup of tea and some breakfast and then carried on toward Camp III. It was a beautiful morning and as we climbed higher the view spread out magnificently beneath us, but we kept watching the steep slopes of Makalu above and suddenly saw two black dots moving slowly upward. We were greatly encouraged and, although my chest was aching abominably, we hacked steps up the last long ice slope leading to the snow plateau and then started trudging across it through the heat and the glare. It was a great relief to me when we came over a last snow hump and saw the tents of Camp III. George Lowe was there to greet us and hot cups of tea were thrust into our willing hands. With some enthusiasm, I collapsed into my sleeping bag.

That night in Camp III was an unpleasant one for me. I had considerable difficulty in breathing and every cough sent a sharp pain through my chest, but I was still stubborn in my belief that the condition would ease. In the morning Charles Evans joined us from Camp IV and gave an enthusiastic account of their climb to 23,000 feet and his optimism that the steep rocky face to the Makalu Col could also be climbed.

In retrospect, I made the unbelievably stupid decision to push on. George Lowe, Brian Wilkins, another distinguished New Zealander climber, Norman Hardie, and I, plus five Sherpas, would go to Camp IV and from there we would establish Camp V. I led off up the steep slope above but, to my considerable disappointment, found I was completely lacking in energy. I was very thankful when George Lowe took over. We reached the snow terrace and started moving slowly across it. The snow was soft and it was a struggle making any progress. I was exhausted when we reached the last steep slope and I only managed to climb it with the remnants of my energy. We dug out a couple more sites on the steep slope and pitched several more tents. Then I tottered inside.

Once again I had a terrible night and in the morning I was too weak to move. I lay there all day while the others worked on the route ahead, but I was fast realizing that I had come to the end of the line. Another difficult night, and by morning I felt terrible and we knew I'd have to go down. I began dressing, but found it impossible to put on my boots. Fortunately, George noted my deplorable condition and swung into action. He helped me with my boots and clothing and lifted me to my feet. I managed to walk down the first long slope but then I came to an uphill grade and I found it impossible to move and everything went completely black. I had a period of terrible hallucinations and imagined myself perched on a great ice slope with avalanches thundering down around me and a voice screaming for help—no doubt my own. I came back into a terrible consciousness to find George strapping me into a stretcher made of backpacks. I was tied inside my sleeping bag, quite unable to move and suffering from awful claustrophobia. Then followed a long period of semiconsciousness, of heat and extreme discomfort, of swinging and bumping.

I have had a number of occasions when I suspected I might be close to death but this was the only time I can remember feeling that it might perhaps be easier to die and I simply couldn't make any effort to survive. The three days it took them to carry me down to Camp I were the most terrible in my life. Dr. Charles Evans looked after me with the greatest care and was determined that I should survive. I was suffering from severe dehydration which caused a swollen tongue with deep cracks across it. I found it impossible to drink but Charles forced me to—he even started feeding me with water in an eyedropper and suddenly I started to swallow. Undoubtedly Charles saved my life. Slowly my health improved and I was able to drink again and even to eat a little. Ten days after my collapse, I was able to walk comfortably down to the green grass of Base Camp. But I was still so weak that I knew my climbing was over for the year.

My illness was headline news in Great Britain and New Zealand. Old friends were approached by editors just in case the worst came to the worst. John Hunt later said: "I was asked to write an obituary which I've still got a copy of actually. It made me realize of course that Ed wasn't by any means tired of climbing and taking risks and pursuing adventure in one form or another and would undoubtedly lay himself open to accidents, possibly fatal accidents."

We had withdrawn from Makalu, but other great climbs were done by our New Zealand expedition—Pethangtse (22,080 feet), Chago (22,590 feet) and finally our ultimate objective, the magnificent summit of Baruntse (23,570 feet).

I turned down valley with the frostbitten Jim McFarlane and a team of Sherpas. It was a long carry to the nearest railway and finally to an aircraft back to New Zealand. McFarlane spent months in hospital but made a remarkable recovery. He carried on his profession as a successful engineer and re-established himself as a competent sportsman. He was a strong and brave man.

I believe my experience on Makalu started the deterioration of the ability I had shown on Mount Everest to acclimatize effectively to extreme altitude. I still remained able to perform adequately above 20,000 feet, but slowly altitude has caught up with me and I am now reluctant to sleep above 8,000 feet. This did not affect my enthusiasm for adventurous challenges—there were still a multitude of interesting things to do in the Antarctic and the Himalayan foothills—or in the wild mountain rivers all over the world. It was only at great altitude that my adventurous ability had subsided.

8

ANTARCTIC PREPARATIONS

THE WORST JOURNEY IN THE WORLD BY APSLEY CHERRY-GARRARD, a member of Robert Falcon Scott's ill-fated last Antarctic expedition, inspired me as a young man. It was a marvelous story and I read it time and again. Even when I was stationed in the Solomons in the Second World War, I often sat at the edge of a perfect tropical shore and wrote letters home saying how I wanted to go to Antarctica someday. At the Auckland Alpine Club dinner where I announced my engagement to Louise I expressed the view that the Ross Sea Dependency under New Zealand's jurisdiction needed to be explored and that I would love to go on such an expedition.

Sitting at the bottom of the world, surrounded by the fierce Southern Ocean, Antarctica is the last great wilderness on the planet. It is the coldest, windiest, driest and also the highest continent on earth—with an average height of 7,500 feet above sea level. Ice up to two miles thick covers ninety-eight percent of the surface. At the Pole the weight of this frozen water has dimpled the earth's crust. Under the pressure of its own weight ice formed on the Polar Plateau grinds continuously outward to the edge of the continent. Ice-free nunataks attempting to break through the endless white mantle are in fact the tips of buried mountain ranges. On the rim of the Polar Plateau the ice moves through the mountain systems and flows inexorably down immense glaciers to the coast, forming vast carpets of ice, hundreds of feet thick, that float on the Southern Ocean. The biggest of these, the Ross Ice Shelf, covers an area the size of France. Captain Cook, the first man to venture into the Southern Ocean and encounter icebergs, was not taken with the place, describing it as, "a land doomed by nature to everlasting frigidness and never once to feel the warmth of the sun's rays, whose horrible and savage aspects I have no words to describe."

But in 1954, just back from Makalu, the frozen continent did not figure highly in my plans. By the end of that year it was as though my adventurous life had never existed. I was working at the beekeeping with Rex and writing my first book, *High Adventure*. On the day after Christmas 1954 my son, Peter, was born and I began sharing with Louise the disturbed nights that most parents experience. I had no premonition, or indeed ambition, that my son would one day climb Everest, too. With our tiny baby we camped in a small tent in the middle of summer on a beautiful beach on the lovely Coromandel Peninsula and there wasn't a single other person in the bay. I was content to live a peaceful family life.

Periodically stories came through from England where George Lowe, who was now teaching geography at Repton School, had been appointed official photographer to the British and Commonwealth Trans-Antarctic expedition. I had met Dr. Vivian Fuchs in London late in 1953. For some reason he was keen to explain his plans to me, and George took me up the grubby stairs to a rather tiny office to meet him. He was an impressive person, strongly built and very serious-minded, but he really came alive as he explained his objectives. He wanted to use modern equipment to achieve what Sir Ernest Shackleton had been unable to do—to cross the Antarctic continent by way of the South Pole. Fuchs' grand plan was for the British crossing party to drive their vehicles from the Weddell Sea coast, through to the Pole, on across the Polar Plateau toward the Ferrar Glacier and down to McMurdo Sound. Any New Zealand involvement would be relatively modest. After establishing a

Base Camp on the edge of the Ross Sea, the New Zealanders would reconnoiter a route up the Ferrar Glacier, using dog teams and establish a single food and fuel depot 250 miles inland on the edge of the Polar Plateau, near Mount Albert Markham, for the British crossing party who would be running low on supplies by then.

Fuchs constantly emphasized the important scientific results for the International Geophysical Year 1956–57 that would flow from the expedition, but to me it just sounded like a rather good adventure. Then, coming to the point, he explained that it would be necessary to establish a support base in McMurdo Sound and he hoped that the New Zealand government would back this financially. I had found our chat all very interesting but hadn't quite seen where I came in until he told me he had worked out the expedition total cost would run to something between a quarter and half a million pounds. As soon as Fuchs said this I realized why I was at the meeting. He felt that if I were involved in the project on the New Zealand side, there would be much more likelihood of the New Zealand government and the people of New Zealand supporting it.

Initially I had no plans to go south myself, but as I did what I could to motivate the powers that be, I started almost unconsciously to develop an enthusiasm for the idea. I talked tentatively to Louise and asked how she would feel if I got selected and was away for eighteen months. Her response was typical. "If you really want to go, then I think you should go," said my astonishingly agreeable wife. But what a miserable husband I was proving to be! However, I had received a substantial publisher's advance for *High Adventure* and an even larger sum for its serialization. Louise's father, Jim Rose, had offered to sell us a half acre of his extremely desirable property at a minimal cost and we were very happy to accept. We employed an architect and soon began building a pleasant house with a beautiful outlook over the Waitemata harbor. At least if I went South I knew that Louise and Peter would have a nice comfortable home to live in, with her family not too far away.

Largely because of the activities of the Antarctic Society public interest in Fuchs' project was now growing in New Zealand and I did all I could to encourage it. Schools adopted a husky and individuals could buy "Share in Adventure" certificates. In the end New Zealanders raised more money per capita for the expedition than the United Kingdom. I meanwhile studied Antarctic literature extensively and developed quite a wide knowledge of polar expedition life. The problems posed by snow, ice, wind, zero temperatures and remote areas didn't seem too different to me from a Himalayan expedition, or even a journey into the untraveled glaciated areas of the New Zealand Alps. In 1955 the New Zealand government had come on board, as Fuchs had hoped, by announcing the formation of the Ross Sea Committee and I was invited to lead the New Zealand party. I was unaware of the arguments that had taken place about my leadership. A respected naval commander had been proposed for the task and I believe it was the influence of Bunny Fuchs himself that swung the Ross Sea Committee in my favor. I sometimes think that the naval commander would have fulfilled Bunny's limited plans perfectly adequately, so perhaps he brought the extensive programs my active imagination created on himself.

The general plan was now taking shape. In the 1955–56 Antarctic summer Fuchs intended taking an expedition into the Weddell Sea to establish Shackleton Base. A small party would stay on through the winter to complete the construction of the Base and get it ready for Fuchs to inhabit with his main party in the summer of 1956–57. In December 1956 I would sail from New Zealand with my expedition and establish Scott Base in McMurdo Sound. Both parties would winter over and then start in the spring to move toward the Pole, Fuchs with three large Sno-Cats on their four-track pontoons, two Weasels, and a converted Muskeg tractor, our party with three modified Ferguson tractors.

By now I had met Bunny enough times to begin to have grave doubts about how effectively he and I would work together. He was clearly very rigid in his views and plans and would carry them through to a very determined conclusion. I, on the other hand, was far more likely to change a program if a better alternative presented itself. The objective that Bunny had set for the Ross Sea party didn't sound all that great a challenge to me—to put a depot out 250 miles from Base on the Polar Plateau would be demanding but not too difficult. Even at that early stage my mind was churning over a grander view. I wrote thoughtfully to the Ross Sea Committee:

> Although the journey objective of the New Zealand end must be the establishment of a dump at Mt. Albert Markham, we should plan to have sufficient supplies and equipment so that if organization and time permits or an emergency occurs, the Party could travel out as far as the South Pole.
>
> Fuchs seemed reasonably happy with these proposals and they are the guide I am using in my discussions with his experts in respect to food and equipment lists, fuel, air support, etc.

Obviously neither the Ross Sea Committee nor Bunny Fuchs took me seriously.

I did most of the selection of the New Zealand wintering-over party, although a certain amount of inevitable horse-trading went on. A brigadier, who was the senior army medical officer, was asked to approve the health of expedition members. When he examined Harry Ayres he turned him down due to his varicose veins. I refused to accept this decision and we agreed to ask for a second expert opinion. Fortunately, the specialist we lighted on had been taken by Harry over a couple of difficult mountain passes the previous summer and had a vast respect for his abilities—so Harry was in. For our senior radio expert we interviewed two very experienced naval chief petty officers. One of them persisted in calling me Sir while the other, Peter Mulgrew, did not. I chose Peter Mulgrew and this was the beginning of a long and fruitful friendship.

To help us with the dogs we would use on surveying trips we obtained two good men from Britain who had each spent two years driving dogs with the Falkland Islands Dependency Survey. Dr. George Marsh was also our expedition doctor and Lt. Commander Richard Brooke was one of our surveyors. They both proved excellent instructors. We had two experienced engineers, Murray Ellis and Jim Bates, who were both innovative and very effective in keeping our machinery going in Antarctic temperatures. In all we had a wintering-over party of twenty-three whose job would be to establish a Base for the main thrust the following spring.

I had my first chance to set foot on Antarctica when Bunny Fuchs included me, my deputy leader Bob Miller and our senior pilot John Claydon in his party to establish the Weddell Sea Base. We sailed aboard the 800-ton expedition ship *Theron*, a battered but effective sealer that was ice strengthened. Expedition supplies were piled high on the decks and living space was limited. I initially regarded myself as being very fortunate to share a small cabin with Bunny Fuchs but I started coming to the unkind conclusion that Bunny had done this so that he could keep a close watch on me. Despite my five Himalayan expeditions Bunny certainly regarded me as an inexperienced observer and I was never invited to attend his frequent executive meetings, although John Claydon and Bob Miller often were. I don't think Bunny had any concept of how irritating I found this—after all I was the leader of the other half of his expedition.

I became very good friends with the *Theron*'s Norwegian captain, Harold Maro, and gained most of my information from him. Bunny didn't ask Harold Maro for many opinions either, so we had much in common. One thing really worried Harold Maro. The traditional approach into the Weddell Sea had been to break through the belt of pack ice on the eastern side of the sea and then enter the channel of open water that usually existed along the ice cliffs of the Caird Coast. But Bunny had a rather unusual plan. He believed that the pack ice in the Weddell Sea was in two sections that rotated independently. If it was possible to strike where the two areas met, he was confident we could have an easy passage to Vahsel Bay at the southern extremity of the sea.

We had very rough water on 22nd December as we approached the pack ice but once inside it became miraculously calm, allowing us to motor south at great speed and in the first twenty-four hours cover 160 miles—it really looked as though Bunny's theory would prove to be a correct one. Even through Christmas Day we made good distance south but slowly and steadily the pack ice became heavier and harder to penetrate and we began the New Year well and truly stuck. It now became a desperate struggle to escape back north. Sometimes we were held immovable and on other occasions we'd break free and make a little distance. But it wasn't until 22nd January—thirty-two days after entering the ice—that we broke free again. So much for Bunny's theory!

It was an exciting moment when the black nunataks of Vahsel Bay loomed up—the first rock on the Antarctic continent I had seen. Twenty-eight miles from Vahsel Bay the tall cliffs of the ice shelf sloped down to the mile-wide strip of sea ice at their feet. The Auster was lowered into the water and reconnaissances flown to the south which confirmed that this spot had the most fundamental requirements—access to it from the ship and access from it toward the Pole. So the site for Shackleton Base was duly chosen.

In the 1980s and 1990s some remarkable adventures have been undertaken in the Arctic and Antarctic. Small teams of men on skis, dragging their sledges behind them, have reached the North and South Poles and returned again. A Norwegian, Borg Ousland, even traveled alone on skis across the entire Antarctic continent without any aerial support. These adventurers displayed tremendous endurance and astonishing courage but they benefited greatly from modern technology. In many cases they were following routes that had at times been crossed before; while on their skis they were towed by quadrafoil parachutes driven by the vigorous katabatic winds; their tiny but powerful radios enabled them if necessary to call for help in a crisis; and their GPS navigation systems advised them precisely where they were at any moment. This does not detract from their achievements.

Our Antarctic expedition in 1956–58 was a slightly different story. We were traveling and exploring in areas where no man had ever set foot before and we also had important scientific objectives to undertake. We were using small aircraft to support us and drove tractors in heavily crevassed country which is always a hazardous procedure. So in a way we were using more sophisticated transport arrangements while at the same time living and working in a more primitive fashion than those adventurers forty years later. But the challenge has basically remained the same.

At Shackleton we were a month behind schedule so we had no time to waste, but a problem immediately became apparent—the vehicles were stowed halfway down in the hold. The only thing to do was to unload large quantities of supplies onto the ice edge and take the terrible risk of a storm sweeping waves ashore to destroy everything there. I was one of the few who realized how dangerous this was. We worked furiously to shift equipment onto the ice and finally the snow vehicles were located—two Weasels and two half-track Ferguson tractors which were lifted out of the hold and quickly made operational. Then we started a desperate rush to drag everything across the bay ice and some of it onto the campsite itself on the high ice shelf.

As Bunny's plan for McMurdo Sound only envisaged our using Ferguson tractors I commandeered one of them and soon found it capable of dragging loads adequately across the sea ice but unable to climb the steep slope up to the ice shelf. Only the versatile Weasels could do that. It became clear that many of the expedition team were not familiar with driving these types of vehicles, or any types of vehicles for that matter. I watched one member get into a Weasel, start it up, put it in the wrong gear and back right over the loaded sledge behind. Despite this it was surprising how many loads were moved across the sea ice to an intermediate depot, although this was still a dangerous spot, being little above sea level. On the third morning 1st February the temperature had risen by nearly twenty degrees and there were many ominous clouds to the north. I talked to Captain Maro who was decidedly worried and forecast a storm.

One of our Weasels had broken down and, of course, all the spare parts were in an unopened hold. Instead of persisting with our three remaining vehicles until the weather conditions improved, to my astonishment a decision was made to take the desperate measure of opening the new hold and unloading the supplies onto the ice until the spares were found. During the afternoon a great storm swept in and waves were breaking over the ice edge. The loads were soon engulfed in six inches to a foot of seawater. By 5 p.m. the storm reached a crescendo of fury, the tow ropes parted and Captain Maro had to move the *Theron* offshore. Those of us still on the sea ice were in a decidedly uncomfortable situation—we had no tents or sleeping bags, so no protection against the elements. Somehow we had to get back on board the ship. We parked the tractors well away from the sea and then crossed to a part of the ice edge that was high enough to be above the waves and watched the *Theron* rising and falling on the rolling waters. Then a great ice floe came bumping along the edge, leaving an area of calm water behind it. This was the chance Captain Maro was waiting for. He nosed the *Theron* into the quiet area and we leaped safely aboard. Next moment we were a hundred yards offshore tossing about in the great waves again. The storm lasted all night and the following morning but then, almost miraculously, the wind changed and the sea immediately calmed down. Captain Maro moved the *Theron* back into its old position and we tied up alongside the ice.

Over the next few days the weather fluctuated considerably with fine periods followed by wind and storm, but the unloading went on. By midday on 6th February the ship was empty and we concentrated on moving the supplies up onto the campsite from the intermediate camp at the bottom of the hill. By this time everyone was rather jittery. Heavy pack ice had been seen to the north and there was fear that the *Theron* might be crushed against the ice edge. When more heavy ice approached, a feeling of almost panic swept through the ship. The wintering-over party of ten men quickly brought their personal gear ashore and then lined up to wave good-bye as we sailed away. I had a terrible feeling that we were abandoning them. For a couple of hours we struggled through moderate pack ice but then we were in open water again and sailing steadily to the north. With almost embarrassing ease, we cleared the ice of the Weddell Sea and rolled our way over the ocean to South Georgia. It is easy to judge in retrospect but there is no doubt we could have stayed a few days longer at Shackleton and this would have made a great difference to the movement of supplies and the construction of the Base hut. Some time after our departure a great storm arose and all the sea ice and the intermediate depot were swept away. The wintering-over party had a struggle to survive and showed amazing adaptability and skill.

As we sailed north up through the Atlantic I could hardly believe how amateurish and disorganized the expedition had been. I had certainly learned a lot, but it was mostly about what not to do and I resolved that no such obvious mistakes would occur in our New Zealand plans. Clearly the first priority was to reach the Base site as quickly and easily as possible, rather than attempt a new and crazy route through hundreds of miles of pack ice. When we came up the river Thames to London we were greeted like returning heroes with every ship blowing its foghorn and crowds waving furiously. In fact I felt there wasn't too much to celebrate. Clearly being stuck in the ice for a month and then escaping appealed to the public and the media, even if it served no useful purpose whatsoever for the expedition. That extra month could have transformed the establishing of Shackleton Base.

On my return to New Zealand our organization speeded up enormously. Suitable huts were obtained and our construction team practiced assembling them in Wellington before our departure. We had the good fortune to have a heavy snow year that winter and I had the whole wintering-over team of twenty-three spend a couple of months on the twenty-mile-long Tasman Glacier. Everyone drove tractors, handled dogs, skied, camped in the snow in tents and at least became familiar with all the skills needed for living in the polar regions. The Royal New Zealand Navy had bought an 800-ton wooden vessel which had been used extensively before by the British Falkland Islands Survey so had been reinforced for use in the ice. It was certainly old but still operational and, renamed HMNZS *Endeavour*, it arrived in New Zealand with its main hold full of equipment and food sent to us by the British expedition. I had a telephone call from the wharf to advise me that unfortunately the pumps on the main hold had become blocked and the hold and its contents were completely full of seawater. At first this seemed a major disaster but when I thought it over I realised that most of the contents in the hold were items which were rather old-fashioned and traditional and could be much better supplied in New Zealand. So Bob Miller and I got onto our telephones and rang manufacturers all over New Zealand. Great support and generosity was shown and we soon replaced all requirements with better equipment and at very modest cost. Only traditional Antarctic Pyramid tents and pemmican had to be airfreighted out from England.

I was determined not to be short of vehicles. After returning to England from the Weddell Sea I had visited the developers of the Ferguson track system in Norway. In the high peaks of the Jotunheimen we tested out half-track and full-track Fergusons against specifically designed snow vehicles. It confirmed my feeling that the full-track Ferguson, despite its weakness in soft snow, was rugged, reliable and adaptable and might well get us a long way toward the South Pole. The manufacturers supplied us with five Fergusons and I was very excited when I obtained a message from Admiral George Dufek, Commander of the U.S. Deep Freeze project based at McMurdo Sound, that he would bring two Weasels south for us. This was typical of Admiral Dufek's generosity and interest throughout the expedition. This meant we had seven vehicles, enough for even my most ambitious plans. I had not made further mention to the Ross Sea Committee of my enlarged intentions as I knew they might not approve. But instead I increased the quantities of most of the important items so that they would be adequate for anything I might decide to do.

The eight months after my return from the Weddell Sea were probably the busiest I have ever spent. Lecturing and fund-raising, planning and training, buying and packing—it was a hectic period but an exciting and enjoyable one, too. It was important for me also as Louise produced our baby daughter, Sarah. I had just built a house with the proceeds from *High Adventure* and I wanted to get our new home into reasonable order.

In the middle of December we started loading the *Endeavour* for the journey south and I made sure we had our tractors, sledges and dogs on deck, plus many drums of fuel. On top of the hold we stowed tents and immediate requirements for food so that we could be self-sufficient without need to put supplies on the ice—and vehicle spares were readily available too. I had learned the lessons of the Weddell Sea.

On 15th December 1956 we had our official farewell in Wellington and the *Endeavour*, laden with cargo and personnel, sailed out of Port Nicholson for the South Island ports and then to the Antarctic. It was in Christchurch that the expedition had its most appreciated farewell. His Royal Highness the Duke of Edinburgh was making a short visit to New Zealand and in Lyttelton Harbour the *Endeavour* tied up at the wharf almost in the shadow of the royal yacht *Britannia*. For his last night in New Zealand the Duke had invited all the members of the expedition to dine with him aboard dressed as we stood. We lined up at *Britannia*'s gangplank in our casual clothing and were welcomed on board by an Admiral of the Royal Navy. Peter Mulgrew who was a chief petty officer in the Royal New Zealand Navy claimed it was the first time in history that a lower rank had been addressed as "Sir" by an Admiral. Our royal host set the lead in informality and we had a superb time. Some of our younger members were uncertain about how to behave at a formal dinner table and they turned to Dr. George Marsh, our English doctor and dog expert, for advice. George Marsh had a somewhat doubtful sense of humor and he advised everyone to watch him carefully and do everything that he did. Not only was the food excellent but there was ample wine and the noise level rose considerably. Finally, finger bowls were placed in front of everyone, something few had experienced before. Then came a plate full of huge delicious strawberries and our young members looked at George Marsh in desperation. But George was equal to the task. He calmly picked up a strawberry, dipped it in the finger bowl and dried it on a napkin then consumed it with relish. His young supporters did precisely the same. I saw a little grin appear on the Duke's face and then he carried on as though nothing unusual had occurred. Everyone was enjoying themselves so much that the *Britannia* was an hour late in leaving. We lined up on the wharf and waved a cheerful good-bye to the Duke who waved back.

Our last farewell and the hardest was on 21st December from the port at Dunedin. Louise and little Sarah were on the wharf, as were the children of the other expedition members. We were to be gone sixteen months leaving our loved ones behind. When a band started playing the sad strains of "Now Is the Hour" I was glad for the darkness of the bridge as tears slowly rolled down my cheeks. Unfortunately, the tide was such that the ship was pushed back to the wharf and the band valiantly continued to play until we finally disappeared into the darkness.

For the first few days the Southern Ocean was calm as a millpond. Then a fierce storm struck us and our little *Endeavour* was tossed around like a cork but remained remarkably stable. When we pushed our nose into the pack ice everything calmed down and we now faced the problem of forcing our way south through the ice. At times we moved freely and sometimes we were jammed tight amongst pressure ridges. The days were passing. I wanted all the time we could have in McMurdo Sound and I didn't feel we were being quite as energetic as we might have been—after all I was almost an expert after being stuck fast for a month in the fiercesome ice of the Weddell Sea eight months earlier. I ventured to talk to our skipper, Royal Naval Captain Kirkwood, but he became almost apoplectic and stormed out of the cabin. Apparently one didn't question the judgment of a Royal Naval captain. However I must admit that our progress south did increase appreciably after my comments.

We entered the open waters of the Ross Sea and motored easily south. Soon the great volcano of Mount Erebus was looming up with its long plume of steam and smoke streaming out from its summit cone. We eased to the right toward Butter Point and the Ferrar Glacier but had trouble pushing through heavy pack ice. Butter Point was the place Bunny had recommended for our Base as he considered the Ferrar Glacier would give us the easiest access to the Polar Plateau. We had helicoptered over there the previous year and had confirmed that Butter Point and the Ferrar Glacier were indeed ideal places. Unfortunately, conditions were very different this year.

The closer we came to Butter Point the more concerned I became. We pulled in at the ice edge, unloaded a couple of Fergusons and reconnoitered the area. First of all we found a deep tide crack between the sea ice and the foot of the moraine hill at Butter Point. Then we discovered that the lower part of the Ferrar Glacier was scoured with great channels of water and was quite impassable for our tractors. Finally there was no suitable flat snow to operate our aircraft. I went back on board the *Endeavour* and, while the others slept, I paced the deck deep in thought. It didn't take me long to make a decision—Butter Point was hopeless—we'd have to look elsewhere, but where? At this moment a fairy godmother appeared in the form of the great American icebreaker *Glacier* which came charging through heavy pack and hauled up alongside us. It was Admiral George Dufek again, just when I needed him most. He invited us on board and I told him my decision about Butter Point with which he thoroughly agreed. "Why don't you have a look at Pram Point on Ross Island?" he suggested. "I'll lend you my helicopter."

It was too good a chance to miss. Bob Miller and I circled over Pram Point, a rocky promontory thrusting out into the Ross Ice Shelf. When we landed I walked around with growing enthusiasm. It had everything we wanted, suitable hut sites on volcanic rock; easy access to the Ross Ice Shelf; and a large area of snow-covered bay ice for our aircraft. It would make an admirable Scott Base. We gathered up our various teams from Butter Point and brought everything together at the ice edge in McMurdo Sound. It was nine miles across the sea ice but good smooth traveling. The first sledge was loaded with tents, sleeping bags and food for a safe camp at Pram Point. At no stage did we unload supplies onto the ice—always onto sledges—a lesson we had learned from the Weddell Sea the year before. These were immediately dragged away to Scott Base. With our five vehicles we operated a twenty-four-hour program of load-shifting and camp establishing. Our construction team was moved to Pram Point and in one twenty-four-hour period we assembled the outer walls of our main mess hut, kitchen and radio room. We now had protection from whatever storm might arise.

It was now time to find a route up onto the Polar Plateau. I remembered that geologist Bernie Gunn had noted the previous year that the Skelton Glacier seemed worth investigating, so on 18th January I did a marvelous flight with John Claydon across the Ross Ice Shelf, up the great trench of the lower Skelton Glacier, over the broad crevassed snowfields at the glacier head, and out onto the wide snowy desert of the plateau itself. I saw crevasses and problems in plenty but I was also able to see a potential way through them all. The next thing would be to carry out a surface examination of the route using dog teams. As it would be much easier if we could fly the dog teams to the bottom of the Skelton Glacier, dog expert Richard Brooke and I did another reconnaissance flight up the glacier with John Claydon. About twenty miles up we saw a smooth stretch of snow beside the main crevassed glacier. We made several low passes over it before John Claydon lowered the flaps and made a careful approach. I watched the snow come smartly up toward us then our angle of vision changed and I realized that the surface was covered with large hard sastrugi, some of them three feet high. It was clear that we were going to crash and I knew it would be the end of us. Next moment there was a resounding crunch as we hit the first iron hard sastrugi. John whipped open the throttle and full power surged from the motor, crash followed crash as we bounced off a couple more sastrugi and then, to our enormous relief, we lifted safely into the air. We looked down at our metal skis and to our astonishment they seemed untouched. It had been a very close shave for us. Still white and shaken, we flew down the glacier to its mouth and this time made a perfect landing on smooth snow. We stepped out of the plane and pranced around in our excitement. We were the first men to set foot on the Skelton Glacier. In the course of the next few days large quantities of supplies were flown into the Skelton Depot—drums of fuel, kerosene, man and dog rations for the crossing party and the surveyors.

February 9th dawned fine and clear but it was colder, -15°C, at Scott Base, the day we were to make our first attempts to land on the Polar Plateau. We flew up the glacier, over the wide snow névé, and then through the pass we called the Portal. It took us some time to find the dog teams but then I caught a glimpse of something black out of the corner of my eye, we wheeled over and, sure enough, it was a camp with four waving figures outside. John Claydon made a careful examination of the snow surface and then with our second pilot, Bill Cranfield, in the Auster circling overhead, John brought the Beaver in for a perfect landing. It was too cold to wait around for long so we handed over some mail, I explained our plans and we were soon back in the air again. Then it was Bill Cranfield's turn in the Auster. The landing was easy enough but Bill was barely able to get his aircraft airborne and we never used the Auster at this altitude again.

In temperatures of −35°C the Beaver did twenty-four-hour flights into the Plateau Depot and three days later it too was fully stocked. Bob Miller and surveyor Roy Carlyon had just completed a trek with dogs from Scott Base to the Skelton Depot, so now the whole route had been covered by dog teams. More important, we had two fully established depots, one at 180 miles and the other at 290 miles from Scott Base. The route we had used was rather longer than the planned one up the Ferrar Glacier, so our Plateau Depot was still a hundred miles short of Fuchs' required 250-mile furthest depot, but it was still only 12th February in the first summer. We had a whole winter ahead of us for organization and then a full summer of adventure. I had a considerable feeling of satisfaction in what we had achieved and how well all my team had performed. On 22nd February the *Endeavour* sailed for New Zealand, taking with it the construction party. We owed a considerable debt of gratitude to them for their efforts had produced a very comfortable and well-appointed home for us. The onset of stormy weather indicated that winter was approaching. A break in the weather on 18th February enabled us to evacuate the dog teams and their drivers from the Skelton Depot and, for the first time, our whole complement of twenty-three men was together at Scott Base.

This was by no means the end of our autumn field activities, but we confined these to the area within fifty miles or so of Base. We had still one big project to do and that was to carry out a major trip with the Ferguson tractors. The Fergusons had done great work for us in the unloading of the ship and they had proved rugged, reliable and easily maintained. Jim Bates had made some massive changes in their tracking systems and had greatly improved their ability to handle soft snow. But just how good would they prove to be? I chose to do a test run to Cape Crozier, the easternmost tip of Ross Island and about fifty miles from Scott Base. This was where Wilson, Bowers and Cherry-Garrard had gone in the middle of winter as related in the famous book, *The Worst Journey in the World*. We set to work to prepare two of our best tractors for that journey.

On 5th March we made our first radio contact with Shackleton Base and I had a brief talk with Bunny Fuchs and a much longer chat with George Lowe. From what I could gather Base Camp life was conducted rather differently at Shackleton. The New Zealand expedition had been donated 500 records (one for every day we were expected to be in Antarctica). On the whole they were rather appalling, but I had no objections to team members playing them any time of the day or night, despite the disadvantage of my bedroom/office being just off the mess-room. According to George Lowe on the opposite coast, they also had a plentiful stock of records but Bunny limited the playing of these to Sunday afternoons. George said Bunny's view was that not everyone had the same taste in music, so it was better to have almost no music. There was no discussion on the matter. As George observed wryly years later, with Bunny you didn't have discussions, you had edicts.

Despite, or maybe because of, this musical deprivation, Shackleton Base also seemed to be in good shape and they had successfully established by air a small advanced base which they called South Ice, some 250 miles south of Shackleton, where three men were installed for the winter. The only thing that rather concerned me was that they had not done any of the planned autumn traveling with their vehicles and very little with their dogs, so that the surface route from Shackleton to South Ice was almost completely unproven. George mentioned that a range of small mountains crossed the route which he hoped would not be too much of a problem.

We had excellent radio communications with New Zealand and I spoke to Louise twice a week. It was wonderful to hear about the family and all that was going on, even if it ended abruptly when the phone was set down and the realization swept in that it was cold and dark outside and we were separated by a couple of thousand miles of stormy ocean. I remember on one occasion talking to Louise when suddenly there was a crash and a scream from a child and then the circuit broke due to sunspot activity. I had to wait a whole week to discover that Peter had only dropped his plate of cereal onto the floor. This was one of the major differences between our expedition and the pioneer ones of Scott and Shackleton. Our communications kept us close to our families and each other and we had all the world news if we wanted to listen to it. We were often lonely, but never really alone.

During the first half of March the weather was very unpleasant but on the 19th I decided we should leave for our Cape Crozier trek before it was too late. Our team was Murray Ellis, Jim Bates, Peter Mulgrew and myself with two tractors each towing sledges. We had quite a job breaking through the pressure ridges on the Ross Ice Shelf and I tipped a track into a concealed crevasse. But finally we made our way on to easier going and had a comfortable camp twelve and a half miles out. When we started next morning we struck deep soft snow—the notorious Windless Bight—and we were only just able to keep moving. But at least we did move and we covered another twelve and a half miles that day. The surface improved next morning and we clattered over the icy surface and climbed up a formidable slope to reach a flat camping spot on the top of Cape Crozier. We had covered twenty-three miles in the day and were now forty-eight miles from Scott Base.

There was wind and drift snow all night and, although it was sunny in the morning, a temperature of −27°C and a strong wind made life rather unpleasant. Our main objective was to locate the stone hut in which Wilson's party had spent such an unenviable time, but we searched the area for four hours without success before returning to our tents. Then Peter Mulgrew and I produced our copy of *The Worst Journey in the World* and argued furiously over where the hut must be. Peter was convinced it must be in one direction and I in another. So we dressed again and crawled out into the wind to examine our particular locations. I was walking down a narrow rocky spur when my eye caught sight of something unusual in the saddle beyond. It was a sledge thrusting up above some low rock walls. I called the others and we examined the site in amazement. Exposed to every wind, it must have been unbelievably uncomfortable in the darkness of mid-winter. Under the snow there was a variety of items, including three rolls of unexposed Kodak film marked "To be developed before May 1st, 1911."

We spent another miserable night and then started back the next afternoon, traveling cautiously down the icy slope, then along the firmer section making very good time. When we reached the Windless Bight the temperature was down below -50°C but we kept going with considerable determination. Even in the darkness we could follow our deep outward tracks with our tractor lights. About midnight we stopped to refuel and to our disgust Jim's tractor wouldn't start again—some water had frozen in the petrol line. Jim and Murray weren't in the mood for dillydallying and took drastic action. They lit a powerful blowtorch and played the flame on the fuel lines and petrol tank until they were successful in warming the fuel up sufficiently to melt the blockage out and permit a free flow again—needless to say, Peter Mulgrew and I stood well back! The lights on Jim's tractor were now fading rapidly as the bitterly cold conditions prevented the battery from recharging and in the dim light we lost the track time and again. But we knew we must be fairly close to Base, so we roped up the vehicles for the last few miles through the crevasses of the pressure ridges. Somehow we found the track again and managed to keep on it, creeping into Scott Base just before four o'clock in the morning. It had taken us four miserable hours to cover the last ten miles.

Although we had spent a long and tiring day, we felt a considerable satisfaction in having covered forty-eight miles in fourteen hours, despite the extended holdups. We had consumed fifty-four gallons of fuel for the ninety-six miles, giving an average of one and three-quarter miles per gallon. This wasn't particularly good, as we had only been pulling light loads, but the soft snow had been a formidable opponent and we had undoubtedly completed the trip with increased confidence in our vehicles. We were all too conscious of their limitations, particularly in soft snow, but they had shown us they could drag modest loads over quite difficult country in very low temperatures—and keep going! We resolved to modify and improve them even further and have them in peak condition to take south on the trail in the spring.

At the beginning of April I introduced a roster system in which everyone took his turn at doing the mess duties around camp—shovelling snow into the snow melters to augment our water supply, pumping kerosene into the fuel tanks of our generators, heaters and stoves, disposing of rubbish down amongst the pressure ridges, collecting cases of food from the rations dump; the daily cleaning of the mess hut and the ablutions and the washing-up of the pots and pans after the evening meal. There was certainly plenty to do. On Sunday the cook had his day off and the "stewards" had to do the cooking as well. Then of course everyone had to take his turn as night watchman. Dr. Trevor Hatherton, our senior scientist, and generally a very genial character, approached me with the idea that his five scientists should be dropped from the roster system, presumably because their work was important or maybe, as technologists, they weren't used to hard physical labor. I cheerfully turned the idea down—it had been worth a try—and Harry Ayres and I took over the first week. From then on everyone did their share without complaint. They were a remarkably good team to work with. For the Sunday night dinner we dipped into our limited supplies of luxury foods and drew on our cellar for table wines. Trevor Hatherton and George Marsh usually performed as waiters, and altogether these were most enjoyable and uproarious occasions.

I was spending a lot of time working out our program for the forthcoming summer season. Two groups of surveyors and geologists with dog teams would explore to the north along the Antarctic mountains. Bob Miller and George Marsh would take two more dog teams to do an exploration of the remote area in the mountains to the west of the giant Beardmore Glacier. I was determined to take a tractor train up onto the Polar Plateau and lay out depots for the crossing party at least 700 miles from Scott Base. And then, all going well, we would carry on to the South Pole. These plans were duly dispatched to the Ross Sea Committee in Wellington. On 8th March I had a radio telephone call

143

from the Chairman. He expressed the Executive Committee's concern at the possibility of me taking a party to the South Pole and "spoiling Bunny's effort."

A few days later I spoke to Bunny Fuchs over the radio telephone and I explained that I expected to put D480 at 80°S, and also hoped to put another depot, D700, at 83°S for our own use. Although D700 would be beyond the direct range of the Beaver aircraft, we planned to stock it by establishing a refueling depot at the foot of Shackleton Inlet. I asked Bunny if he would like us to attempt to stock D700 with petrol for his vehicles, too. I sensed a hesitation in his reply—perhaps a fear that we might be overreaching ourselves—and then came his answer, "First stock Depot 480 and then examine the possibilities of stocking D700."

That was safe conservative advice, no doubt, but I needed to plan well in advance for such a large-scale operation so I just included the stocking of D700 for the Trans-Antarctic party in my routine objectives. A number of times during the winter I asked Bunny for details of what supplies he would like at the various depots but he never gave me any positive information. In the end I just worked out what I considered he would need and put that in place. It did prove in fact to be considerably more than he ever required, so the extra was left at the depots and may still be there to this day.

There was so much expressed and unexpressed opposition to my making any effort to get to the South Pole that for a while I lost heart. I knew that even my deputy, Bob Miller, didn't like my plans and was more loyal to what he felt Fuchs would want. That was OK with me. It just meant I didn't take too much notice of his advice. Most of my team were very adventurous and seemed enthusiastic about some of the lively programs we agreed to undertake. Somewhat with tongue in cheek, I chose an even more difficult challenge—we'd establish D700 and then travel hundreds of miles west to the Pole of Inaccessibility where the Russians were planning to establish a base. I sent a long report to the Ross Sea Committee suggesting this, plus the many other field activities we intended to carry out and actually did complete. I received an equally long reply approving of the establishing of D480 and D700 but more or less turning everything else down. The orders were delivered with the authority of Antarctic experts which I was fully aware few if any of the Committee could claim to be. I wasn't too surprised at their response, but from then on I decided I would largely ignore the instructions of the Ross Sea Committee and, as leader in the field, make whatever decisions I regarded as appropriate.

On 14th May Scott Base was struck by its first real storm. We had a warning in the form of a rapid rise in temperature, and then for several days the wind rarely dropped below forty miles an hour with long periods when it remained between sixty and ninety miles an hour. Outside in the darkness all visibility was obscured by blinding sheets of drifting snow, and activity was restricted in times of lull to brief visits to the dogs and hasty examinations of the wire ropes holding the huts down. The Base vibrated to a continual roar and I spent most of my time checking everywhere for weaknesses and damage and watching the wind speed recorder. The wind was whistling up the slope in front of the Base and creating a powerful suction with the result that the ceilings of the two New Zealand–built huts were flapping up and down several inches in rather alarming fashion. Fortunately, they survived without damage, but we used the first decent lull in the storm to construct a powerful truss for each of the roofs and then tied them securely down with wire ropes. When the storm blew itself out and the starry skies and cold temperatures returned we breathed a sigh of relief. The Base had stood up to fierce winds without difficulty. We rarely had more than one storm a month during the winter, but when they came they could last for up to a week. The maximum gust of wind we experienced was ninety-five miles per hour; our minimum temperature was -50°C. In general, however, we enjoyed crisp clear weather and when the full moon was up it was almost like daylight.

During the winter I made many plans in cooperation with our various field parties, including aerial support. They were full of fiery enthusiasm for the tasks ahead. But the emphasis still lay on our main objective of reaching and stocking D700 and for this I intended to use tractors supported by aircraft.

Perhaps the biggest task during the winter was preparing our vehicles and sledges for the southern journey. Murray Ellis and Jim Bates completely overhauled the three Fergusons; they constructed a stout crash bar over the driver's head to protect him in case the vehicle rolled over, and improved the canvas cabs to try and give the driver a little more protection against the wind and drift. We did a great deal of work on the tracks and the tracking system, trying to get the maximum performance out of the vehicles in soft snow, and we removed the steel soles from the runners of most of our sledges and replaced them with the much more efficient Bakelite plastic, Tufnol. Remembering the discomforts we suffered on our Cape Crozier trip, I started the construction of a caravan on skis which we called the caboose. With a framework of welded piping and angle-iron, covered in a sheath of plywood and an outer skin of heavy green canvas, the internal dimensions were only twelve feet by six feet, but we installed bunks, cupboards, a cooking bench with primus stoves, and our radio equipment. Despite its ludicrous resemblance to a horse trailer, we were very proud of it.

On 23rd August we had our first sight of the returning sun. It was a fine day with a temperature of −35°C and by eleven o'clock the Western Mountains were glowing with a glorious pink as the sun hit them. By 1:30 p.m. the sea ice beyond Cape Armitage was alight and the sun was shining on Observation Hill. As Scott Base was still in the shade we all gravitated out into the sunshine like moths toward a candle. We started our preliminary journeys by tractor and dog team early in September when the ice in McMurdo Sound was firm and the temperatures decidedly low. October 4th saw the departure of the first of the field parties on the main summer operation. This was the northern party who carried out a long and successful journey of geology and mapping.

Our primary task remained the same—to get D700 established as soon as possible. This depot would be beyond the direct range of the Beaver aircraft from Scott Base, so John Claydon would have to establish an intermediate refueling point on the Ross Ice Shelf. I became very concerned about what would happen to my plans if the Beaver should come to grief during one of these complicated operations. While the dog teams could travel considerable distances when supported by aircraft they had limited usefulness as load-carriers. But by using the tractors we could be doubly sure of completing the task. I was convinced that by starting fully laden from the Plateau Depot we should be able to establish D700 with the tractors alone. My whole planning turned in this direction. The tractors would be the major thrust and the dog teams would be useful for reconnaissance and for support in emergency. Once the tractors reached the Plateau Depot we could head south fully laden with fuel and the establishing of D700 would be assured. But first we had to get the tractors to the Plateau Depot.

During the winter four of us had become closely involved with the tractor operation—the Old Firm we called ourselves. It was the group that had driven to Cape Crozier: Jim Bates, Murray Ellis, Peter Mulgrew and myself. Peter had done a very good job running our radio communications at Scott Base but he was never satisfied with staying there. Increasingly he infiltrated into field activities, and I think he had appointed himself to the southern tractor party almost before I was aware of it. Certainly his technical skill with radio equipment proved invaluable to me on long journeys and we were always able to maintain close communications with Base and the outside world—at times I felt we were almost too efficient in this respect. Jim Bates was quite a contrast. Lean and hungry-looking, Jim was an expert skier and had a notable disinterest in how he looked and dressed. He was also something of a mechanical genius and a successful inventor and I have never met anyone with more imagination and resourcefulness in mechanical matters. Murray Ellis was large, strong and very reliable; an engineering graduate who might grumble a little at times but who would tackle any job however unpleasant it might be; a mighty useful chap to have around in adverse circumstances.

9

To Depot 700

ON MONDAY 14TH OCTOBER THE LIGHTING WAS FLAT AND CHEER-less as we hitched up our sledges and started up our four vehicles—one Weasel and three Ferguson tractors. We had already established a route through the pressure ridges with a couple of empty tractors but it made all the difference towing our overloaded sledges. Two miles out one of my sledges broke through into a crevasse and we had to unload the twelve drums of fuel, haul the sledge to the surface and load the 350-lb. drums back on board again. We changed sledges around between vehicles but still had major problems. After five and a half hours we had traveled only eight miles and were only a mere six and a half miles in a direct line from Scott Base. Our progress had been pathetically slow. That night we could actually see Scott Base. I felt rather mortified that the team at the Base would all be nodding their heads and saying, "Told him so!"

Next morning we struck deep soft snow and had to relay our loads, dropping half of them off and then going back for them. In two hours we covered only one mile. I at last accepted what had been obvious from the beginning—we were overloaded. We took eight drums of fuel off our sledges and piled them into a depot to be picked up later by the people at

Scott Base. We started moving now, although slowly, but at least we didn't need to stop. We were doing a big swing out to the left to dodge the massive crevasse areas at the tips of White Island and Minna Bluff and as a safety measure we tied all the vehicles together with an eight-ton breaking strain Terylene rope. After a long day we camped—we had covered twenty-three miles—we were on the move and my confidence had grown considerably.

I was steering the tractor train with the assistance of an astro-compass. I had become familiar with this useful little instrument when navigating in aircraft and had decided to use it in preference to the traditional but more limited sun compass. Setting it up involved finding the latitude, declination, local hour angle, and true course on to four different dials and then turning the tractor until the shadow cast by the sun on a front sight came between two black lines on an opaque screen. This may sound rather complicated, especially as the knob twiddling had to be done in very cold temperatures, but in practice it wasn't really difficult. The main task was to draw up a list showing the local hour angles for every half-hour during the traveling day, and this usually involved me in forty minutes' struggle each morning with my astronomical tables. This list was kept in the lead tractor and the driver would use it to make the necessary half-hour changes of local hour angle. I also used the astro-compass for fixing our position, for it was quite an easy process at this stage of the trip to take bearings on a few known mountains and plot the results on my chart.

We were now moving much better, despite mechanical problems with the Weasel. On the third day we did thirty miles; on the fourth thirty-two, and on the fifth thirty-eight. We were only fifty miles from the Skelton Depot but to our disgust the Weasel wouldn't start. Murray struggled with the problem all day and finally at 5 p.m. the motor burst into life. By 6 p.m. we were ready to leave and decided to keep going all night—it was of course daylight for twenty-four hours—hoping to reach the depot before we stopped again. By 4 a.m. we were approaching the entrance to the Skelton Glacier and were rather concerned about possible crevasses. I fixed our position accurately on the local peaks with the

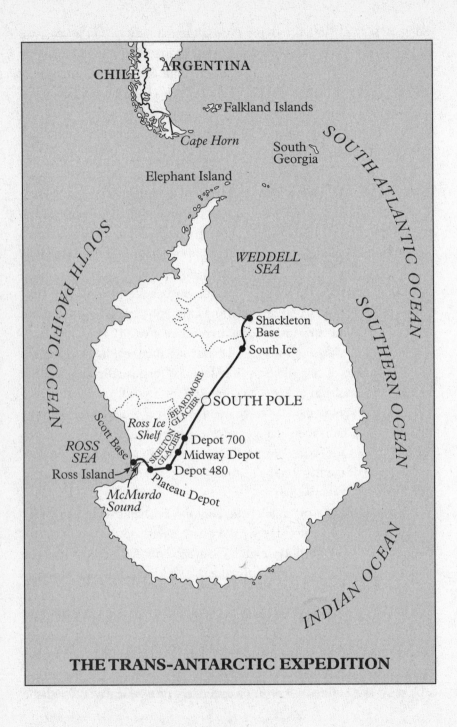

THE TRANS-ANTARCTIC EXPEDITION

astro-compass and drove straight down the middle of the glacier. At 6 a.m. we picked up a black dot ahead and swung toward it. At 7 a.m. we were being welcomed by eighteen dogs, plus Bob Miller, George Marsh and Jim Bates who had all flown in the previous day. The fifty miles had taken thirteen hours and we were very pleased to crawl into our sleeping bags. We spent two days at the Skelton Depot while Jim Bates and Murray Ellis erected a bipod, lifted the engine out of the Weasel and repaired it—all done in temperatures of -37°C. Murray in particular seemed to be immune to the cold.

Late in the afternoon of 22nd October we started up our vehicles and began moving up the rough ice of the Skelton Glacier. For the sake of safety we roped the three Fergusons together and the Weasel followed along behind. These were the conditions that the Fergusons reveled in but it was hard work for the more tender Weasel. Bob and George had left with their dogs many hours before and we reached their camp at 9:15 p.m. They had covered eighteen miles but it had been a terrible day for them on the hard rough surface and between them they had experienced thirteen toss-outs, so were rather battered and bruised. In the morning it was gusting up to fifty knots and there was dense drift snow which even blanketed out the other tents. But amazingly by midday it was sunny again and we made preparations for departure. The dog teams drove off into a blanket of drift snow and we soon followed behind into a renewed storm and in just over an hour covered five miles. But we had lost the dog teams and simply couldn't find them. I was confident they could look after themselves so we carried on into the teeth of the wind on a hard icy surface. Suddenly the whole surface of the glacier was split with crevasses and our tractors lurched around, punching many holes in their snow bridges. It was decidedly unpleasant, as some of the crevasses were very wide and we barely succeeded in crossing them. I felt a tightness in the pit of my stomach—when would we hit a crevasse which could absorb a tractor?

Following the advice of the autumn reconnaissance party, we swung down to the right into a broad trough that ran up the glacier. The crevasses here were mostly only a couple of feet wide but they gave way with unfailing regularity, leaving a line of black holes behind us. But at least we could handle this size. After we'd crossed a hundred or more crevasses the surface spectacularly improved and we started climbing upward amongst magnificent peaks and superb scenery. Clearly the storms were not just bad weather, but katabatic winds periodically sweeping down from the cold high places. We kept driving toward a prominent rock feature we had called Clinker Bluff. A vast icefall came tumbling down to the left of Clinker Bluff but we were hopeful of finding a route around to the right where gradually ascending snow slopes steepened some distance ahead and merged into the great buttresses of Mount Huggins. This was the way the autumn party had gone.

At 8 p.m. we stopped and camped—we had covered nineteen and a half miles of really rough traveling. Over the next two days we clawed our way up the steep snow slopes between the great crevasses on either side of the Lower Staircase and finally past Twin Rocks where we camped on a comfortably flat snow plateau we called the Landing at an altitude of 3,000 feet. After a radio schedule with Base and some food I went for a worried stroll outside in a relatively mild temperature of –25°C. Where on earth were Bob and George I wondered? I wasn't able to raise them on the radio. We decided we'd have an extra day here while Jim Bates tuned up the Fergusons.

By midday there was still no sign of the dog teams. Peter Mulgrew and I took the lively Weasel and retraced our tracks leading down the hill. We drove through the Lower Staircase but I could see no one and I was starting to feel desperate. We stopped briefly and next moment I heard the strident commands of a dog driver to his team. Peter and I walked over to the edge of the slope and 200 feet below us were Bob, George and their teams. By evening they were with us in our camp. We had driven past them in the storm, despite their shouts, and they had started running after us until they realized they might well lose their dogs and that would be the end of them.

Some miles across the Landing loomed the rock buttress of Stepaside Spur. It required a long detour around severely crevassed areas before we reached the Spur and then climbed steeply up the Upper Staircase.

With some relief we emerged on the Skelton névé and drove vigorously on. When we camped at 8 p.m. we were in an area of heavy wind and drift and at an altitude of 7,000 feet. John Claydon flew over us in the Beaver and radioed that he had just flown Harry Ayres and surveyor Roy Carlyon into the Plateau Depot with their dogs. The weather on the Plateau was clear but cold. We couldn't afford to waste fine weather so before long we were on our way again, climbing up the steep slopes leading to the Portal. During the night the caboose rocked and swayed as the wind freshened to a gale. By 10 a.m. next morning there was a rapid clearance in the weather. The improvement only looked temporary but we decided to leave. We hadn't gone more than a few hundred yards before the wind and drift hit us again. The only thing that enabled us to keep going was the pale gleam of the sun barely visible through the mist above us which let me steer by astro-compass. When we camped we'd only done two and a half miles in the day and what a struggle it had been.

It was cold during the night with the temperature down to close on −40°C. We had a clearance after starting again and I took advantage of it to fix our position accurately from the local peaks. Then the weather closed in again with fierce winds but we drove on with considerable determination. At the end of an hour Jim Bates took over my lead tractor and I moved to the Weasel in the rear. I knew we must be somewhere near the Plateau Depot but in this visibility how could we be sure? Then with amazing suddenness the mist cleared and directly ahead of us I could see a black triangle. It was the Plateau Depot! I am not one to display great emotion on important occasions—whatever I might feel— but this was the most exciting moment I can ever remember, certainly more exciting than reaching the summit of Everest. I actually shrieked and yelled with joy! It had been a monumental struggle up the Skelton Glacier with our Ferguson tractors and heavy loads but we had done it. It was just too much!

I lay in bed on that night of 31st October at the Plateau Depot and thought about the other members of the Old Firm—Murray, almost a professional pessimist, Peter, madly optimistic, and Jim, going from the depths of one to the heights of the other. But they were a tough trio—capable, resourceful, hardy and loyal. And what about me? Slightly crazy, frequently terrified and not a bad navigator—that about summed it up. I turned over and slept peacefully.

One potential weak link in our lines of communication once we reached the Polar Plateau was what we would do if anything happened to the Beaver aircraft. The Auster could operate to some degree at lower altitudes but not high up. I decided therefore to fly extra supplies into the Plateau Depot and then move on from there with fully laden tractors and dog teams. Then if anything happened to the Beaver at a later stage, we could establish a good southern depot with tractors alone. At this point the Old Firm received two body blows. Murray strained his back (an old rugby injury) and Peter fell off the caboose roof onto a trailer bar and cracked three ribs. Both had to be evacuated. I needed four drivers to take the tractor train on from the Plateau Depot. In desperation I flew back to Scott Base and telegraphed Admiral Dufek in Christchurch to see if there was any chance of getting Derek Wright down to the ice any earlier—the National Film Unit movie cameraman had proved an adept tractor driver the previous summer and was scheduled to come south again. To my relief and delight Dufek informed me that Wright would be on the next Globemaster flight, and in place of Peter there was Ted Gawn. Ted was an expert radio man, though hardly an outdoor type, but he bravely agreed to come with us.

With this fixed, my main ambition was to get back to the Plateau Depot and prepare for the onward journey. When I arrived I was accosted by a serious Jim Bates who said that he and Murray Ellis had discussed things before Murray was evacuated, and that neither of them was keen to go beyond D700. They felt the tractors would be worn out by then and we would be moving beyond the range of the Beaver. I consoled Jim with the reflection that we had to get to D700 before worrying about going beyond it. I had more confidence in the vehicles and my mechanics' ability to keep them going than they had themselves, so I decided not to be unduly influenced by their misgivings. But there was no doubt that our time at the Plateau Depot was the lowest point on our journey south.

Once our flying operations were completed the weather unexpectedly took a turn for the better and on 11th November it was brilliantly fine as we loaded sledges and made our last checks of the vehicles. It was fine again on 12th November as we completed the lashing of the loads on our seven sledges. We had a gross load of eleven tons and we knew this would take a powerful lot of pulling. We often found it easier to travel at night when the sun was to the south of us, as this helped our navigation. But we always traveled when the weather was fine, day or night. At 6:30 p.m. we pulled ourselves free from the drift snow and started moving, but we were soon bogged down. We tried all sorts of methods to keep moving but the most successful was when the lead tractor had no sledges but it threw all its weight onto the tow rope attached to the second tractor which had two sledges. Then there was a rope to the third tractor with three laden sledges. The Weasel pulled two sledges easily in the soft snow.

By 8:30 p.m., after much desperate work, we had covered four and a half miles. We stopped for our radio schedule with Bob Miller. He and George and the dogs had left ahead of us with twenty days' supplies. They were now miles out and able to assure us the surface improved considerably after the twenty-fifth mile. This was good news. We started again with renewed vigor but the farther we went the steeper the slope became and the softer the snow. The more we struggled the more we became bogged and I bitterly regretted the loss of Murray and Peter. My new team could hardly hope to have the acquired skill and timing of the old one and we sank in time and again. It was with reluctance that I decided we'd have to revert to the time-wasting and fuel-consuming system of relaying. When we camped we had covered only seven miles and it had been a struggle all the way. Before I crawled into my sleeping bag, I checked the temperature. It was –36°C—fairly normal I thought.

My personal temperature wasn't too good either—it was 39°C. After ten months in the Antarctic we were not immune to the flu, which had traveled down by plane from New Zealand, and I felt terrible. Jim Bates tried to keep things going but it was hopeless. A few hours later I was feeling a little better so I crawled weakly out of bed, pulled on my clothes and went outside. A scene of chaos greeted my eyes—tractors and sledges deep down in the snow in every direction plus three flushed faces and strained tempers. Obviously a new approach to the problem was needed and we attacked the job methodically, concentrating on getting one tractor or sledge clear at a time and onto more solid ground. In half an hour order had been restored and I retreated to the caboose. Jim and the other two relayed over very soft snow for the first two miles. The surface then improved a little and Jim reported that there was a fair chance of the vehicles pulling the total load at once. I decided I'd better ignore my ailing flesh and get on with the job, so emerged again and took over the driving of the Weasel which was by far the warmest and most comfortable vehicle. I hoped this would give me a chance to recuperate.

And now the Weasel started proving its true worth in soft snow. To ease the burden on the Fergusons I unhitched a two-ton sledge from their load and attached it behind the Weasel. This made the Weasel's load up to five tons, but it towed it magnificently and was able to keep up with the other three vehicles pulling a total burden of six tons. By this means we moved fairly continuously, although every now and then we were forced to halt as a tractor or the Weasel bogged down in a soft patch. In my somewhat hazy mental state I had worked out the necessary LHA Table for operating the astro-compass and Jim Bates was steering on the sun in the lead tractor. When we halted and camped we had covered thirteen and a half miles, not a great distance perhaps, but a big step toward the twenty-fifth mile where we could hope for improved surfaces. I went to bed feeling fairly contented.

It was a superb morning on 15th November with a temperature of −27°C and not a breath of wind. I'd had a good night but decided to take it easy and go on in the Weasel. We didn't get away until 1:30 p.m., but we soon reached the twenty-fifth mile and noticed the promised improvement in the surface which allowed us to change the loads around again and let the Fergusons drag their full share. Our immediate objective was a cairn established by Bob and George's dog party thirty-five miles out from the Plateau Depot. At this cairn the course changed sharply onto a southwesterly heading.

Steering on the astro-compass, we continued on over a good surface and by 8:30 p.m. we had covered fifteen miles. We should by now have been in the vicinity of the corner cairn, but there was nothing to be seen. We stopped for a while and I did a careful sweep with the glasses and I managed to pick up a snow cairn shining in the rays of the sun. Something had gone very wrong with our navigation and we'd made an error of six miles in thirty-five. We discovered that the base of the astro-compass was loose but I don't think this was the only reason. Clearly in my fuzzy condition I had made errors in the settings and I resolved to take more care with this but also to keep a closer watch on the use of the astro-compass in the lead tractor. I sensed that my new team had a slightly different approach than the Old Firm. As expedition leader they expected me always to drive in the lead tractor which was unquestionably the most dangerous position in crevasse country. At an appropriate time when we were all together, I pointed out that we were a team. I was prepared to do my share and more, but we all had to take our turn in front and in the future we would change every hour. But in fact with this team we were all happier with either Jim Bates or me leading.

On 16th November we heard that Bunny Fuchs and his party had reached South Ice after a very rough trip and they were considerably behind schedule. That day we covered thirty miles over a very rough surface which suited the Fergusons but not the Weasel. It was a wild wind and drift the next day but we kept going. There wasn't enough sun for a shadow but enough for a rough sight on our instruments and that was sufficient for us. By the end of the run we were 105 miles from the Plateau Depot. I had taken several sun shots with my bubble sextant and the fix coincided very closely with our dead reckoning position worked out with the sun compass and the distance meter on our trailing bicycle wheel. I talked to Bob on the radio and he'd been held up for two days by wind and drift, so we had passed him six miles to the east. We agreed to meet at Depot 480.

The next day we did thirty miles over a rough surface and very cold conditions. Our radio schedule produced two surprising messages:

> Hillary
> Scott Base
> Owing to thirty-nine days spent forcing route to South Ice our start delayed ten days giving 200 miles to catch up to maintain twenty miles per day. This will be attempted. Distance run to South Ice 300 miles but will be 330 next time. Seismic Sno-Cat and one Weasel at South Ice. One Weasel abandoned and one returned to Shackleton early on journey. Leaving (Shackleton) 24th with three Sno-Cats, two Weasels, one Muskeg. Air reconnaissance to 85° S indicates Shackleton to South Ice most difficult section to Pole. Not certain twenty miles per day can be maintained to South Ice but expect over 20 miles per day thereafter. Could be up to fortnight late arriving Scott Base, but will endeavor reduce this though possibility remains we do not arrive till 9th March. Hope improve this pessimistic statement on passage. If conditions difficult we can accept intended D700 at 600 miles, but would then appreciate proportion of fuel you save in addition to twelve drums. Time so gained may be useful to you for your works on mountains. As it seems unlikely we can meet at D700 would appreciate guide from Plateau Depot if possible. Delighted you have vehicles on plateau and going so well. Congratulations from all.
>
> Bunny
> Shackleton, Nov. 19

For some reason I had thought that the previous message indicating that Bunny had reached South Ice meant that his whole team had arrived. I didn't realize that the main group wouldn't actually be leaving Shackleton until 24th November which was almost a week away. But the most surprising point to me was Bunny's lack of appreciation of the momentum we were getting behind our southern tractor journey, as indicated by his suggestion that we might prefer to put the final depot at 600 miles instead of 700 miles. As we were only 250 miles from D700, I considered our arrival there in some force was a foregone conclusion. It was what would happen beyond D700 that occupied my thoughts and plans.

However, the most amazing message was from the Ross Sea Committee, relayed to me by John Claydon, our pilot.

> Helm rang saying following the Committee meeting Monday it appears greatly increased public interest in expedition and stocks particularly high. Committee interested in your prospects reaching Pole and whether you have considered this. If you are prepared to go for Pole Committee will give you every encouragement and full support following formal approval from London. If you intend to proceed Helm requests you seek Committee approval for the venture following which they will get OK from London. Could you wire Helm re this on same day as you send "Times" dispatch from D480. Good work.
>
> Claydon

To say that I was astonished by this message was putting it mildly. As an expression of opinion from the full Ross Sea Committee, it was in direct contrast to the usual message from the Executive Committee with their emphasis on playing safe. In actual fact, I misunderstood the message. It was scribbled out by Ted Gawn on a rough piece of paper and I thought that "following formal approval from London" meant just that—we had been given approval. In fact the Management Committee in London had never even been approached.

In very poor weather we only covered eighteen miles in our next run and bad weather continued the next day. We were preparing to camp down when suddenly the sun appeared and it was possible to travel so we shrugged off thoughts of bed and pressed on. As we drove, the nature of the country started to change. We seemed to be climbing steadily upward and in every direction ice hummocks were appearing, growing larger and larger the farther we went. Our course became a sinuous one, twisting in and out amongst the hummocks and even over them when no other way presented itself. As we only had about eighteen miles to cover to get to D480 we pushed on as hard as we could and were delighted at the speed we were making. The only disturbing feature was the increase in size and number of the ice hummocks and far ahead they loomed up on the horizon in formidable proportions. In the first two hours we covered nearly ten miles. Jim Bates was now in the lead tractor and I was following along in the Weasel some hundreds of yards behind the Fergusons.

Then I noticed that the vehicles ahead of me were breaking through a series of small crevasses and leaving behind them regular holes about six inches or a foot wide. These weren't enough to be troublesome but they were an indication that we might be approaching a bad crevasse area. I accelerated in the Weasel to overtake the tractors and warn them, but Jim was in full flight and I had difficulty in catching up. I shot around a hummock at full speed and then came to a halt as I almost overran the last sledge of the train. The three vehicles had stopped and I noticed that the middle one was leaning over at an unaccustomed angle. I parked the Weasel and walked carefully forward to join the others.

An unpleasant sight met my eyes! The lead tractor was now on firm ground but behind it was a great open hole, so big that it was hard to see how the tractor had managed to get clear of it. The second tractor was lying over at a sharp angle with one of its tracks deep in a crevasse. This was a blow to my complacency. I had been expecting to reach D480 within a couple of hours and here we were now in serious difficulties. I carefully investigated the surface with my ice axe and made my way forward to join Jim at the lead tractor to gaze with some dislike down the icy depths of the crevasse behind it. It had only been his speed that had carried him across.

The first thing to do was to get the lead tractor out of danger. I probed over a wide area of snow around the vehicle and soon discovered a number of other holes running in a regular pattern across our route. The bridges over many of these crevasses were very thin and we had strayed into a very nasty area. I carefully marked out a route across all the crevasses I could find and then untied the lead tractor from the rest of the vehicles and climbed aboard. With my nerves a little on edge, I swung the tractor around and then carefully inched my way back over the snow bridges, my imagination expecting them to crumble underneath me, but finally arriving safely back beside the Weasel. It was quite clear now that the whole area was a mass of holes, both small and large, and even the small ones could engulf a man. I noticed Ted Gawn wandering around in a somewhat aimless fashion and realized that he had neither knowledge nor experience of crevasses so was quite unimpressed by them. For his own sake, I suggested he should go and sit in the caboose until we needed his help.

The big task ahead of us now was to get the number two tractor free. The left-hand track was deep into the crevasse, but it did appear that a really concerted pull by the other three vehicles might drag it clear. First we had to move all the laden sledges out of danger. Thoroughly investigating any new piece of ground before we drove over it, and getting back into our old tracks as soon as possible, we made two trips of it and dragged all the sledges about a mile back onto safer ground. This constant passage over the same track was now opening up all the crevasses and the route was liberally supplied with them. Fortunately, none were of any size. Then we returned to the rescue of the helpless Ferguson. With our thick Terylene ropes we hitched the three vehicles together and then attached them to the crippled vehicle. As we would probably only get one chance it would have to be a good one and coordination would be all important. I gave the signal, let out the clutch of the Weasel, and accelerated forward as hard as I could go. The strain came on with a jerk, and for a moment the tracks skidded in the snow and I thought, we're not going to do it! Then we shot forward again like a cork out of a bottle and I knew the tractor was out or the rope had broken. I jumped out of my vehicle and walked back to see what had happened. To my delight the third Ferguson was on an even keel again. We gathered around it but could see no particular damage. The Fergusons were tough all right!

Jim seemed rather excited and called out, "Take a look at the hole we left behind." To my amazement I saw that an enormous area had completely sunk away, leaving a huge void large enough to absorb a house. We crept over to the edge and looked in. It was a most unpleasant sight with sheer icewalls dropping away to vast depths and enough room to put a hundred Fergusons. I realized how extraordinarily lucky we'd been in striking this crevasse at a narrow spot, for another ten feet to the left and there was no doubt that Jim's tractor would have plunged into this hole with certain loss of the tractor and only the tow rope to save his life. We were a subdued party as we drove our four vehicles back along our tracks to the sledges, and there was no doubt that our faculties had been sharpened by this close call.

But we were not by any means out of trouble. We struck another huge crevasse area and the only way to negotiate it was by me going ahead on foot and testing the surface with my ice axe. I found dozens of crevasses but succeeded in locating adequate bridges. Somewhat shaken we carried on south and, as I knew we must be somewhere in the vicinity of the position I had chosen for D480, I kept a careful watch out for an area that would be suitable for an aircraft to land. After traveling for nearly an hour, we came over the crest of a long slope and found a promising position in a broad easy basin. I waved to the others to stop and we walked around examining the area. There were still a few large sastrugi dotted around, but we decided we could shovel these away if necessary to provide a suitable landing strip. It was with a distinct air of excitement that we drove our vehicles into position and pitched our tent to mark the establishment of D480—the end of the second long stage in our journey.

On that same day, still heartened by the misunderstood message from the Ross Sea Committee, I cabled them:

Not for publication. On establishment of D700 the tractors carrying sufficient fuel to reach Pole will continue south to meet Fuchs. Unless Fuchs requires the assistance of the vehicles which

is unlikely, we will continue on after meeting him and leave our
vehicles at the Pole where they can be of some use. Admiral Dufek
has agreed to evacuate us by air to Scott Base. I will join Fuchs at
the Plateau Depot and guide him down the Skelton and across the
Ross Ice Shelf. Hillary.

My tone was, I felt, very reasonable and was based on the rather questionable assumption that Fuchs would reach the Pole well before us,
which had certainly been the original plan. However my message rang
alarm bells in some quarters when it was circulated to members of the
Executive Committee a few days later.

The first three days at D480 were overcast and there was no possibility of any Beaver flights. But we had plenty to do. First we erected
a tall aluminium ladder mast for our low-powered radio homer which
we hoped would enable the Beaver to find us. Then Jim had plenty of
maintenance to see to on the vehicles and there was more stowing of the
loads on the sledges. On 28th November we welcomed Bob Miller and
George Marsh, plus Harry Ayres and Roy Carlyon, so the camp was
alive with noisy dogs. Bob told me we were at present six miles out of
position and they'd been lucky to find us. I did a series of sun shots with
my bubble sextant and found I'd been making an error of four nautical
miles in my calculations so I needed to compensate accordingly.

On Friday 29th November we had a really superb morning, warm and
windless with a temperature of only −24°C. The weather at Scott Base
was fine too so everything looked right for the arrival of the plane. For
a couple of hours we hovered over the radio and followed the flight
of the Beaver across the Ross Ice Shelf, up the Darwin Glacier and over
the Polar Plateau toward us. It was a relief when John Claydon's deci-
sive voice told us over the radio telephone that he had picked up our
homer on his radio compass and was winging toward us. Five minutes
later he called out that he had sighted the depot and at 1 a.m. he was
circling around overhead. To see our gallant little orange plane again
brought a lump to my throat. John made a couple of low runs over the
strip we had marked out for him and then came in for a perfect landing.

We were all there to greet him when he taxied up to the depot, and also to welcome back Murray Ellis who was looking fit and strong again. We unloaded half a ton of supplies and a big bag of mail. John didn't delay for long as he was anxious to take full advantage of the fine spell of weather. Ted Gawn was to resume his radio duties at Base, so he clambered aboard with all of his equipment and waved farewell. His help had been invaluable on the tractor train but, although he had enjoyed the experience, I think he was glad to be returning to familiar tasks.

We were nine days at D480 as the Beaver continued flight after flight, stocking the depot and our sledges. On the third day it brought back Peter Mulgrew. It was amazing how much I enjoyed having the Old Firm all together again. The dog teams had already set off and I talked on the radio to Bob and George who had covered fifty-three miles in three days which was excellent going. But they warned of a number of crevasse areas. So the Old Firm pointed itself toward D700, making excellent time and when we stopped for the radio schedule we were in a very cheerful frame of mind—but not for long.

There was a message from the Ross Sea Committee Executive and it was the same negative story. A team must always stay at Depot 700 in case Bunny Fuchs' party couldn't find it and generally we must hang around and see what Bunny wanted us to do. I was unaware that on 3rd December the London Committee had sent quite a constructive message to Wellington saying that it was up to Bunny Fuchs and me to decide if we should carry on to the Pole. I, in fact, never received this message and, although Bunny never gave approval for my going to the Pole, he didn't try to stop me either until it was too late! It didn't help, of course, that we had no communication with Bunny at this period. He was so tired of press messages asking for his exact position that he stopped all radio communication for several days. I certainly can't blame him for this, although it made us feel even more clearly that we were almost a different expedition.

Somewhat in a fury, I got us rolling again in firm conditions. We passed through an area of ominous hummocks but still kept going. When we finally stopped we'd covered over fifty-two miles, the best day's run we had ever done. The next day was very tense as we had a most unpleasant time with sledges breaking through into crevasses but in the end we still completed forty-one miles. Peter and I helped the others pitch their tents and then we scrambled inside the caboose, cooked up some food and, after eating, crawled into our sleeping bags. The alarm woke me at 2 p.m. and I went outside half-clad to take an altitude sight on the sun with my bubble sextant. I plotted it on my map, grunted with satisfaction when it coincided with my dead reckoning position, and then snuggled back into bed. I seemed to have barely gone off to sleep again before the alarm clanged at 5:30 p.m. for the radio schedule. This time it would be Peter's turn to get out of bed half dopey with lack of sleep to sit at his little radio table and pound away on the Morse key to Scott Base. Then we had our breakfast and made all our preparations for departure. At 8 p.m. I took a longitude shot on the sun to combine with the middle of the day sight and so gain an accurate fix of our position. I then worked out the bearings for our astro-compass for the next twelve hours. This was pretty much our daily routine.

We were now ready to go, but it was Sunday evening, the evening each week on which Radio New Zealand broadcast to our expedition a special half-hour program. It was worth waiting for, so from 8:15 p.m. to 8:45 p.m. all of us crowded into the caboose and listened. We enjoyed the summary of world news, although international troubles and conflicts seemed very divorced from our own. Undoubtedly the things that appealed most were the tidbits of information about activities in New Zealand and in our home towns. The new Prime Minister, the Right Honorable Walter Nash, spoke to us and wished us all well. For half an hour we were back in the familiar green countryside of New Zealand, and it was something of an effort when the radio session finished to drag our minds back to the barren, knobbly waste of snow which was our environment.

We rolled on at great speed and covered six miles in the first hour. Then the clutch on the Weasel packed up and it took Jim and Murray six hours to replace it, and even then there were still ominous sounds coming from the transmission. We moved all the loads onto the

Fergusons, dragging only the caboose behind the Weasel and, despite increasingly soft snow conditions, we managed to keep going. We still did twenty-seven miles that day. I felt that the Weasel's days were numbered and doubted if the three Fergusons could continue hauling the full load. Bob and George had asked for a small intermediate depot about a hundred miles from D700, so I decided to make it into a full depot. We kept going and I must have been navigating rather well because we came onto a tall cairn with a flag on top. This was where Bob and George wanted their depot to be and this was where we put it— we called it Midway Depot.

We unloaded six drums of fuel, eight tins of pemmican, two man ration boxes, and a jerrycan of kerosene. I also decided to abandon a sledge here, and we tipped this up on its end with a flag lashed to the drawbar so that it could be seen at a considerable distance. At half-mile intervals on either side we built five snow cairns with flags on them to help the crossing party locate the depot when they came through. In the process we discovered many small crevasses which confirmed our view that it wasn't an ideal area. This took most of the day, so I decided to camp the night at the depot and start off afresh with the ambition of doing fifty miles in each of the next two nights to reach D700.

We started off from Midway Depot at 8 p.m. on 10th December all set for a good run after receiving a message from Bob saying, "Crevasses ten miles south of cairn are harmless." We had only gone a few hundred yards before we had to stop as the Weasel was making terrible noises. Our mechanics burrowed into the vitals of the engine and discovered a worn thrust bearing which we couldn't replace. We would just have to run the Weasel until it dropped. The "harmless crevasses" proved to be rather devastating and we made our way cautiously across them for several hours. In one frightening corner with deep crevasses coming from three directions, we had to repair a tractor tread and Murray and Jim did an absolutely fantastic job. We finally cleared three miles of crevasses, having spent eight and a half hours amongst them.

I took over the lead tractor again and drove toward a very knobbly looking slope. Fifty feet up I lurched violently through still another crevasse, a really bad one, and I was lucky to get to the other side. It was a rather strange crevasse area, some of them seventy feet wide, but generally with huge plugs of snow. It all looked mighty unstable. Somehow we managed to get across just in time for the Weasel to give up the ghost. We left it behind, looking extremely lonely. Now our three Fergusons had to tow the full load of eight tons over a plateau of soft snow, barely managing to keep going. We were fifty-eight miles from our site for D700 and it was a fifty-eight miles that I will never forget. It hadn't helped that a message had come through from Bunny Fuchs that their estimated time of arrival at South Ice had now been put back to 16th December, six days off. Crevasse areas were followed by soft snow and then crevasses again. Murray and Jim went ahead to investigate and then waved me through.

I gave the signal for the tractor train to start and then revved up my motor and headed toward the snow bridge. My nerves were tense with expectation as I clattered onto the near side and then into the center. All seemed to be going well, when suddenly there was a thud beneath me and my tractor tipped steeply backward. I almost fell out of my seat but had sufficient presence of mind to lean forward and flick the throttle full on. The bridge had gone and I was going with it! For a few awful moments we teetered on the lip of the crevasse, with the tracks clawing at the edge and the nose high in the air. Then the extra bit of power told and we seemed literally to climb up the wall of the crevasse and thump to a level keel on the far side.

Somewhat shaken, I turned off the motor and scrambled out for a look. The hole was a beauty, plenty big enough to take the tractor, and I couldn't quite see how I'd managed to escape from it. If the motor had stalled I wouldn't have had a chance. I knew it wasn't any use brooding over these things, so I started looking for a better bridge. After a bit of investigation, I found one a few yards to the east, but we were a silent and moody party as we brought the two vehicles and sledges across it and there was a certain tenseness in the air. We'd been going strong for fifteen hours and now everybody was deadly tired. Although we were only a frustrating ten miles from D700, the sensible thing to do was to camp and get some sleep before tackling the problems ahead. The others agreed, but before pitching the tents, Murray, Peter and I roped up and went ahead for half a mile to see what the area was like. There were large numbers of big crevasses, some of them very big, but we didn't seem to have much difficulty in picking what looked like substantial bridges over them. We returned to the tractors, and were soon engrossed in the tedious and mundane task of preparing our food before crawling into our sleeping bags for a much needed rest.

We awoke refreshed after a good sleep. I went ahead with Peter Mulgrew on the rope and prodded carefully about, finding crevasses in every direction and testing the bridges over them. Only on a few occasions did any bridges give way and then it was nothing of great consequence. We came to a wide flat area and discovered innumerable crevasses. The signs were minute—an almost invisible crack winding its way across the hard surface—but investigation with the ice axe soon opened up a hole and we could look down into some vast cavernous tomb, only insecurely bridged. We began climbing up a long slope where the crevasses were even bigger, but were more securely bridged, and our progress, though at no stage casual, now at least became more confident.

Three and a half miles from the first crevasse, we came to the last one at the head of the slope. This was large and easily identifiable. To my surprise, I found the bridges over it were of a less stable character than the ones we had been crossing, and there were signs that the crevasse had been opening wider fairly recently—the bridges were light and flimsy and showed no signs of consolidation. Most of the area around seemed unstable and there were many small transverse cracks. Peter and I tramped around searching for a safe route but, prod as we did at every likely prospect, the bridge would either ring hollow or collapse under the questing point of the ice axe. We worked our way 400 yards in one direction and the same distance in the other, but saw nothing that appealed to us. Only in one place was there a thicker portion of bridge which seemed more stable than the rest and we examined this once again. It wasn't perfect, but it didn't seem too bad. Our success so far had bred a certain amount of confidence in these bridges, so I decided it was worth a try. I waved to the tractors to come on.

Jim Bates was doing a spell on the lead tractor, for we were back to changing drivers every hour to give each man a share of both the risks and the rests. Peter and I drew back a little from the crevasse and watched the tractors grinding steadily toward this last barrier. We had convinced ourselves that the bridge was satisfactory, but I know that in the back of my mind was still a little lurking worry, as there was with every crevasse crossing. Just before he reached the bridge, Jim stopped and his rather anxious face appeared over the top of the cab. He gave a few suspicious glances around and then disappeared down onto the seat again. Next moment his tractor motor revved up violently and he shot forward onto the edge of the bridge—it was obviously a do-or-die effort. Our attention intensified as he moved out onto the middle of the bridge. Then the front wheels reached the far side and the heavy drive wheels ground into the center. Next moment there was a tearing sound, the bottom dropped out of the lid, and in almost slow motion, the tractor sank back into the crevasse.

For one horrifying moment I thought it was going right down! Then the last few inches of the cab caught on the edge of the crevasse and the tractor remained poised over the hole. My first thought was for Jim. Jim was a determined driver, but he probably disliked crevasses even more than the rest of us. He wasn't going to like being down one! I dashed over to the edge and called out, "How are you, Jim? Are you all right?" There was a momentary silence and then, in a rather strained voice, Jim spoke. "Yes, I'm all right, but I don't like the view!" From his seat he could look straight down into the depths of the crevasse and it wasn't a reassuring sight. Next moment Jim's head appeared as he struggled out of his seat and hastily climbed up onto the surface once more.

The crevasse was certainly huge—sheer icy walls dropping away to black depths—and I couldn't see how we were going to get the tractor out this time. We gathered together and discussed the problem. The only way it could come out was from the front, as the back was much too far down. The first thing to do, therefore, was to find some way of getting

169

our two remaining vehicles onto the far side of the crevasse. I set off on foot to make a more determined hunt for a bridge, and this time it had to be a good one. Several hundred yards farther to the east than I had been before the crevasse suddenly petered out, or went deeper underground, and even most exhaustive proddings couldn't find it again. However, the area was a mass of crisscross small crevasses, so we didn't waste any time bringing the two tractors across onto the south side of the big crevasse, and hitching them on to their helpless companion with a little strain on the rope so it couldn't fall any farther.

We decided on our plan of action. We would dig away the snow in front of the tilted vehicle and make a sort of ramp for it to climb out. It wouldn't be safe to start its motor, but we hoped that our other two tractors would have enough power to drag it to the surface. Keeping a tight rope on the tractor, we shoveled away the snow under the front wheels. With quivers and jerks the vehicle started settling down onto a slightly more even keel, but it seemed more precariously balanced than ever. After much hard work we had produced a steep ramp and decided to have our try at pulling the tractor out. The first thing to do was to get the vehicle out of gear. Despite its unstable position, Peter volunteered for the task. He swung actively into the cab and dropped from view. Next moment, the tractor gave an unpleasant lurch and sank back a few more inches, as Peter put the gear into neutral. It looked to me as though it might be going for good at any moment, so I called to Peter to get out as quickly as he could and he nonchalantly scrambled to the surface. Peter certainly wasn't lacking in courage!

Now we were ready. We knew we'd only get one chance. If we didn't succeed this time the vehicle would undoubtedly drop down beyond any chance of recovery. Murray got into the tractor next to the stranded vehicle and I climbed into the leading tractor. We had worked out our respective tasks. Murray's job was to supply a steady pressure on the victim and hold it in place until the crucial moment. In the lead vehicle I was to give the sudden jerk which we hoped would bring it to the surface. I started up my tractor and warmed the motor. Then drove backward until I was practically touching Murray's tractor and the tow rope was a slack loop. I had decided to use second gear in order to get up greater speed before the weight came on, so I whipped my vehicle into gear, signaled to Murray, and then with maximum throttle, I roared ahead to the full length of the rope. Next moment there was a fearful tug on the tractor which almost jerked me out of my seat. We seemed to hesitate for a second and then surged forward again. Something has broken or the tractor is out, was my thought—and out it was. Murray had timed his driving to perfection. Just as the weight of my vehicle came on the rope he had given his vehicle full throttle, and the combined strength of the two vehicles had wrenched the sunken tractor up our rough ramp and out onto the level ground. Feeling decidedly jubilant, I clambered out of my vehicle and went back to inspect the damage. Despite the fearful jar there must have been on the rear tractor, it seemed to have come to no harm whatsoever—a distinct compliment to its rugged construction.

So we set to work to reassemble the tractor train. All the sledges had to be collected from the northern side of the crevasse and brought over the shaky ground and the safe bridge. In the process I walked onto a different spot and put a leg down an unseen crevasse, which only served to reinforce my decision to get clear of this area as soon as possible. A reconnaissance on foot confirmed that we were at the end of the crevasses, and we set off at a good pace over rough going. We were now only seven or eight miles from D700 and we were anxious to get there as soon as possible. We drove up a broad high ridge, keeping our eyes open for some indication of the dog camp. It was many hundreds of miles since we had seen a prominent land feature of any sort—only the wide rolling swells of the plateau—but now we were permitted one last glimpse of a mountain. From the crest of the ridge we caught sight of a great massif far to the east—it was Mount Markham (15,000 feet) on the south side of the Nimrod Glacier. A few moments later we saw before us a wide snowy basin—and some miles away the black dot of a tent.

We would have liked to have made a brave showing by sweeping up to the dog men with great speed and all flags flying. But it was not to be. A couple of miles from their camp we bogged down once again and had to resort to the ignominy of relaying. Dropping the two-ton sledge, we drove on again in low gear and ploughed a deep furrow across toward the camp, from which we could soon pick out the figures of Bob and George coming out to meet us. It was great to see them again, and before long we were circling their tent in our tractors and picking a suitable place for our camp. The dogs gave us a vociferous welcome, and we all felt an enormous sense of satisfaction in having reached D700 at last. It was the last depot for Bunny Fuchs—almost the reason why our expedition had originally started. To reach it in such force and in reasonably good time seemed to justify all our efforts and plans. We had reached D700 at 1 p.m. on 15th December 1957.

10

To the Pole and Back

T HE ROSS SEA COMMITTEE DISPLAYED THE RELUCTANT SUPPORT that had been such a feature of their messages. Why didn't they just send us a complimentary message for a job well done instead of worrying about what naughtiness we might get up to next?

18.12.57

To Hillary:

Please accept heartiest congratulations from Committee and myself on reaching D700 in such good time. We hope that the depot will be successfully stocked. Operation to date reflects greatest credit on all concerned.

In considering your future program, you should know that the Committee recently agreed that if Fuchs or London Committee requested you should carry on toward Pole the Committee would raise no objection provided this could be done within existing resources. My telegram of 5th December nevertheless indicated that Committee would be loath to approve any extension of your program which would place strain on men and resources.

In these circumstances the Committee feels that you should now make every endeavor to discuss your next steps as fully as you can with Dr. Fuchs personally. If you are unable to make contact messages could be passed through Scott Base and London. You should then be able to make a joint recommendation to Committee and to London.

For the first two days at D700 I was too tired to worry much about the future—certainly not until the Beaver was able to reach us again. I did, however, have two quite important discussions. Bob and George didn't want us to go on to the Pole, but to use the tractors to travel out a hundred miles to the east and put in a depot for their dog teams near the Beardmore Glacier for their future mapping program. I was not entirely sure of Bob's motives. He was a great supporter of Bunny and I felt he would do almost anything to stop us getting to the Pole first. So I turned his idea down but agreed to have John Claydon put in a depot for them with the Beaver. Then Murray Ellis came to see me. Murray said he had been invited by Bob to join his dog team for the exploration of the Nimrod Glacier and he wanted to do it. "Better than sitting on an old tractor that never gets up and wags its tail in the morning," he said. "I'm a dog man not a tractor man," he later told me. Considering the great job he had done with the tractors I could hardly believe him. I told Murray that if he didn't agree to go farther south then Jim would refuse to go, too.

It was time for a counting of heads. I gathered the Old Firm together and told them I planned to head for the Pole, even if I went alone. I knew, of course, that Peter Mulgrew would stick with me. It was a direct challenge to their loyalty. They reluctantly agreed to continue, despite the 500 miles of formidable Polar Plateau ahead of us. I wasn't joking either. I was fairly sure that Peter and I could get two tractors a long way toward the Pole.

On 17th December a message came through that Bunny Fuchs expected to be at the Pole between Christmas and New Year. I found this impossible to believe. On 18th December to our delight, the Beaver arrived and with its third load brought a disturbing message—the crossing party didn't expect to leave South Ice until 15th December. It was very confusing and I decided that my only course was to be completely self-sufficient and expect to see the crossing party when we saw them and not before. The last flight came in late on 20th December and this completed our depot stocking and gave our tractors sufficient fuel, I felt, to reach the Pole. My formidable team now comprised the extended Old Firm—Murray Ellis, Jim Bates, Peter Mulgrew, plus cameraman tractor driver Derek Wright. I sent a message to Bunny Fuchs that we were pushing out at a hundred miles to note crevasse areas and would then await his instructions.

At 8:30 p.m. on 20th December I gave the signal to start and we rolled out of Depot 700. We were on our way again and we all felt a bit lonely and exposed so far from anywhere. We had three vehicles, the minimum needed if any one of them fell down a crevasse and needed rescuing. If we ran low on fuel I was prepared to abandon one tractor and risk going on with only two. In the event of an emergency we were carrying a man-hauling sledge, so if all else failed we could walk the last hundred miles. I felt we were covered for all eventualities. By 6 a.m. we had covered twenty-seven miles and hadn't seen a crevasse. In the radio schedule there was a rather cheerful message from Bunny Fuchs, confirming that they'd had lots of trouble with crevasses and now expected to arrive at South Ice either today or tomorrow. So I sent him another message:

Personal to Fuchs:

Have completed stocking of depots as arranged. Left D700 yesterday with three Fergusons and twenty drums of fuel with the intention of proving the route out another 200 miles and then, if the going proves easy, doing a trip to the Pole. Did twenty-seven miles yesterday in heavy going before being stopped by small area crevasses. Will scrub southward jaunt if vehicles and fuel can be used in any way to expedite your safe crossing either by a further depot or anything else you suggest. In the interim until I get a reply we will continue on out a hundred miles from D700 and will cairn crevasse areas . . .

Best wishes for a speedy onward trip from South Ice.

Ed Hillary

Then we carried on again, getting another nasty fright in an area of crevasses, but making our way through them. Crevasse area followed crevasse area, but we flagged them all for the benefit of the crossing party. By 8 a.m. on 24th December we had completed forty-six miles for the day and we were now only 390 miles from the Pole. I obtained a more promising note from Bunny Fuchs, giving specific details—something I'd hardly ever received from him before:

Personal to Hillary:

We arrived South Ice 21st December after severe crevasse trouble and three or four recoveries of Sno-Cats. Distance traveled in twenty-nine days 349 miles. Consider this worst stage of journey and expect rapid travel from here on. Thanks for your information and proposed crevasse reconnaissance. Hope you will be able to make route through or limit area with snow cairns or flags. We have arrived here with four Sno-Cats three Weasels one Muskeg. Two dog teams will travel ahead. We expect leave South Ice 25th then Otter and four R.A.F. fly there to await suitable day for flight to Scott Base. Hope for radio contact as arranged 26th onward. Happy Christmas to you all.

Bunny

I sent a message back to Bunny:

Personal to Fuchs:

Glad to hear of your arrival South Ice and hope your troubles are over. We are 390 miles from Pole. Have cairned two areas of crevasses since D700 but last fifty miles has been clear going. Waiting one day here then will push on. Will attempt contact you as arranged and advise you of progress. Best of luck, happy Christmas and an early New Year at the Pole.

Ed Hillary

We spent Christmas day in slightly festive conditions. Things were going well for us and we were making excellent time. As promised, after we had surveyed the route a hundred miles further south, we had camped for a day, awaiting instructions from Fuchs. When they were not forthcoming I made my own decision and issued a press release on Boxing Day 1957: "Am hellbent for the Pole, God willing and crevasses permitting."

Unbeknown to us, we were becoming involved in national politics. The Prime Minister of New Zealand had asked for a report from Foreign Affairs and they concluded with the following words:

> The most important considerations in the present situation are that:
>
> (a) Hillary has carried out his primary obligations with notable success;
>
> (b) if he were to wait for Fuchs at Depot 700 he might have to wait many weeks doing nothing;
>
> (c) a further reconnaissance would obviously assist Fuchs if and when he reaches the area;
>
> (d) Hillary is confident—and no one in New Zealand can question his judgment—that he can reach the South Pole with his present resources;
>
> (e) if Fuchs makes no faster progress and if a successful crossing becomes impossible, the Trans-Antarctic Expedition may be glad of the prestige arising from Hillary's own achievement;
>
> (f) Hillary has recognized his obligation to assist Fuchs over the last stages of the crossing.
>
> It appears, therefore, that there are no good grounds for instructing Hillary to return to Depot 700 there to await Fuchs' arrival—nor would such an instruction be easily explained to the New Zealand public.

I had a great respect for the Right Honorable Walter Nash and I would have greatly appreciated this message if I'd ever seen it.

On the day after Christmas we achieved fifty-seven miles, the next day forty-four miles and the next, forty-one miles, although we were now at an altitude of over 10,000 feet. We were just over halfway from D700 to the South Pole. Then on the radio schedule we had an earth-shaking message from Bunny Fuchs.

Urgent personal Fuchs for Hillary:

Leaving South Ice with 109 45-gallon drums and 320 gallons in vehicles' tanks. With D700 this takes four Cats and one Weasel over direct route to D480 provided we have three other vehicles to be abandoned at optimum distances. Our only fuel safety factor is to abandon extra vehicles. If our planned abandonment of three vehicles is followed by any breakdown among remaining five, our only means of augmenting fuel would be by further reduction of numbers at time when mechanical condition and weather are deteriorating. Already two Cats have track trouble. This risk was accepted when we thought you would have difficulty stocking D700. In the interests of whole expedition I do not feel we should continue to accept this risk, and am in difficult position of feeling I must accept your offer to clear present crevasse area then establish additional fuel depot at appropriate position from D700 thus abandoning your idea of reaching Pole. Know this will be great disappointment to you and your companions, but the additional depot will enormously strengthen the position of the crossing party which cannot afford at present to deviate from the direct route. How do you propose to return to Scott? What quantity of fuel will be available for new depot? Have you reason to suppose crevasse areas become more frequent or extensive south of you? Please give magnetic variation at D700, D480, and Plateau Depot, also approximate altitudes. Request you date time group your messages to ensure sequence is known.

Bunny Fuchs

To hear Bunny say he was worried about his supplies of fuel was a stunning surprise to me. Once he reached D700 he would have all the fuel he could require. If he didn't think he had enough fuel to get from the Pole to D700, he simply shouldn't leave the Pole at all. We had enough fuel to go to the Pole or back to D700. The only place we could establish a depot was where we were and we didn't have the food to sit around for a month or more. I had the feeling that it was a final gesture to stop us from getting to the Pole. It is interesting that of the total of fifty drums of fuel the New Zealand party placed in the depots, only twenty drums were actually used by Bunny. It was then that I recommended to Bunny that he should consider stopping at the Pole Station and complete his journey the following year—a view that Bunny understandably rejected.

We started off again, determined to get to the South Pole as soon as we possibly could. Now we were entering a vast area of deep soft snow and once again it became a fearful struggle. Despite this, we drove very long hours and covered forty-five miles. The soft snow became even worse the next day and we ground along in low gear, leaving great channels in the snow behind us and fighting to keep the tractors moving. The consumption of fuel was horrendous and the navigating almost impossible but once again we'd put thirty-six miles behind us. We wouldn't have thought it possible but the snow got even worse—heartbreaking stuff, loose and bottomless. In six frightful hours we only covered six miles. We left a huge pile of excess gear and then moved on again, barely able to keep going. The altimeter showed 10,900 feet, the temperature was -33°C and, after another great struggle, we had covered only twenty-two miles, but our petrol was draining away before our eyes. A message from Scott Base indicated that Bunny Fuchs was now only 315 miles from the Pole—a tremendous jump forward. We decided to just keep on going until we got there.

It was hard work for the next two hours, but then it became apparent that we were moving a little more easily and a check on the altimeter showed that we were starting to lose height, a good sign as the Pole Station was at 9,300 feet. For twelve hours we drove grimly on and covered thirty miles, stopping only for a meal and a radio schedule. We could actually hear Bunny's voice through the static saying he was now 380 miles from the Pole. "Gawd, he's going backward," someone muttered. Then on we went again.

It was time to change drivers when I noticed a black speck far in the distance and a little to the right of our course. Almost without thinking, I swung the tractor over toward it. Surely enough it was a flag and a row of them stretched away on either side of us. "The flag is good enough for me," I said. "I'm going to bed." We'd been driving for twenty-four hours and had covered exactly sixty miles.

The Ross Sea Committee had asked us to notify them when we were within a few miles of the Pole so that they could break the news to our supporters, the London *Times* and the BBC. Peter called up Scott Base and uttered the cryptic word "Rhubarb," then switched off his radio and crawled back into his sleeping bag.

At 9:30 a.m. on the morning of 4th January we drove on again over a series of great folds. At 10:30 a.m. we could see a round dome on the horizon. At 12:30 p.m. a Weasel flying the American flag rolled out to meet us and we were warmly welcomed by the two Commanders of the Pole Station—Dr. Houk and Major Mogesson. We followed their Weasel to the circle of drums and flagpoles which marked the South Pole itself, and then we were greeted by batteries of cameras and friendly faces.

I turned off my motor for the last time and scrambled wearily out of the seat to be swept into a confusion of congratulations, photographs and questions and then led off by friendly hands toward the warmth and fresh food of the Pole Station. But before I descended underground I took a last glance at our tractor train—the three farm tractors, tilted over like hip-shot horses, looked lonely and neglected like broken toys cast aside after playtime. The caboose which had been a haven of warmth and rest to us now seemed more like a horse trailer than ever, and the two sledges had only the meager load of a half-full drum of fuel. Yes, there was no doubt about it, our tractor train was a bit of a laugh! But, despite appearances, our Fergusons had brought us over 1,250 miles of snow and ice, crevasse and sastrugi, soft snow and blizzard to be the first vehicles to drive to the South Pole.

Two U.S. Navy Neptune aircraft flew in from McMurdo Sound on the evening after our arrival. As our communications with Bunny Fuchs had been so spasmodic I had agreed with Peter Mulgrew that he should stay at the Pole Station and operate the radio in the caboose. The Americans were very happy with this as their communication equipment had not been performing well and they could now use Peter to send important messages to McMurdo Sound. Peter and I were still convinced that Bunny had been restricting his contacts both with us and the outside world.

I flew with a Neptune back to McMurdo Sound and found that our journey to the Pole and my recommendation to Bunny to complete his journey the following year had caused a press uproar worldwide. I talked with Admiral Dufek who was very concerned about the possibility of the crossing party coming to grief. He had no duty whatsoever to worry about Bunny's party but he was such a nice person that he felt a responsibility to see the expedition safely through. He made a most valuable decision when he delayed the departure of the icebreaker USS *Glacier* until at least 10th March at the earliest. This was a great relief to me, as it made it very unlikely that we would be forced to winter over again.

On 13th January I received a message from Bunny saying they were now 170 miles from the Pole and he requested me to ask Admiral Dufek if he would be prepared to fly the expedition dogs out to McMurdo Sound. I was decidedly uncomfortable about asking the Admiral to do this, but in his usual generous fashion he agreed. Five days later he and I took off from McMurdo Sound, flew up the Beardmore Glacier and then fifty-six miles beyond the Pole to see if we could locate Bunny Fuchs' party. Sure enough, there they were, sleeping in their tents beside the five vehicles. Only one person emerged to wave and that was George Lowe as I found out later. The plane flying at a couple of hundred feet must have made a tremendous noise and I wondered if it was a deliberate slight.

The Admiral and I were there to greet them when at midday on 20th

January the crossing party came sweeping in to the Pole, and what an imposing sight they were! The four great Sno-Cats gave an impression of enormous power, and the Weasel and the two dog teams made up an extensive entourage. Every vehicle and sledge had a flag flying and they swept up at high speed to come to a halt beside us. Bunny jumped out of the leading Sno-Cat and we shook hands and exchanged a warm greeting. I don't know how Bunny really felt but I was mighty pleased to see him. I had no desire to spend another winter in Antarctica. We drove back toward the Pole Station in some disorder but in high spirits, and all the vehicles and heavily laden sledges were parked together beside our three Fergusons. I have to admit that there was quite a contrast in the vehicles.

I managed to get Bunny aside from the media for a few moments, gave him a map with the depots and crevasse areas plotted on it, and we agreed we would meet again at D700. Then I boarded a plane with George Dufek and flew back to Scott Base. Why was it, I wondered, that I always felt slightly uncomfortable with Bunny and yet completely relaxed with Admiral George Dufek?

After a useful period of refitting in the workshops at the Pole Station the crossing party left at 4:50 p.m. on the evening of 24th January. They were now spacing out their seismic shots from the original thirty-mile intervals to between fifty and seventy miles which was a great saver of time. Following our tracks they averaged far in excess of anything they had done before. Their sledge dogs were flown out to Scott Base in a considerable effort by the Americans and then on 28th January there was another emergency call from Bunny. Geoffrey Pratt had collapsed with carbon-monoxide poisoning and needed large quantities of breathing oxygen to ensure his recovery. The crossing party were far beyond the range of our small aircraft, so once again I crossed over to the American Base, told the story to Admiral Dufek, and a rescue operation was soon put under way. The weather over the whole Antarctic continent was very unsettled but nothing stopped our dashing friend, Commander Coley, in his U.S. Navy Neptune. With magnificent navigation he found the tractor train but couldn't land beside it, due to the awful weather condi-

Louise, the mainstay of our family, on the verandah of our new house in Auckland.

Belinda was a special child.

(*Left*) Peter, Belinda and Sarah with Tenzing in Darjeeling; (*above*) enjoying a Nepali bazaar.

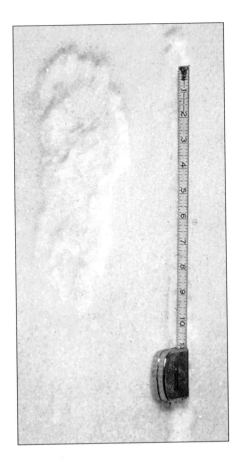

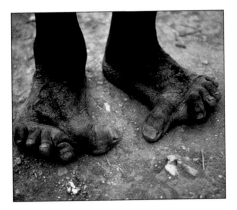

(*Left*) A perennially interesting question: Were these yeti tracks?

(*Above*) Prints from deformed Sherpa feet might account for some sightings.

(*Below*) The Khumjung yeti scalp comes home from its American travels after being identified as belonging to a Tibetan blue bear.

(*Above*) The Silver Hut, base for our 1960–61 high-altitude physiological program just below the Ama Dablam Col.

(*Left*) A laden Sherpa reaches the top of the Ama Dablam Col.

(*Below*) Peter Mulgrew, who was to pay a terrible price for his attempt on Makalu.

(*Above and below right*) The first children to attend the very first school we built at Khumjung. (*Below left*) Senior pupils in Khumjung High School today.

The hospital building program at Kinde, with Kangtega and Tamserku beyond, and (*opposite bottom*) at Paphlu.

Carrying in aluminum roofing to
a remote village.

The bridge built by the Himalayan
Trust at the foot of Tengboche Hill.

Mingbo airfield with the hill
to test the nerves of visiting
officials (and ourselves)
rising above the end of the
runway. Tamserku is
immediately behind.

(*Opposite right*) The strip at
Lukla was flattened by
dancing Sherpas well
supplied with chang.

Mingma Tsering Sherpa (*above left*), who had been a young porter on Everest, became our indomitable sirdar. His wife Ang Doule (*above right*) wore all her finery for the photograph.

In the next generation, Ang Rita, our chief administrator, and his wife Ang Jangmu. Ang Rita is a very important member of our Himalayan Trust operation today.

tions. Instead he expertly dropped the oxygen bottles into the soft snow beside the vehicles. Geoffrey Pratt breathed oxygen for several days and completely recovered. I found it slightly ironic that Bunny who had often expressed his determination not to accept any assistance from the Americans was now calling on them whenever a problem arose—incidentally always using me as an intermediary.

Meanwhile the dogs from the British expedition were posing a real problem. The Ross Sea Committee advised me that due to agricultural regulations the dogs would never be permitted to return to New Zealand. After much exchange of messages it became clear that the only alternatives were to let the dogs loose ultimately to die or to put them to death now. None of my dog drivers would consider doing this unpleasant task, although Harry Ayres reluctantly offered to give me a hand. So despite feeling awful about it, Harry and I shot them and threw them into the tide cracks. What a miserable end to a great journey for these great dogs. I rather felt that Bunny should have thought of this problem at a much earlier stage instead of leaving the task to me and I didn't sleep too well for a couple of nights. Our own dogs remained in the Antarctic for a number of years and were used extensively on survey and geological journeys.

Bunny Fuchs and his four powerful Sno-Cats covered the 500 miles from the Pole to D700 in fifteen days—the same time it had taken us—and most of the time they just trundled along in our old tracks. They crossed the first crevasse area without any problems but damaged two of the Sno-Cats in the second area and this held them up for a while. On 9th February I took off with John Claydon in the Beaver and we did a most complicated and daring flight across the mountains finally to home in on the beacon at D700.

Then began one of the most bemusing three weeks of my life. It was like going back into the Weddell Sea again. I was no longer the leader of a large expedition. I shared a tent with Bunny but wasn't a decision-maker anymore—unless we were lost or passing through crevasse areas. The first day out from D700 I actually sat in Bunny's seat in the lead Sno-Cat and helped guide the vehicles through two major crevasse areas. I was a little surprised that our tracks, made two months before, were still clearly identifiable despite storms and drifting snow. The pressure of the Fergusons passing over the snow had compacted it and made a hard ridge and, although the loose snow around them had been blown away by the constant wind, the tracks remained as a prominent and semi-permanent feature. Once back in the old tracks navigation became very much of a formality. So after that first day I rarely sat up front on the Polar Plateau. For day after day I lay in my sleeping bags in the gloomy uninsulated freezing back of the Sno-Cat, unable to see anything or even know what was happening, until they lost the tracks again or came to another crevasse area when I was called out of the darkness, put on some skis and went forward to make some decisions. But once the problem had been solved, there was no room for me in the front cabin and I crawled back into my cold dark home. I very much doubt if Bunny realized how miserable I felt.

One lot of crevasses that had taken us eight and a half hours to negotiate in the Fergusons we crossed in an hour and a half. Having a broad road ahead made all the difference, even if it did have some large potholes in it! When we camped at Midway Depot I jotted in my diary: "Covered 53 miles today and felt pleased with having got the chaps through 105 miles and four crevasse areas in two days. The boys say they have never made progress like this before." On 23rd February we had a remarkably smooth surface and at times were doing ten miles per hour. I knew we must be fast approaching the Plateau Depot as I had caught a glimpse of the surrounding mountains, but it was quite a thrill when the tall framework structure and waving flag of the Plateau Depot loomed up. At 8:30 p.m. we drew up alongside it. Next morning there was a terrific roar and the Otter and the Beaver swept overhead to land beside the depot. They had brought fresh food and, best of all, the mail. We pushed on in the evening with the temperature at −38°C and I wasn't at all surprised when we had to camp in the Portal in a raging blizzard. This was an area I knew very well.

When we awoke next morning the tents were still rocking and swaying under the wind. There was a strong feeling in the group that we shouldn't start but I was convinced that down on the Skelton névé the weather would be fine. Somewhat doubtfully Bunny agreed to give it a go and we struggled down in drift conditions and constant icing up of our engines. Then, almost miraculously, the level of high drift dropped to only a few feet above the surface and we looked out on to the stupendous sweep of the Western mountains. We reached the névé in bright sunlight and a gentle breeze. Back behind us on the Portal the snow was still writhing and twisting in the grip of the fierce wind.

We set course across the smooth surface of the névé and made excellent time. I was most anxious to reach the Staircase at the correct spot because this was the key to the descent of this extremely tricky middle portion of the glacier. Hitting the right spot wasn't going to be easy, for not only was it difficult to see the start of the Upper Staircase from the névé, but when I had come up this way before we had been feeling our way through fog and bad visibility and I had no opportunity to get a clear mental picture of the surrounding country—although I'd seen enough to know that a wrong course could get us into a ton of trouble. We rolled steadily across the névé with Midway Nunatak starting to loom up ahead, until we came to a halt on the edge of the névé and looked down the steeply descending slope of the Upper Staircase, liberally supplied with wide areas of crevasses. In the far distance we could see the lower trunk of the Skelton Glacier sweeping out on to the misty expanse of the Ross Ice Shelf.

I examined the area thoroughly with my glasses. It looked all right ahead, but there was something that didn't quite fit in with my mental picture and I felt a little uneasy. I decided to do a reconnaissance on foot and flag the route down for a mile or so. Hal Lister accompanied me, and we tramped down the steep slopes keeping an alert watch for anything suspicious. On the right the crevasses were almost continuous, from the top of the Upper Staircase down as far as we could see, but this didn't worry me—it was what I had expected. My main concern was the large group of crevasses quite close in on the left. These I didn't remember! We continued on a long way down the slope, flagging a route and keeping more or less central between the dangerous areas. We were perhaps a mile down from the crest before I realized what was wrong. We could now see the whole broad slope spread out above us, and from my memories of the upward route it was clear that we'd entered the Upper Staircase too far over toward Midway Nunatak.

Two courses were open to me. We could either go back up and cross the névé to the old route or try and work our way across from where we were. I decided on the latter course and we veered to the left, leaving a line of flags behind us and trying to get on to the proven ground skirting Stepaside Spur. When we ran out of flags we went on for a quarter of a mile and then waited for the Sno-Cats to come down to join us. It was an impressive sight to watch them grinding slowly down the steep slopes above. When the leading vehicle arrived I jumped in the front with David Stratton and directed him down toward the cliffs of Stepaside Spur and down onto the old route.

This was now familiar ground to me and we rolled steadily downward, losing a great deal of height, until we reached the point of Stepaside Spur where we turned sharp left, to swing around the corner and head toward the beetling ice cliffs of Mount Huggins. Below us now was the wide expanse of the Landing, but in order to get onto it we had to do a tremendous dogleg around extensive areas of crevassing. A mile from the corner we turned sharply to the right again and then roared down onto the wide-stretched Landing and raced over its superb surface at high speed. We soon picked up the empty drums that denoted our old Landing campsite and came to a halt beside them to enable the rest of the vehicles to join us.

The weather was absolutely superb and with our considerable loss of height there was a marked increase in warmth—in fact with a temperature of -23°C it seemed decidedly balmy. When the other vehicles arrived we moved on together, dropping down the steep snow gut to Twin Rocks. Here an unpleasant surprise awaited me, for the exit from the gut had all the signs of hidden crevasses which I certainly didn't remember. I went ahead on foot and probed the surface, but didn't find anything more than a couple of feet wide, so waved the Sno-Cats through. We coasted down the long slopes of the Lower Staircase, keeping well clear of the widespread crevassing on our right and descending fold after steep fold. All the great peaks around were glowing crimson from the setting rays of the sun, and we seemed to be descending into the dark bowl of night. Down on the lower trunk of the glacier I could see billowing snow plumes writhing up, clear indication of a very strong wind. As we approached the black cliffs of Clinker Bluff we entered the windy area and were soon enveloped in drifting snow. The further we went the stronger the wind became and the worse the visibility, but we fumbled our way on, hoping to get right down onto the floor of the Skelton Glacier. The wind was now approaching gale force and I knew we'd have little hope of getting much further. I was less concerned with finding a way down the glacier than with the problem of getting somewhere suitable to camp, for below Clinker Bluff the glacier was hard polished ice for many miles. So I advised Bunny that the wisest move would be to camp on the last bit of snow off Clinker Bluff itself.

We kept looking through the screaming drift for an ideal campsite, but nothing very attractive presented itself and it soon became apparent that we were getting off the snow onto a hard, patchy surface. So here we decided to stop. David Stratton swung our vehicle across the wind to give some protection when the tent was pitched and the other vehicles drew up in similar fashion. We still had a fearful struggle getting our tents erected in what was now a full gale. Vast quantities of snow were shoveled on to the tent flaps, the guy ropes were well and truly anchored down and in the more exposed places we built protecting walls of large snow blocks. Despite all these efforts the tents were still flapping like mad things, but it was very pleasant to crawl inside and astonishing how protected you felt with two flimsy walls of fabric between you and the outside world. It had been a wonderful day for me. Not only had we covered fifty miles down one of the great glaciers of the Antarctic but we'd dropped over 5,000 feet and gone from the approaching winter of the Polar Plateau to the late summer of almost sea level. I felt proud of my efforts but, strangely enough, I can't remember a single soul saying a complimentary word. Maybe they had no idea of what we had just done—that's the kindest thing to believe anyway.

It was still blowing furiously in the morning but it was easing off at midday and I suggested to Bunny that we should strike camp and move on. We left at 2 p.m. and descended the blue ice of the glacier, clattering over ice and small crevasses for some hours, with regular minor damage to our vehicles and sledges. At 8:30 p.m. we came to the end of the bare ice and, much to our relief, drove on more easily over firm snow. This coincided with a return of cloudy conditions and whiteout. I navigated on judgment of eye, roughly estimating our position from the peaks and rock bluffs around. At 1:30 a.m. we drove into the Skelton Depot.

In the next four days we roared over the Ross Ice Shelf and covered 180 miles. On Sunday 2nd March we could see the tall masts and yellow buildings of Scott Base, and welcoming vehicles racing out to meet us. We twisted our way through the pressure ice, roared around Pram Point, and came to a halt on the smooth sea ice in front of the Base. The welcome was tumultuous and it must have been a great moment for Bunny Fuchs and his team. A great journey had been successfully completed!

My New Zealand expedition had been successful, too. We had initiated a wide and continuing program of scientific research which is being energetically carried on by the New Zealand government to this day. We explored and carried out extensive geology over vast unvisited areas of the Antarctic continent. And I suppose it is some sort of feat that we drove three farm tractors to the South Pole.

As for my recommendation that Bunny should stop his journey for the winter at the South Pole—well, he proved me wrong! I had not known that the crossing party would be able to follow my tracks so easily for seventy-five percent of the way—and I don't believe that Bunny did either—that was a great bonus for him. And so was my guidance down the complex Skelton Glacier. Without these two factors the crossing party would undoubtedly have spent an extra winter at Scott Base. It had been close, very close!

I politely refused Bunny's friendly invitation to go back to London with him for another jaunt on the lecture circuit. I just wanted a peaceful time at home with my family and some green grass and trees. I was very happy for Bunny to go back home to receive all the credit he undoubtedly deserved. He had proved himself to be brave, determined and incredibly stubborn and, with a little help, he had completed his journey in his hundred estimated days.

On 19th December 1998 my son Peter and two robust companions were feeling their way nervously up the giant Shackleton Glacier that no one had ever climbed before. On skis and by foot they had battled across the great Ross Ice Shelf—as wide as France—their objective being to man haul unsupported to the South Pole and return.

From my home I talked to Peter on his sophisticated Iridium communications system and the circuit was clear as a bell. It had been mighty hard work he told me with storms and sastrugi. Now the tough climb up through the heavily crevassed glacier lay ahead of them. Then it would be over the Polar Plateau to the South Pole and return.

In my heart I wished them well! There was much potential danger ahead and a mighty challenge to overcome. I accepted that the spirit of adventure burnt as strongly today as it had ever done.

Peter's party were battered by long storms and unexpected health problems but they pressed on and finally reached the South Pole. They were too late now to travel back on foot to Scott Base so returned in a Hercules aircraft. I felt that their first ascent of the Shackleton Glacier and their reaching of the Pole had been a reasonable reward for a magnificent effort.

11

Yetis in Thin Air

I HAD BEEN INVOLVED IN ANTARCTIC MATTERS FOR A FULL THREE years and I greatly enjoyed returning to family life in New Zealand. Louise had made this very easy for me. While I was away she had always involved the family in everything that happened. Every day she would talk about where I was and what progress we were making and what we were doing, in such a way that when I returned after fifteen months the family were very much aware of everything that had been going on. I discovered that due to her efforts I wasn't an outsider at all and was quickly absorbed back into the family group as though I'd never been away.

I worked on the bees, for the last year, as it happened, and wrote a book on the Antarctic and Louise had our third child, Belinda, who was to prove a joy to us all. After Everest people kept telling me that I would never have to work again, dozens of companies would want me as a public relations director and money would just keep flowing in. I would be a rich man in no time at all. It didn't turn out quite that way. Certainly I was invited to be a director and patron of many worthy causes but none of them paid any money. I had to raise my finances in a quite different manner. In the middle of 1959 I received a letter from the editor of *Argosy* magazine in the United States saying I had been chosen to receive their Explorer of the Year Award. Would my wife and I come to New York at their expense to give a talk at an award banquet and receive a check for U.S. $1,000—a rather tidy sum in those days. Our trip to New York was a happy and successful one and was made more exciting by a telephone call from Chicago inviting us to visit there on our way home and do a program for educational television with all expenses paid and a useful honorarium as well. It was a considerable difference from New Zealand where I had never received any money for a lecture—the honor of being asked was regarded as sufficient reward in itself (fortunately this attitude has improved somewhat over the years).

Field Enterprises Educational Corporation was a very large company that published World Book Encyclopedia and they had an extensive part-time staff spread all over the United States, largely selling door to door. I had never experienced such an organization before. They treated me in a very friendly fashion and I was interviewed on film for their series of programs called "Beginnings," which tried to show young people how they, too, could become successful and even famous!

We had dinner one evening with their public relations director, John Dienhart, a very confident and effervescent person who seemed to have an unending supply of beautiful girlfriends. John started asking me about my future expedition plans. I got rather carried away and said how I would like to do another Himalayan expedition that would be a happy blend of science and mountaineering. We would investigate, I said, the secrets of high-altitude acclimatization, about which little was known, and also search for the yeti, the Abominable Snowman, to prove whether it really existed.

John Dienhart became very interested, particularly about the yeti, and suggested that maybe his company could help financially, but I did not take him too seriously. We returned to New Zealand after a much happier time in the United States than we had enjoyed on our 1953–54 lecture tour. At John Dienhart's request I did work out a plan for the expedition when I got home and sent it off to him. Somewhat to my astonishment I received a cable almost immediately saying, "Can you come Chicago soonest our expense discuss expedition." For someone who had expressed a desire to spend some years with my young family, I headed off to Chicago rather promptly.

I was asked to give a presentation to the Board of Field Enterprises and was invited in to meet the Chairman, Bailey K. Howard. I had a rather battered briefcase with me containing all my papers, the clasp of which had broken, so I'd obtained a bit of twine and tied it firmly together. When I undid the twine and produced my papers in the Chairman's office there were some raised eyebrows amongst the directors. Bailey K. Howard asked me how much I considered the expedition would cost. I told him the figure I had worked out—U.S. $125,000, a very considerable sum. Mr. Howard asked me if I would mind going outside while the Board discussed the matter. It couldn't have been more than ten minutes before I was invited back inside and the Chairman announced that the Board had agreed to support the expedition. And then he uttered some words that I will always remember. "Tell me, Sir Edmund, what would you like us to do with the $125,000? Will we pay it into your bank account in New Zealand?" For a moment I visualized the reaction of the manager of my bank in Auckland if a check for $125,000 should suddenly appear in my modest account. He was the person who, some years before, had been reluctant to lend me £400 so that I could take Louise with me to London. I didn't know if Bailey Howard was joking or not. "No," I sensibly replied, "it would be more helpful if the money was just supplied as the expedition requires it."

Bailey K. Howard's final words were also a surprise. "I do not wish you to be offended," he said to me, "but we would also like to present you with a new briefcase." I wasn't the slightest bit offended and left for home with a very fancy new briefcase.

The search for the yeti created tremendous interest in the United States. While everyone agreed that little was known about the supposed creature, there were some rumors that it was half-animal and half-human. One newspaper in Chicago humorously suggested that if the yeti were brought back to that city a decision would have to be made

192

whether to put it in the Lincoln Park Zoo or check it into the Hilton.

I had always been a little skeptical about the existence of the yeti myself. There had been quite a lot of evidence that I could not explain: footprints in the snow; a scalp in the Khumjung Monastery; a bony hand at Pangboche Monastery; stories of sightings by monks in their monasteries and by Sherpas in lonely shepherds' huts. Several expeditions had already gone looking for the yeti but had not been able to provide any positive results. It would be interesting to see what we could find.

On the more seriously scientific front, I had kept in touch with Dr. Griffith Pugh, the physiologist on our 1953 Everest expedition, and we had often discussed the need for more research into what actually happened to people who spent long periods at high altitude. Griff Pugh became the expedition's senior scientist and we agreed that an insulated hut would be built at 19,000–20,000 feet and extensive testing would be carried out on a group of physiologists over a long period. We felt the ideal location for the hut would be on the Ama Dablam Col that Eric Shipton and I had crossed in 1951. It was indeed a very exciting prospect.

We started in the remote and spectacular Rolwaling valley, which Earle Riddiford and I were the first foreigners to descend in 1951. We had two animal experts with the expedition, Marlin Perkins, Director of the Lincoln Park Zoo in Chicago, and a U.S. biologist, Dr. Larry Swan, who was an experienced Himalayan traveler. It took us a week to walk from the broad Kathmandu valley into the steep narrow entrance to the Rolwaling and its main village of Beding. For eight days after our arrival we were held up by torrential rain. All we could do was talk to a number of local people, who all assured us that the yeti certainly existed.

The long delay irritated us all and tempers grew shorter. It all came to a head—literally—one afternoon when a group of senior local Sherpas arrived at our camp bringing a porter who appeared to have his brains surging out of his skull. They claimed that our sirdar Urkein had drunk too much chang (beer) and as a consequence had become very annoyed with this particular porter who was slow to carry out some specific order. They were standing on the steps of the Beding Gompa (monastery) when Urkein had picked up a great chunk of wood and hit the porter over the head, splitting his skull open. We could not understand how the man could stand, let alone walk, but when our doctors examined him they found his skull was plastered with ash, a lama remedy for bleeding, and he had in fact suffered only a five-inch head wound. A modest payout of rupees sent the group and the porter away reasonably happy, but we always thought that *Blood on the Gompa Steps* would have made an excellent title for a book.

Our press correspondent, Desmond Doig, proved a considerable asset. Artist, author, romanticist, he had a fluent grasp of the Nepali language and a remarkable imagination. Every day he came back from the village with a new yeti story, although some were a little hard to believe. He heard there was a skin in the village and after much persuasion we managed to buy it. It looked remarkably like the descriptions I had read of the Tibetan blue bear, but at least we could study it now.

In early October the weather cleared and we moved up valley amongst the glaciers and great peaks. We discovered many tracks on the Ripimu Glacier at 18,000 and 19,000 feet which our Sherpas were quite convinced belonged to the yeti. But when we followed these for any distance, we came to an area where the snow was in the shade and then the large tracks would disappear and be replaced by the small footprints of a fox or wild dog, grouped together as the animal bounded over the snow. We saw much evidence of the effects of sun on these small tracks, melting them out, running them together, and making as fine a yeti track as one would wish to see.

One evening, a group of us were huddled around a smoky fire on the Tolam Bau Glacier and the conversation turned idly to the future welfare of the Sherpas. "What will happen to you all in the future?" I asked sirdar Urkein. He thought for a moment and then replied, "In the mountains we are as strong as you—maybe stronger. But our children lack education. Our children have eyes but they cannot see. What we need more than anything is a school in Khumjung village." For the first time there rose in my mind the determination to build a school for the Sherpas. It would be the least I could do for my very good friends.

Later that evening we had an amazing experience. It was dark in the valley, but the sky was still bright. The Sherpas made some comment and I looked up to see something whizzing across the eastern sky. A bright round object swept up from behind the wall of mountains separating us from Tibet, leaving a distinct vapor trail behind it. This trail curved upward into the sky, then bent over backward toward Tibet again, making an almost complete circle. Was it a Chinese rocket, I wondered? (A month or so later, when I was briefly at a hotel in Chicago, there was a knock on the door and two very large somber gentlemen appeared, identifying themselves as CIA agents, to question me exhaustively about this happening. I never heard anything further from them.)

I decided to move on into the Khumbu area over the Tesi Lapcha Pass that Earle Riddiford and I had crossed in 1951. We managed to recruit some reluctant porters from Beding and put 80-lb. loads on their backs. When our expedition members and the porters had disappeared up valley, Peter Mulgrew and I remained behind with our 40-lb. rucksacks. To our disgust, we discovered that one 80-lb. load still remained. There was no alternative but to carry it ourselves. Peter labored up valley with a hefty 70 lbs. and I had a mighty 90 lbs. Somehow we scrambled up and down over the moraine-covered glacier to reach our next camp at the bottom of the icefall leading to the Tesi Lapcha Pass. It was a considerable struggle next day to climb up a steep rocky bluff beside the icefall to camp on the ice on the crest of the pass. Most of us had tents to sleep in, but many of our hardy Sherpa porters just shivered all night beside their loads. Next morning we moved over the pass and descended a long steep snow slope that funneled into a narrow rock-strewn gully. I was halfway when there was a great rumble from the cliffs above and an avalanche of rock came pouring down. I managed to squeeze under an overhanging rock, but some of the party were still exposed. By some miracle little harm was done and we carried on down the 5,000 feet of descent to reach Thami village in the Khumbu.

Thami was an amazing sight. Camped on the broad flat area below the village were thousands of Tibetan refugees who had escaped over the Nangpa La with all their yaks. Food for the yaks had quickly disappeared so the Tibetans had butchered the animals and hung the meat out on hundreds of lines to preserve it in the sun. It brought forcibly home to us the desperate situation produced by the Chinese invasion of Tibet.

In the Khumbu valley we interrogated monks and local Sherpas but, although they all expressed their belief in the existence of the yeti, there was only one Sherpa, Sen Tenzing, who actually claimed to have seen one. He told me the story of how he had been attending an important festival at Tengboche Monastery which concluded with much ceremonial drinking of the local chang. He admitted that he was slightly the worse for wear when he started down the steep snow-covered track to the river on his way to his home village of Phortse. He was alone and halfway down when he suddenly saw a hairy yeti approaching up the track toward him. Sen Tenzing immediately dropped behind a rock and waited with bated breath as he heard the footsteps approach closer, hesitate for a while, and finally retreat down the track. After a long wait, Sen Tenzing got to his feet and continued cautiously downward, to see large yeti footprints in the snow, outlined in the bright moonlight. Sen Tenzing did not catch up with the creature but always maintained he had indeed seen a yeti.

Probably the most interesting relics were the yeti scalps in the monasteries at Khumjung, Pangboche and Namche Bazaar. They were all remarkably similar, a high pointed skull covered with coarse reddish-black hair and they certainly looked of considerable age. Desmond Doig and Marlin Perkins carried out an experiment with skins of the Himalayan serow which had hair that was similar in texture to the scalps. They softened the skins and molded them over shaped wooden caps and, although the results were different in many ways from the originals, they were close enough to indicate we might be on the right track. But some sort of authoritative answer was needed on the scalps, else they would remain a constant source of conjecture. The only scalp that was not in fact a religious relic was the one at Khumjung and after much debate, in which a large sum of rupees played a part, the village agreed to let us take the scalp away for a maximum of six weeks, with the proviso that one of their senior village elders must travel with it to protect it. Desmond Doig, Marlin Perkins and I, together with village elder Khunjo Chumbi, covered the 170 miles of steep country to Kathmandu in a vigorous nine days. From there we flew to Chicago, Paris and London and at every stop Khunjo and the scalp attracted more attention than a film star. The scalp and our blue bear skins were examined by zoologists, anthropologists and other scientists. All agreed that the scalp was very old, but their decisions were unanimous. As we suspected, the scalp had been molded out of the skin of the serow, a rather uncommon member of the antelope family. Our yeti skins were confirmed as Tibetan blue bear.

In Chicago, Field Enterprises was reveling in the worldwide publicity and generously made a further financial contribution which went toward the Khumjung school project which was already taking shape. While in Calcutta I had approached Indian Aluminium for help with a building and they kindly donated an aluminum structure and even preassembled it to show me how it went together. Then it was shipped to Kathmandu.

We concluded that the yeti was a mythological creature, probably based on rare sightings of the Tibetan blue bear, although even now I would be happy to be proved wrong. In the last thirty-seven years tracks have been reported many times and there have been claims of sightings, but always in dim and misty conditions. Despite the many people who wander through the Himalayas these days with excellent camera equipment, no authentic photograph has yet been produced of a yeti. It seems to be as elusive as the Loch Ness monster.

The search for the yeti had been a fascinating experience, but our main expedition objective was our extensive physiological program. An insulated tubular building had been constructed in England in pieces large enough to be carried on a porter's back and this had been shipped to India and trucked to Kathmandu. It was 13th September when I left Kathmandu with my party for the Rowaling valley and a day later the major train of 310 porters set off for the Everest area and the Mingbo valley to start building the scientific huts. In charge of this party was Norman Hardie, a Himalayan mountaineer of wide experience whose greatest feat was the ascent of Kangchenjunga (28,150 feet), the world's third highest summit. Assisting him were Dr. Jim Milledge, Barry Bishop and Wally Romanes, who were all experienced mountaineers, while Romanes was also a builder. Their journey into Tengboche was carried out in appalling weather conditions and their cumbersome loads of building materials only aggravated the situation for the porters. It was a very considerable relief when the monsoon rain ceased and they were able to arrive intact at Tengboche Monastery and pay off their porters.

Norm Hardie set to work to move nearly 400 loads up the Mingbo valley and it proved quite a struggle as there was a foot of soft snow down to low levels. At a height of 17,500 feet, Wally Romanes started building our "Greenhouse" and the rest of the party reconnoitered up toward the Ama Dablam Col. On 29th October our two parties gathered in Khumjung in beautiful weather and we were joined by Dr. Griffith Pugh, who had arrived from Kathmandu a couple of days earlier with fifty loads of scientific equipment. We moved up valley and on 3rd November started up the Mingbo valley. I was in fine form, and pleased to be marching along with Peter Mulgrew, one of the Old Firm from Ross Base. We reached the temporary Base Camp on a grassy shelf at 14,500 feet, and after a quick lunch carried on again, mostly over grassy slopes. I made the idle comment to Peter Mulgrew that it would almost be possible to put a little airstrip in the gentle hollow beneath us. Then we were crossing rough moraine and clambered up to a little pass. A hundred feet below us beside a lake was the green square of the hut with the terminal ice cliffs of the Mingbo Glacier looming above it. Wally Romanes had done an excellent job on this intermediate hut. It was warm and comfortable, and seemed capable of withstanding the coldest temperatures and the strongest winds. But now we had to establish the Silver Hut where the main scientific work would go on. The plan was to erect it on the Ama Dablam Col.

The next morning we set off up the glacier, following Hardie's route along ice cliffs and gullies and around crevasses, trudging over the snowfield at the top of the glacier to the foot of the steep face running up to the Ama Dablam Col where we admired the large pile of hut sections that had already been carried there. We roped up, climbed the steep fluted slopes and emerged on the col at 19,600 feet into a terrific wind. It was bitterly cold and we had a tough job just pitching our tents. Hardie and I examined possible hut sites but weren't impressed with what we saw and feared the col might be cut off by dangerous winter snows. It was now blowing like fury and we were happy to retreat into our flapping tents. Four of us spent a miserable night on the col and were very glad when morning came and we could abandon this exposed camp, cramponing steeply down the fluted ice.

After a careful search, we decided on a pleasant location for the Silver Hut on a small snowfield with excellent access to the Green Hut and protected from avalanche danger by a large open crevasse. Its altitude of 19,100 feet was rather lower than we had hoped but still high enough for our purpose, so we spent the next day making a substantial snow platform, assembling the foundation beams, and carrying all the hut sections into position. With remarkable smoothness and efficiency the shell grew rapidly into the giant drainpipe that was the Silver Hut and I descended happily into the valley only to receive a tongue-lashing from Griff Pugh. Griff always had his own agenda and, as he had not been around when I had decided to assemble the hut, I had gone ahead without him. Now he was absolutely furious and reeled off a long list of my various inadequacies, while George Lowe listened with amusement. Later Griff came to accept the Silver Hut and its site as ideal and quickly started an elaborate physiological program that continued right through the winter and resulted in considerable profitable research.

Several of us returned to Kathmandu in early January to organize a second lift of supplies and while we were there I was approached by a Swiss pilot, Captain Schrieber, who wanted somewhere he could drop International Red Cross relief to the Tibetan refugees. They were in a pitiful condition, for on the 10th March 1959 there had been a Tibetan uprising against the Chinese in Lhasa. The Chinese retaliated with great force. Thousands of Tibetans were killed by Red Army troops. Seven days later the young Dalai Lama fled Lhasa to seek political asylum in India, followed by over 80,000 Tibetan refugees, some of whom crossed the border into the Everest region. Captain Schrieber had a Pilatus Porter aircraft with an outstanding high-altitude performance, but he didn't know of any place to land in the Khumbu. I remembered the site I'd pointed out to Peter Mulgrew up the Mingbo valley, but warned Captain Schrieber that it was at 15,000 feet. This didn't seem to worry him, and we agreed that, if I could devote expedition effort to clearing the Mingbo landing strip he, in return, would fly in several loads of aluminum sheets to build a school at Khumjung. So at my request, the Silver Hut wintering group put a team of men on to leveling the site at 15,000 feet, chopping off the frozen clumps of snow grass, filling in the worst of the holes, and rolling away the large boulders. Snow sometimes restricted their activity but it rarely lay for long once the sun was shining again. When the strip had been cleared to 400 yards the first landing was made. Unfortunately, the aircraft damaged its tail wheel on a rock and had an unscheduled stay of some days while being made airworthy again. Work on the strip continued for some months and we finally enlarged it to 500 yards and generally improved it.

At the takeoff end were two huge boulders weighing many tons and standing six feet above the ground. We had no explosives and the boulders were singularly unresponsive to the blows of our sledge-hammer. The problem was finally solved in a highly ingenious fashion by our Sherpas. They dug enormous craters beside each boulder and then used long heavy poles as levers to tip the boulders out of the way into the holes. Altogether we paid $900 for the labor used on building this strip, which possibly made it one of the cheapest as well as one of the highest airfields in the world. Due to the skill and experience of Captain Schrieber, large quantities of refugee food was transported safely into Mingbo and we for our part were helped considerably with the rapid freighting of personnel, scientific equipment and our school building.

Peter Mulgrew and I returned to Nepal in February with large quantities of supplies for the restocking of the Mingbo valley huts and the requirements for our final project, an assault without oxygen on Makalu (27,790 feet), the world's fifth highest mountain. With us were temporary additions to our team—my wife, Louise, and Peter's wife, June. Our journey into Tengboche was a source of great pleasure to me. It was Louise's first visit to the Himalayas and I saw this familiar route afresh through her delighted eyes. More than anything it was the flowers that made our days so wonderful. The crimson rhododendrons were in full bloom and our path would often cling to a hillside which was a blaze of color in every direction. As we climbed up to each pass the air would be heavy with the scent of daphne and the grass was hidden by a thick carpet of primulas. The magnolias were just coming into bloom; and in many shady spots were clusters of graceful orchids. Louise and June were very good friends and a lively pair. I can remember one pleasant camp when after dinner our Sherpas commenced their vigorous traditional dancing and dragged the two girls in to join them. They danced with much élan and a great deal of laughter, while their two husbands glowered from beside the campfire.

At a camp beside the Dudh Kosi river I received a message that team members Mike Ward, Mike Gill, Barry Bishop and Wally Romanes had reached the summit of Ama Dablam. From the climbers' viewpoint this was wonderful news, a triumph for the expedition. Ama Dablam had seemed impossibly steep and difficult and when I had given my support to an attempted reconnaissance I had no conception that they could possibly reach the summit. But now there was a nagging worry at the back of my mind. The Nepalese had recently instituted a system of permits and peak fees for mountains—something quite new to the Himalayas—and we certainly didn't have permission for Ama Dablam.

On 22nd March Griff Pugh flew into the Mingbo airstrip from Kathmandu with disturbing news. The Nepalese government was getting very difficult about Ama Dablam, they required an official explanation. A moment's reflection and I realized I would have to return to Kathmandu and clear the matter up. I snatched my satchel of papers and joined the expedition wives on the plane. We were short on seats so June Mulgrew was put on the floor in the back of the plane and tied down with a piece of rope, facing sideways like in a tram. Captain Schrieber calmly told her, "If anything happens just undo the rope." Louise didn't like small aircraft and she was very nervous and upset. I could understand this, as there was no second chance, but it didn't stop me from subjecting her to small plane flights.

We were loaded to the maximum. Captain Schrieber started up the motor and revved it fiercely, while the two large rocks wedged under the wheels for brakes were removed and we rolled forward onto two smaller ones. The motor was given full throttle and the plane shuddered with power as the wheels inched over the small rocks and then rolled suddenly down the other side. With the motor blaring like a demon we surged into our takeoff run. To my startled eyes the short strip ahead of us seemed quite inadequate for our needs and the hill at the end loomed up with frightening rapidity. At the last moment Captain Schrieber pulled back on the stick and we lifted sluggishly off the ground. Next moment he had tipped up onto one wing to dodge the hill and we were slipping through the gully to the left, to be precipitated out into free air as the river valley dropped sharply away beneath us. With a sigh of relief, I unclenched my hands as we soared high over Tengboche and set course for Kathmandu.

The news in Kathmandu couldn't have been worse—the government was instructing us to withdraw immediately. We were to be punished as an example to others. For nine days I trudged around government buildings seeing officials and ministers and trying desperately to change the decision. But it all seemed hopeless. Finally I was called to the office of the Foreign Secretary who gave me a ten-minute lambasting about the responsibilities of experienced mountaineers which I, he said, had gravely breached. Then he carried on to say that the government had come to a decision. I waited nervously. "We have agreed that you can go ahead but you will have to pay a very substantial fine." I immediately thought of thousands of dollars as he continued, "We have agreed that you should pay a fine of 3,000 rupees." Which was $60 or so. I must admit I had to keep the smile off my face and I hastily paid over the money. It was an enormous relief and I was emotionally exhausted. It was only the fact that I had Louise with me that nightmare nine days that enabled me to keep going.

The return to Mingbo on 5th April was a terrifying experience. Civil aviation in Kathmandu had only just become aware that the Mingbo airfield was operating, even though it had been in action for several months. They demanded that one of their experts should fly in with us and check it out. It was quite turbulent as we made our approach toward the hill at the bottom of the Mingbo runway. As Captain Schrieber headed down there was a fierce sideways gust of wind and the aircraft started sliding toward the left-hand edge of the field. Captain Schrieber's reaction was immediate—he just dropped the aircraft from thirty feet to land with a huge thud and then rolled upward close to the rocks on the left-hand side where we stopped safely at the top. We were all severely shaken. The Civil Aviation gentleman staggered out of the aircraft and vomited noisily. Then he declared the airfield closed for all time. When he was informed that this would involve him in a seventeen-day walk to Kathmandu, he re-opened the airfield for one last flight. Captain Schrieber wasn't too concerned—he'd flown in all the food for the Tibetans and our Khumjung School material had been brought in, too.

The damage-control trip to Kathmandu meant we had lost two weeks of valuable time and our approach to Makalu was a technically demanding one—probably more demanding than any other approach I had heard of to a really high mountain. I planned to use a high-level route, crossing from the Mingbo over the Ama Dablam Col (19,600 feet), then across the Hongu Glacier, up over two 20,000-foot passes on either side of the Barun Plateau and finally down to the Barun Glacier. For ten days we concentrated on getting all the loads into the Hongu and then up the very steep face of the West Col at 20,000 feet. I led the first team up to the foot of the West Col and there was no doubt that my acclimatization had weakened during those awful two weeks in Kathmandu. We stopped for a rest and I took off my 40-lb. load wearily. Beside me was Pem-batharkay, one of the strongest Sherpas I have ever known, and he was carrying over 60 lbs. With a sigh I reached down for my load but it wasn't there. I looked up in amazement—well ahead of me now was Pembatharkay and my load was perched on top of his own. He was carrying over 100 lbs. at close to 20,000 feet. No wonder I had admiration and affection for my Sherpa friends. At times I had forty-seven Sherpas carrying loads on one sector or another, and by 16th April we had 133 loads on the West Col.

The next day we started the second phase of my plan. With a large group of climbers and Sherpas we left our Base on the Hongu Glacier, climbed the fixed ropes to the West Col, trudged slowly across the broad Barun Plateau to the East Col and then descended abruptly down a tributary valley toward the main Barun Glacier. It was a tremendously hard day with heavy loads. Camp I was eventually established at 17,500 feet and we began relaying loads down to it from the West Col. I had promised myself a few days of rest to recover from my efforts in Kathmandu and on the high route, but problems had arisen in the Mingbo that needed urgent attention. With Peter Mulgrew for company I did a mad rush back to the Green Hut and then returned to Camp I with some more loads. I seemed to be traveling as well as anyone, but felt very tired on the completion of this trip.

We now devoted all our efforts to establishing and stocking the camps on the flanks of Makalu. Camp II was established at 19,000 feet, and by 1st May Camp III at 21,000 feet was in full use. Wally Romanes and I set off to complete the route to Camp IV. We made good time across the terrace and worked hard on the couloir, cutting steps and putting in fixed ropes to complete the work done by the team on the previous day. The sense of exposure in the couloir was quite terrific as it drained out over a 1,000-foot precipice. In thick fog and driving snow we came to the top of the couloir and, although I was feeling rather tired, we pushed on to find a suitable place for the camp. After a steepish traverse, we dropped over a little ridge onto a flat piece of snow which seemed an ideal location. The altitude was somewhere around 23,000 feet. We returned in thick visibility and heavy snowfall and there was three inches of new snow around Camp III. The wind battered our tents and it was just like the Antarctic with drifting snow and high sastrugi. I was awake most of that wild night with a miserable headache which seemed reluctant to go away. Despite the weather, Camp IV was established next morning and quickly stocked, and on 5th May we watched with great excitement as Mike Gill and Mike Ward forced their way onto the Makalu Col at 24,300 feet.

The pains on the left side of my forehead wouldn't go away. I now realized that I'd been grossly overdoing it, so I decided I'd better go down to Camp II at 19,000 feet for a break at lower altitudes. Mike Ward and Mike Gill deserved a rest too and came down with me. At Camp II I had a reasonable night's sleep, although I didn't feel too comfortable in the morning and wasn't really happy all day. In the evening I once again had a frightful pain on the side of my head, and when a Sherpa brought my meal I just couldn't speak to him properly. It all came out as gibberish, a very nasty feeling. Our doctors, Mike Ward and Jim Milledge, put me on oxygen for the night (we had brought a little oxygen for medical purposes) and gave me a shot of pethidine. I went off to sleep rather later in the night and when I woke I was human again—but rather fumbling in speech, shaky in hand, poor of balance and seeing double. It sounds awful but I really wasn't too bad, although I realized my time on the mountain was finished. Late in the afternoon I walked down to Camp I without too much difficulty.

Mike Ward called it a cerebral vascular accident, and over the radio with Mingbo there was some very negative talk from Griff Pugh, who insisted I should be helicoptered immediately to Kathmandu. I had no intention of doing that as I still had the school at Khumjung to build, but I agreed to follow the long way around to Mingbo via the Arun river so as to keep at an altitude below 15,000 feet. Dr. Jim Milledge generously agreed to abandon his chances on the mountain and came with me. That same day twenty-one loads were carried up to the Makalu Col. I recast my assault plans and handed them over for Mike Ward to use. The expedition was in such good shape that I was hardly needed anyway, or so I told myself. What could possibly go wrong?

In actual fact, while Jim Milledge and I were walking back to the

Khumbu a great deal did go wrong and I think my presence might have helped. At first progress was excellent. Some good physiological work was done on the Makalu Col and on 13th May Mike Gill, Wally Romanes and Leigh Ortenburger, a renowned American mountaineer, established Camp VI at 25,800 feet. Next day, in very unpleasant weather, they established a depot at 26,300 feet and it was rather a grim struggle back to Camp VI in the heavy wind. Gill and Romanes had a fall which could have been disastrous. The weather remained terrible, so next day they battled their way back to the Makalu Col. Mike Gill said that I probably had the experience and wisdom not to have let them get into the troubles they got into later "because we tried to climb the mountain too early. It was absolutely dreadful. It was some of the worst days of my life really. It's like being terribly, seriously ill all the time. While you rested, it was not too bad, but you take about five steps and you are out of breath. You just can barely breathe at all."

After much discussion, the next plan was made with Tom Nevison and Peter Mulgrew as the assault team. With six Sherpas they climbed to Camp VI in improving conditions and spent the night there. When they started the next morning the Sherpas carried the loads and broke trail to save the strength of the two climbers. The Sherpas were tied together on one rope, something I would never have permitted, and had almost reached the depot when one of them slipped, pulling all the others off in a devastating slide. By sheer chance two of them broke through a bridge into a crevasse and this pulled the whole team up with a jerk, otherwise they would all have fallen to their deaths. Two of the Sherpas had been rather battered but felt they could get back to Camp VI by themselves. The two climbers and the remaining four Sherpas continued to the depot, shared out the loads and carried on upward, going very slowly. At 27,000 feet they established Camp VII on the edge of a crevasse and Nevison, Mulgrew and Sherpa Annullu stayed there while the others descended.

They had quite a restful night's sleep in this spectacular position. When they started in the morning they were moving very slowly indeed and after four hours were only 400 feet above the tents—but this meant only 400 feet from the top. They continued on again, determined to reach the summit, when suddenly Mulgrew doubled up and collapsed on the snow. It was discovered later he had a pulmonary edema in his right lung, which probably should have killed him at this altitude. Somehow, Nevison and Annullu got him down to Camp VII and by then Annullu was very weak too, as he'd broken a rib in the Sherpa fall. Mulgrew's second night at 27,000 feet was a bad one and he coughed up quite a lot of blood. Yet in the morning he was able to move slowly downward with Annullu and Nevison belaying him. He only got to 26,300 feet before blacking out, and here Nevison decided they would have to stay, sending Annullu down to Camp VI for help. Later in the afternoon, Pemba Tenzing and Pasang Tenzing arrived with a tent and food and the rescue operation slowly got under way.

How Peter Mulgrew managed to survive the trip down the mountain is hard to know. It was a nightmarish operation with desperate efforts by many men, spearheaded by Leigh Ortenburger and John Harrison, a New Zealand mountaineer. Urkein and his Sherpas were absolutely magnificent. Somehow Peter reached Camp I more dead than alive and was helicoptered back to Kathmandu. During the descent he had also suffered severe frostbite to his feet and fingers and was put straight into the United Mission Hospital, the best hospital in Kathmandu.

Much had been achieved by the expedition. We had failed to climb Makalu without oxygen—but only just. We had carried out the best high-altitude physiological program undertaken to that time, and maybe even up to this day. In a lighter vein, we had certainly formed an opinion on the possible existence of the yeti. But there was still one thing left to do—we needed to build the school for Khumjung.

It took Jim Milledge and me fifteen days of vigorous walking to reach Mingbo again, and by that time I was as fit and normal as I ever was. When the party returned off Makalu we saw them safely on the way to Kathmandu and then concentrated on dismantling the Silver Hut and bringing all the equipment down from the Mingbo. Wally Romanes, Desmond Doig and Bhanu Bannerjee, a friend and interpreter from Calcutta, stayed behind with me and together we tackled the erection of

Khumjung school. Captain Schrieber had flown the aluminum building into the Mingbo airfield and it was carried by porters to Khumjung. It was a great advantage having our builder, Wally Romanes, with us. We built wooden foundations in a flat empty valley near Khumjung village and in misty monsoon conditions we assembled the aluminum building ready for occupation.

The opening ceremony was a remarkable occasion. Surrounded by clouds and fog, with frequent showers of rain, the villagers celebrated this important moment with great enthusiasm. The Head Lama and his musical entourage carried out the official blessing and I was invited to cut the ribbons and open the door. The forty pupils had bare feet and scruffy clothes, but their rosy cheeks and sparkling eyes were irresistible. It was a happy and satisfying occasion. When I left Khumjung on 13th June I little realized I was leaving behind what was to become a new way of life for me.

We completed our long damp monsoon walk back to Kathmandu to find Peter Mulgrew in hospital and his wife, June, there with him. Peter was still incapacitated and had severe frostbite, but was as determined as ever. "I wish we'd got to the top of Makalu," he said grimly, and then more softly, "and I wish you'd been there."

I wrote in some distress to Louise: "As soon as I arrived in Kathmandu around midday I went out and saw Peter at the hospital. Poor boy! It's a terrible shock when you first see him—just skin and bones, pretty lethargic from all the drugs they are giving him for the pain and with hands and feet black and shriveled from frostbite. I could have wept he was so pleased to see me."

The hospital agreed that Peter should return home to New Zealand for better treatment as soon as possible. So June and I loaded him on a succession of planes and we headed for home. I had only known June for three or four years, but we had become good friends. Now I saw a different June. She had been taught to give injections and gave Peter painkillers with great regularity on our long journey home. She was patient, reliable and friendly.

In hospital in New Zealand Peter had a very tough time. Both of his

legs were amputated six inches below the knees and replaced with pros-
thetics. It took all his determination to overcome his addiction to
pethidine, but he did that, too. He learned to walk again, so well that
most people would not have realized that he had artificial limbs. Four
years later he even went back with me to the Himalayas. Peter retired as
a serving naval officer and it was in the business and sporting world
that he really excelled. He became manager of a succession of large
companies and a world-class yachtsman. He could jam himself in the
cockpit of his boat and steer the craft very expertly. He inevitably
became more aggressive and competitive—and more grumpy too, I
guess, so June had to bear with quite a lot. But he proved himself a rather
remarkable man and was always a loyal and effective friend for me in
the Antarctic and the Himalayas.

My second illness on Makalu spelled the end of my career as a high-
altitude climber. But I think it is very true to say that as one thing seemed
to become impossible for me, other opportunities and other interests
certainly developed. And although these interests were perhaps not as
dangerous or exciting as some of my previous ones, yet they were in
many ways just as important challenges.

12

TENT-TESTING, SCHOOL-BUILDING

THE SUBSTANTIAL CONTRIBUTION BY FIELD ENTERPRISES TO OUR Himalayan expedition was not by any means just a generous gift. I had agreed to bring my whole family to Chicago at the conclusion of the project and spend a year lecturing about it to their branches all over the country. Soon after Christmas 1962, Louise and I rented out our house in Auckland, packed our gear and flew to Honolulu. At this stage Peter was just eight years old, Sarah was six and Belinda only three. We were met in Honolulu by Bailey K. Howard and some of his senior staff who wanted to see for themselves if I had fully recovered from my ill health on Makalu. Mr. Howard was greatly relieved to find the whole family in the best of shape.

We attended a big party on New Year's Eve and stayed celebrating until midnight, something I don't think I had ever done before. When the bells rang there was much rejoicing and one mature but handsome World Book lady leaned over and deposited on me the sloppiest kiss I had ever experienced. I found it rather revolting but it made me realize that I was entering an entirely different way of life. We traveled to Chicago and moved into a house they had rented for us in the suburb of Park Ridge. It was an adequate home, although nowhere near as comfortable as our house in Auckland. It had a rather empty feeling about it, which was understandable when we discovered it had been unused ever since there had been a murder there. However, it was very close to O'Hare Airport and this was important for me. Almost every Monday morning I flew out of O'Hare to some U.S. destination, lectured all week and then, after a lunchtime lecture on the following Saturday, I flew back again to O'Hare. It was an extremely busy life and a lonely one, particularly for Louise. But with her warm and gregarious personality she soon had many friends up and down the street. Altogether I did 106 banquet lectures in eighty different cities during the course of the year, and shook hands with 17,000 World Bookers, as they called themselves.

John Dienhart seemed to lack any confidence in my ability to travel alone around America, so he always sent one of his many beautiful young ladies along to organize and plan things—or maybe he couldn't understand anyone not wanting to have female company every evening. I actually enjoyed these bright young women and they certainly came to no harm with me. On one occasion I was lecturing in Salt Lake City on a very snowy evening. My companion was called Darlene Odell and she was indeed exceptionally beautiful. Unfortunately, she tipped my magazine of slides out onto the floor just before my presentation commenced. I told her that I would entertain the audience with a few anecdotes until she had the slides correctly mounted. It seemed to take quite a long time, but then to my relief the magazine was put in place and the projector turned on. "First slide please, Darlene," I requested. Immediately 200 pairs of cold eyes swung in my direction accusingly. From then on I took great care to call her "Miss Odell." As it happened, all the slides were back to front anyway.

Soon after our arrival in Chicago I was invited by the colossal American operation, Sears, Roebuck and Company, to join their Sports Advisory Staff as an expert on camping equipment. Sears was making a vigorous attempt to improve the quality and status of their sporting gear and for this purpose they had recruited a famous baseball player, Ted Williams, who was also a fishing and hunting enthusiast. Various other experts were added in a wide diversity of sporting activities—skiing, athletics, football, swimming, tennis and so on—they formed a redoubtable group, dripping with Olympic gold medals and famous names. Endorsement by a renowned sporting figure isn't always much of a recommendation—sporting heroes can become depressingly human when money and principles are involved. However, I learned that the members of the Sears Sports Advisory Committee were actually meant to work on the design and testing of their equipment, so I agreed to become part of the team and I am still, after thirty-five years, a camping advisor to Sears, Roebuck. It has been a happy and successful arrangement for me, and over the years I've been involved in the production of some excellent family tents, and tested them, too, on all sorts of expeditions and in many parts of the world.

Sears decided that in the summer they'd like to do a film of us family-camping in Alaska. It sounded like a great idea to Louise and me. Sears supplied us with a large and powerful Ford station wagon and we towed a small experimental "camper trailer"—an ingenious device that opened into a large and comfortable tent. This became our first major family adventure. We camped in the beautiful mountains and forests of Colorado; raced at eighty miles per hour across the wide deserts of Nevada and looked open-eyed, but without envy, at the throbbing gambling towns of Reno and Las Vegas. We admired Lake Tahoe and thought San Francisco was beautiful, too, but we weren't interested in cities. We drove happily north to mighty redwood forests and great volcanic cones.

I had also been commissioned by the U.S. Secretary of Agriculture to produce a report on the campgrounds of the National Forest Parks. They had asked an experienced Antarctic traveler, Mat Brennan, to look after us and make sure the campgrounds gave us full cooperation. We enjoyed the company of Mat and his family, but I think they found our camping and traveling habits something of a strain. Following the routine of our Himalayan trekking we were up at daylight, loaded the sleeping children into the back of the station wagon, packed up camp, drove past the sleeping Brennan tent, and dashed on for three or so hours through the cool of the morning. When the children complained of hunger we'd stop in some beautiful place for a leisurely and substantial breakfast. By mid-afternoon we had usually covered 300 or 400 miles to reach our destination and the children had plenty of time to play and explore while we set up camp. Poor Mat and his family inevitably woke to find us gone and then desperately chased after us, but as they traveled at least ten miles an hour more slowly than we did it was a hopeless struggle for them. We were very impressed with the National Forest campgrounds which were roomy and peaceful—in marked contrast to the cramped conditions in the National Parks.

Mostly the children behaved extremely well but now and then they would start acting up amongst themselves. When I could stand it no longer I'd pull off the side of the road, jump out and rush around to the back of the station wagon with the intention of quieting things down. But I was always too late—with remarkable speed they would leap forward and huddle giggling around their mother. Louise and I would just laugh and I'd drive on in the best of humors.

In Vancouver we loaded our vehicle on the *Princess Louise* and sailed north up the Inside Passage toward Alaska. We had glorious weather and reveled in the calm waters and the innumerable pine-clad rocky islands. In the Juneau area we watched glaciers carving icebergs into the sea and fished for trout on mountain lakes. In the fjords I caught a 14-lb. silver salmon on a rod and line heavy enough to land a swordfish. I thought it was a huge fish, although my host curled his lip in scorn. We helicoptered over rocky mountain summits and deep crevasses. On a high mountain pasture we buzzed a huge brown bear who reared upright and waved his mighty paws at us in anger.

At Haines we joined a Sears filming crew and drove together across Alaska to Anchorage. They were an agreeable group and we enjoyed their company as they filmed us around the campfire and on the road. Most evenings I gathered the children around me and told them stories about Jimmy Job, tales which my father had related to us many years before. In Anchorage a train was chartered to carry our vehicles and ourselves inland to Fairbanks. I doubt if I will ever have another train trip quite like it. We rattled over the tundra through forests and lakes, marvelously free of man and his works. At every promising stream we'd stop and thrash the waters for fighting salmon and beach them on clean washed pebbles. We unloaded our cars at Mount McKinley Park and camped on the flanks of the mountain, seeing few humans but plenty of caribou and bears. There was no time for mountaineering, but I did a plane flight with a famous bush pilot and climbed the mighty glaciers and ridges in super-heated comfort. I felt the old urge, half excitement, half fear, to pitch my tent on the snow and join battle with the great peak.

As a treat, I suppose, the film team had organized a moose-hunting trip for me, even though I get little pleasure out of hunting. In a two-seater Piper Cub equipped with oversized wheels we flew across the roadless tundra and landed on a shingle bank in the middle of a meandering river. The hunting camp was a series of battered tents, simple but adequate. They had found a herd of moose, I was told, and one of them was a fine head, maybe a record head? All day we drove over the tundra in tracked Weasels—the same as the Weasel I had driven toward the South Pole. We were in constant radio communication with our reconnaissance aircraft which checked the movements of the herd. Late in the afternoon we hid our vehicles beside the river and walked forward for half a mile or so. Our guide waved us to stop and then beckoned me forward. I crept up and looked through the brush. Two hundred yards away a herd of moose was grazing quietly, and in the middle of them was a magnificent bull.

"Shoot him," instructed the guide.

With a feeling of reluctance I raised my rifle and fired. The animal jumped and then stood quivering.

"Quickly, shoot again! Shoot again!" shouted the guide.

And shoot again I did—a fusillade of shots and the moose dropped to the ground. I knelt beside the animal, holding up the noble head and the great spread of antlers so they could take my picture. It was forty-eight inches across I was told—very good indeed but not quite a record. I felt no triumph, only shame and disgust with myself. What right had I to destroy such a beast? We had used aircraft and tracked vehicles to chase it down. What courage, strength or skill had I shown? I resolved never again to carry out such senseless and cold-blooded slaughter in the name of sport.

When we said good-bye to the film team we drove into the Yukon and down the gravel road of the Alcan Highway. We loved the feeling of wide open spaces and the beautiful lakes and mountains. Names like Dawson City, Klondike, Whitehorse reeked of adventure and romance. Banff National Park was superb. Our camp in the forest was visited by bears and I had to crawl reluctantly out of bed to drive away a cub that was pushing its nose into Peter's small tent. Beside Diamond Lake a fall of snow warned us that summer was over. We headed east across the Canadian prairies, covering vast distances each day. We were drunk with the joys of camping and traveling. We had established our simple routine, life was free and unpressured, and nature very beautiful. We could have gone on forever—it was with immense reluctance that we drove down the expressway into Chicago and accepted that our dream was over.

Field Enterprises had paid me a comfortable retainer and we had been careful with our spending. At the end of 1962 we had accumulated a nest egg of U.S. $20,000. I had become friends with a successful and wealthy stockbroker and asked his advice on what I should do with the money. "Give it to me to invest," he told me, "and I will double it in value every seven years." He lived up to his promise. So that year we spent in Chicago was both an interesting and profitable undertaking.

My association with Sears, Roebuck went from strength to strength. We carried out a variety of annual camping trips in which the Sears buyers and their tent manufacturers took part, testing prototypes in all sorts of weather conditions, making recommendations for improvements and selecting the lines of tents for the following seasons. It also enabled us to get to know each other better in relatively primitive conditions, and I have always regarded this as a very useful method for maintaining communications.

I've had thirty camping trips with Sears and enjoyed every one of them, but there is one that particularly stands out. The main manufacturer of tents for Sears was American Recreation Products and their large parent company had a number of private executive jets. We often used one of these small jets to get us close to our destination and I found this the greatest luxury as far as air travel was concerned. The plane didn't leave until all were safely on board, we chose our own destination and were picked up at the end of our adventure. I can always remember one of my first flights by executive jet when we landed at Denver airport to refuel. As we got out to stretch our legs the fuel tanker rolled up and our Captain said, "Four hundred gallons in each wing, please!" For some reason I found this casual comment rather impressive.

In June 1971 we did one of our longer flights. With several stops for refueling we flew from Chicago to Anchorage in Alaska and then an easy flight across to Kodiak Naval Base. Here we boarded a Grumman Goose, a rather useful amphibian aircraft, and were flown across the desolate tundra, sighting a number of brown bears on the way, and finally landing smoothly on Karluck Lake which sits high in the north-western end of this legendary home of the great brown bear. Karluck river drains from the lake for thirty miles to the sea and this was our objective, for in late spring multitudes of huge salmon come up the river to spawn. The challenging terrain, frequent rain and fog, the mountains to climb, the virginal wilderness, prospects of good fishing and the opportunity to see many bear and wild fowl combined to make this an ideal field-testing location for our development tents, sleeping bags and backpacks. But we also had rods, reels, freeze-dried foods, insulated wear and fishing jackets to be evaluated.

We spent that first night on marshy ground at Karluck Lake, then next morning pumped up our inflatable boats, loaded all our gear on board and tentatively paddled our way into the entrance to the Karluck river. Next moment we were swept down into a violent rapid; paddling madly to keep stable we were being carried steadily toward the sea. That first day was an exciting one in the swift-flowing water but very few fish were caught. We were told that the season was a couple of weeks late and few big fish had come upriver yet, so we would have to go downriver to meet them. We floated down next day, still with little fishing success. Then the river widened into a lake and the current disappeared almost entirely. There was a strong up-valley wind and our boats were almost going backward. I jumped overboard into thigh deep water and slowly dragged my laden boat down the lake. Dan Sullivan from Los Angeles sat comfortably aboard surrounded by six-packs of beer which he consumed with some enthusiasm. Finally a portage cabin came into view—the only building on the river—and it was a thorough disgrace; everyone had dumped their refuse there. There was no way we were going to use it as a campsite. We explored and found an area above the cabin that was clean, but we had to search around to find a few square feet suitable for a tent and elevated enough to keep us out of the thawing tundra. A few more fish were caught here but nothing very exciting.

A fast breakfast and we were glad to leave this disreputable portage cabin area. Now the fishing was greatly improved. We made many stops and soon had steelheads up to 10 lbs. in weight bending our rods. It was an exciting day and we luxuriated in an evening meal of fish and steak. Next day we floated into the Karluck Canyon and our luck improved considerably. The king salmon were there in great numbers but they were very hard to catch. We had overlight tackle—only 8-lb. breaking strain—and we lost fish after fish. We soon learned the technique, cast upstream, let the weighted lure bounce along the rocky bottom, steel yourself for the strike—then set the hook—getting ready to run down-stream, struggling to keep the king's head upstream. Usually there were broken lines and broken hooks, and leaping salmon spitting out lures. Most of us fought more than three apiece that evening and we lost them all, but it was incredibly exciting.

After a great round of drinks, followed by a fish and steak meal, we went out after them again. Someone struck into a large king salmon but couldn't land it. I waded out into the fast-flowing water with a big gaff hook and made a wild swipe, which luckily connected. Next moment we had this magnificent fish ashore—a 26-lb. beauty. Early next morning two more 26-pounders were landed and delicious salmon steaks became our food for breakfast, lunch and dinner.

We devoted one day to climbing one of the local peaks with the excuse that we were testing out our backpacks. We climbed up onto a long sloping bench of quite hummocky terrain with soft Arctic vegetation underfoot. Then the slope steepened and we scrambled over rocky sections with much panting and puffing. I wouldn't have called it mountaineering, but when we reached the summit at noon the party celebrated as though we had just climbed Everest. Certainly the view was spectacular. Several bends of the river swept ahead of us and we could see the lagoon, the Indian village, its Russian Orthodox church, the great headland of Cape Karluck and the sea beyond. Far to the north was the volcanic Aleutian range, white with snow and cone-shaped. Behind us and before us two ranges of snowy mountains stretched off into the distance, and I think that all of us were exhilarated by the height and the sense of lonely, massive grandeur.

We returned to our camp to find that the non-climbers had departed. We were soon afloat and then three sweeping bends and fast-running water brought us to the end of the river and the start of the Karluck Lagoon where our other rafts were pulled up on the shore.

As we set up camp below a willow thicket, a much-needed windshield, we were startled by a low rumbling growl. Up on a grassy slope 800 yards away a great brown bear rolled his head, sniffing the wind blowing in from the bay—cold, moist and full of the smell of the sea. He could hear us but couldn't actually see that far we decided. For thirty minutes we watched him edging closer. He was a huge animal— possibly 1500 lbs. in weight—with massive shoulders, a deep body and great legs. Our guide blew two sharp blasts on his whistle to frighten him away. The bear turned sharply toward us. Another blast on the whistle and he veered away and slowly climbed back up the slope toward a thicket. But he had been close enough for me.

At the end of 1962 we left Chicago and returned to our comfortable home in Auckland. Reports from Khumjung had indicated that the new school under headmaster Tem Dorje was proving a tremendous success. The word had spread around Solu Khumbu and I started getting petitions from other villages asking for help with more schools and with water pipelines and bridges. Both Field Enterprises and Sears, Roebuck had shown sympathy for these projects so I was able to use their backing to return to Nepal in March 1963. In my team I needed men who combined construction ability with a wide experience of technical mountaineering, and preferably I wanted some of them to have been with me on our expedition before. I had Desmond Doig, Bhanu Bannerjee, Murray Ellis, Michael Gill, Phillip Houghton and Jim Wilson, who had been there before, and the two expert American climbers, Tom Frost and Dave Dornan, who had not. Our first task was to put a freshwater pipeline into the village of Khumjung but, although it worked well at first, it proved rather erratic when the source started drying up during several periods of the year.

Then we moved up to Pangboche village to combine the construction of a school and an attempt on the impressive summit of Taweche. We were forced to abandon our mountain when the assault party was only 200 feet from the summit due to the unusual feature of the narrow summit ridge being heavily corniced on both sides. But Pangboche school we did complete.

We had a most unusual experience at Pangboche. One of our young Sherpas, Purbu Chundu, was a favorite nephew of the famous sirdar, Pasang Dawa Lama. He now appeared before us in the grip of fierce emotion and asked permission to tell his story. He explained that in 1962 he had been a member of a German expedition of which his uncle was sirdar. This expedition had tackled the formidable peak, Pumori, a mountain which had rebuffed a number of previous expeditions. The German party was not to be denied and they forced a difficult and spectacular route to the summit. On the descent of the mountain the assault team was very late and the weather had become cold and thick. On one rope were two men, the only Swiss climber in the party and an experienced Sherpa. Tired from their climb and baffled by the bad visibility, the two men strayed too close to the edge of a bluff and when the snow underneath gave way they plunged thousands of feet to their deaths. Purbu explained how next day they had started the search for the bodies of the two men and had found them on the glacier at the foot of the mountain. Two graves were made for the men in a deep crevasse. The expedition leader placed in the Sherpa's grave his down jacket as a bed, and in the grave of the Swiss his colorful wool sweater. Then the bodies were lowered gently into place and, after a short ceremony, rocks were piled high above them. Over the Swiss a cross was erected and over the Sherpa a Buddhist chorten.

Quite a number of high-altitude Sherpas and ordinary porters were present at the funeral, said Purbu, including a man from Pangboche, the village elder we called the Nike, who was now helping build the school. Purbu quickly came to the heart of the matter. Yesterday he had seen the Nike wearing a jersey that was far too big for him. "Even the sahibs noticed the jersey and made jokes about it," said Purbu. He had recognized it as the jersey from the grave.

I sent Mingma Tsering to see if he could get the Nike to come to our camp, but he proved hard to find. It wasn't until we were crowded around the campsite after tea that he was led up to us. Desmond Doig started to question him quietly.

"Yes," he admitted quite freely, "I was wearing the pullover that belonged to the dead sahib."

After further prompting he conceded that he also had the down jacket belonging to the Sherpa.

"How did you get them?" asked Desmond. The response was glib and well prepared. "I was given them by sirdar Pasang Dawa Lama."

At this accusation against his uncle, Purbu Chundu sprang to his feet and with eyes full of fire asserted that this was an outright lie. "I was with my uncle all the time after the accident," he said, "and at no time did he go near the graves. In fact he warned everyone (including the Nike) that if the graves were disturbed he would come back and kill them with his own hands. Already in Darjeeling the wife of the dead Sherpa has heard rumors that a man has been seen in Pangboche wearing the ring she had given her husband on their wedding day!"

At this fierce denunciation the Nike hastily withdrew his story and replaced it with another. Some time after the accident, he said, he happened to be strolling up on this lonely glacier and he'd come upon the opened graves. To his astonishment he'd found the pullover and down jacket stuffed carelessly under a rock. They were too good to waste and he'd brought them home.

The man was so obviously lying that my anger rose mightily. When he cracked a hearty joke with the silent ring of Sherpas round about, I could stand it no longer. I leaped up and thumped him vigorously around the ears and knocked him down. He scrambled about on his hands and knees, trying to escape, and presented the seat of his pants to my irate gaze. Next moment I had delivered a mighty kick to send him tumbling down the hill into the darkness. There was a roar of laughter from our Sherpas.

I, however, felt slightly embarrassed at my violence, as there was no way that a Sherpa would have responded physically. But Desmond Doig and I were still determined that the Nike should be punished by the authorities for his crime of stealing from a grave. When the Senior Headman suggested that the Nike should not be handed over to the police but should be subjected to the village "disgracing ceremony," I was only too happy to agree. We gathered in the courtyard of the gompa and a miserable Nike was brought stumbling in with a bandage around his head. He sat in the gloom of a corner with his head between his hands, but Desmond refused to allow this—the man must face his punishment standing up in the open.

The tension built up to a high pitch as the proceedings commenced. First a document was read to the assembled gathering, a confession from the Nike in which he admitted his guilt but pleaded for mercy and forgiveness. Then another longer document signed by all the senior men of the village, in which they condemned the Nike's action and guaranteed that such a thing would not happen in the village again. I was then called on to say a few words to be translated into Nepali by Desmond, and into Sherpa by Mingma Tsering. By now I was feeling rather sorry for the Nike, so my words were brief: a suggestion that he had been punished in the sight of his equals and it was now up to him to rehabilitate himself by his actions over the next few years. Desmond, too, had few words to say, but they were telling ones.

"We can forgive your crime," he declaimed to the crouching man. "But you will have to make your own peace with God!"

There was a deathly hush after this statement, broken only by the sobs of the Nike's sister, and there was no doubt that these last words had made a strong impression. We later heard that the man had disappeared from the village and had not returned again. I sometimes wondered if we had judged him by Western standards rather than by the attitudes of his own community.

To my great pleasure we were to be joined in the final stages of the expedition by Louise, accompanied by Ann Wilson and Doreen Del Fium, a young geologist from Los Angeles. The fourth member of the party was Ralph Wyeth, who, as the United Nations–appointed general manager of the Nepal Bank, had been extremely helpful to us. Louise and her party were flown into Jiri—halfway in those days to Khumjung—and then walked the rest of the way to join us. They arrived just before the sports day we had organized for the Khumjung School, and it proved a very happy and successful event.

Our next major project was to build a school at Thami, up toward the Tibetan border. Timber was very scarce here and had to be cut and carried from far down valley. The walls were constructed of rock and the framework of the roof was in rather fragile timber, covered with very light corrugated aluminum sheeting. After a couple of years a huge windstorm largely destroyed the building and we had to construct it all again, tying the roof down this time with No. 8 fencing wire. Even this did not prove adequate, and before long the building was destroyed once again. I realized then that the location was quite unsuitable, so we chose another position on the protected side of a great ridge. Our final Thami school ended up with the rocks tied together with concrete and wire netting and with a heavy corrugated iron roof.

Opening ceremonies are always happy occasions, and it certainly was at Thami. I was firmly placed on an appropriate rock and the senior village elder came forward and removed from his bakhu (the Sherpas' traditional robe) a bottle marked Johnnie Walker Red—it no longer contained Johnnie Walker but the Sherpas' distilled firewater. He also removed a large dusty glass and filled it to the brim. He handed this to me and gestured to me to drink it. I had no wish to offend the gentleman, so I poured it down and felt it burn its way into my stomach. I handed the glass back and he filled it up again and gestured once more. Once again I poured it down. A third time he filled it—but I knew the local custom, I didn't have to drink it this time. I could just wet my lips or dip my finger in the rakshi and flick a few drops in the air in case some minor god should be passing by and enjoy it. Then the senior elder stowed the bottle and glass back in his bakhu and stepped aside. Now it was the turn of the next most senior elder and the same procedure was followed. By the time five or six village elders had carried out this formality I was in a very jolly frame of mind indeed. Then all the young students stepped forward and presented us with white scarves (kartas as they are called) or leis of flowers. By the time they had concluded this, we were a most unusual sight.

Our last challenge on the 1963 expedition was an attempt on the impossible-looking Kangtega at 22,340 feet. From Tengboche the mountain was an array of grim black precipices overhung by a fringe of breaking ice cliffs. But we knew there was a different side to the mountain which was a good deal more feasible. On 29th May 1963, the tenth anniversary of the ascent of Mount Everest, Mike Gill, Jim Wilson, Tom Frost and Dave Dornan headed down valley to Chaunrikarka and then over the pass into the Inukhu valley.

Meanwhile, Louise, Desmond Doig and I were being feted by the people in Khumbu. Annullu gave us a magnificent breakfast and at the conclusion made a short speech. We had, he said, lightened their darkness, saved their lives, and eased their domestic problems. We were indeed the father and mother of the village. A little exaggerated perhaps, but still very nice to hear. The day concluded with a dinner at the house of our very good friends Mingma Tsering and Ang Doule. Mingma was now unquestionably our most important sirdar. Their house was magnificently decorated for the occasion and we had a real Tibetan dinner.

Piles of tukpa (handmade noodles) and a lovely thin soup were handed to us in dainty Chinese bowls. We put the tukpa into the soup and added a mixture of fresh chopped yak meat, spring onions and fresh butter. It was a very tasty repast, and we washed it down most pleasantly with Ang Doule's very good home brew. Vigorous Sherpa dancing followed and we finally departed for bed well satisfied with a most unusual day.

After a long and emotional farewell we made our sad departure from our friends in the Khumbu. The monsoon showers had now started and the paths were slippery as we made our way down the Dudh Kosi to Ghat, then crossed the river and started the great traverse that would take us over a 15,000-foot pass and ultimately down to Junbesi village. In the high pastures there were flowers in profusion, masses of primulas and many beautiful Himalayan poppies. We had just camped after crossing the pass when we heard a shout, the Kangtega team, with Mike Gill and Jim Wilson in the vanguard, came rolling into camp with their teammates close behind.

They had an exciting story to tell. In pouring rain they had crossed from Lukla into the Inukhu valley, whose upper slopes were red with rhododendron flowers. For two days they traveled up valley and Base Camp was established at the foot of Kangtega. The first problem was a massive icefall, but Mike and Jim managed to force a way through it. On the next day they made their way up long steep slopes, often unstable from soft snow, and reached the base of the 800-foot summit cone. It was only noon and they had time in hand, but the slope was very steep. Jim Wilson led upward at first in firm conditions, but the surface softened and the steps broke away. Mike was in the lead now and only twenty feet from the top when an avalanche broke and surged over and around Jim, but fortunately his belay held. The avalanche missed Tom and Dave down below, so with a bit of good luck they all remained safe on the mountain. Another urgent scramble up to the ridge and Mike found he was looking down the incredible precipice of Kangtega into the Khumbu valley. The actual summit was nearby, perhaps three feet above their location, but that meant their heads were three feet above the top, and that was near enough for them. They cautiously descended down the dangerous area of soft snow and then raced back to camp. And here they were a few days later, back with us on the high traverse. It had been a spectacular end to a busy expedition.

13

FAMILY ADVENTURES

THE NEXT TEN YEARS, FROM 1964 TO 1974, WERE A VERY HAPPY period in my life. We formed the Himalayan Trust to organize our programs of school, hospital and bridge-building in Nepal and the membership was a group of very good friends, all with Himalayan experience. There was Max Pearl and Mike Gill, Jim Wilson and Murray Ellis, Peter and June Mulgrew, John and Dianne McKinnon, Norm and Enid Hardie, my brother Rex, Neville Wooderson and Wally Romanes. Most of all I had Louise who enjoyed the Himalayas enormously and was very patient with my plans and ambitions. Sirdar Mingma Tsering Sherpa and his wife, Ang Doule, were a tower of strength, as were many other Sherpas. Later, Zeke O'Connor from Toronto became heavily involved, as did Larry Witherbee from Chicago. They were a formidable group.

In all this school- and hospital-building activity sirdar Mingma Tsering was indispensable. I had first been with Mingma when he was a young porter on the 1953 Everest expedition. Then, during my 1960–61 Yeti, High-Altitude Research and Khumjung School expedition, Mingma had been one of my assistant sirdars. In 1963, the first of my many expeditions devoted primarily to school- or hospital-building,

I asked Mingma to be sirdar. This involved organizing all the load-carrying from Kathmandu to the Khumbu, all the expedition Sherpas and all the labor and local materials on the projects. He and I would negotiate rates of pay and assign loads in the midst of a seeming chaos of up to 200 porters. Then, at the end of the carry, and at intervals throughout the building activity, it would be Mingma who would know how long each person had carried or worked and how much each was owed. As each individual was called forward, he would quietly confirm the amount and tell me how much and what bonus he recommended. I would then reach into the large bag of small-denomination notes Mingma carried round for me, count out the money to Mingma, Mingma would re-count it into the porter's hand, then call for the next. If disputes arose—and they often did—Mingma was firm but fair in resolving them. He seemed always to have the respect of all he dealt with.

Increasingly, also, he became invaluable to me in sorting out the many requests for new schools or other projects. He accepted the petitions and commented on their merits so I could make informed decisions, then conveyed my responses to the village delegations. Though his English was fairly basic and my Nepali and Sherpa even more so, we seemed able to communicate with ease and fluency. However, newcomers to the scene, whatever their native tongue, often had difficulty understanding either of us. For after a period of months talking with Mingma in our curious mixture of tenseless English, smattered with Nepali and Sherpa, I would sometimes fail to adjust when talking with English speakers until I noticed the look of astonished incomprehension in their eyes and hastily reverted to more standard English. As projects increased in number and complexity, I would often send Mingma from New Zealand lists of local materials needed for the next expedition: rock and timber on the site, nails and other hardware from Kathmandu. Always he would have the materials bought and assembled and be able to tell me where they all were and how much they had cost. All this required formidable organizational skill, in which Mingma certainly excelled. But even more impressive to me was his prodigious memory. I would be armed with endless written lists and plans,

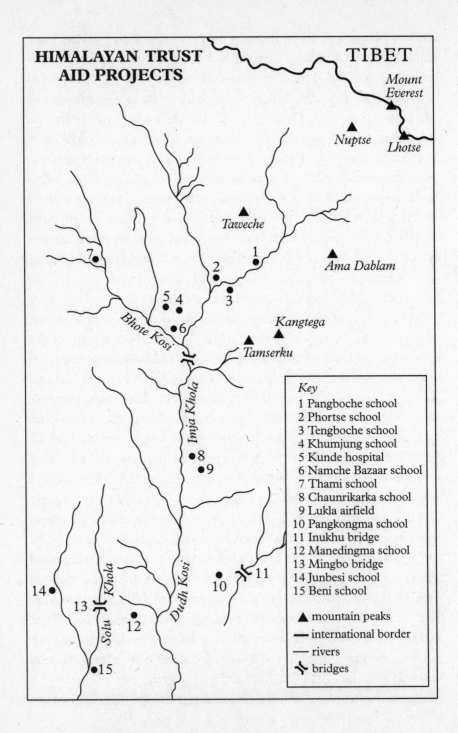

HIMALAYAN TRUST
AID PROJECTS

TIBET

Mount
Everest

Nuptse

Lhotse

Taweche

7

2

1

5 4

3

Ama Dablam

6

Bhote Kosi

Kangtega

Tamserku

Imja Khola

8

9

Key
1 Pangboche school
2 Phortse school
3 Tengboche school
4 Khumjung school
5 Kunde hospital
6 Namche Bazaar school
7 Thami school
8 Chaunrikarka school
9 Lukla airfield
10 Pangkongma school
11 Inukhu bridge
12 Manedingma school
13 Mingbo bridge
14 Junbesi school
15 Beni school

▲ mountain peaks
— international border
— rivers
⊁ bridges

11

10

Solu Khola

Dudh Kosi

14

13

12

15

and during our pay-out sessions would be noting everything down. Mingma kept it all in his memory, writing nothing down—indeed not able to—yet I never knew him to make a mistake.

Mingma and his wife, Ang Doule, became close family friends, and our projects had a considerable impact on their family life. Before we knew her, Ang Doule had had thirteen pregnancies, but only two had resulted in live births, and, of these, one was a complete cretin and the other deaf. All these difficulties were the result of iodine deficiency. Once we got her onto a course of iodine injections she gave birth to two perfectly healthy and normal sons, much to her delight.

Mingma, and the other Sherpas he recruited to build and climb with us, tough and competent themselves in their mountain environment, never really believed we could cope on our own. They would try and ensure we "sahibs" carried only light loads, and would worry if we were going any distance without Sherpa guidance. Their concern was greatest when we were in a jolly mood through having chang and rakshi pressed upon us at ceremonies and parties. I remember particularly a party at Pembatharkay's house in the rather remote village of Phortse. His house was on a very steep slope and the courtyard ended at a high rock wall with potato fields below. Feeling the need to relieve myself of the pressure of too much chang, I indicated to Mingma my intention to go outside. He said he would come with me, lest I fall over the wall, but I shrugged off his offer, convinced I was reasonably sober, and swayed out. Mingma must have silently signaled to two other Sherpas, because as I balanced precariously on the top of the wall, I suddenly realized strong arms were supporting me on either side.

On another occasion Jim Wilson was returning to Kunde from a party at Khumjung, a ten-minute walk along narrow uneven tracks between high rock walls. It was very dark, and he admitted he was not especially sober. "But," he said, "it was no problem, my feet never touched the ground." A Sherpa on either side kindly gave him the dignified impression that he was walking upright while in fact carrying him all the way home to Mingma's.

It was no wonder that Louise and I, and all the members of the

Himalayan Trust, developed a great affection for Mingma and Ang Doule and indeed all the Sherpas. They gave us much help and friendship and in return we felt the need to assist them in obtaining the schools and medical facilities they urgently needed.

I was still energetic but no longer the lead climber. I was the planner and organizer and ran the whole operation. We built a hospital at Kunde and it was operated by a volunteer New Zealand doctor. In response to petitions from local villages we constructed half a dozen new schools. We built a number of bridges over foaming mountain rivers and brought fresh water to villages with plastic pipes. To save carrying hundreds of loads on men's backs for the seventeen-day walk from Kathmandu, I decided to try and find another suitable site for an airfield.

In 1964 I was in the Khumbu again with Jim Wilson, Peter Mulgrew and quite a large group of our Himalayan Trust members. I had noticed that below Chaunrikarka there was a large area of almost flat land pushing out into a curve of the Dudh Kosi. I asked Jim Wilson to investigate it and he reported that it just might do, but that it was barely long enough and also very fertile land, so that the local people might be understandably reluctant to sell. Then Jim had a rather amazing experience. He was approached by a group of farmers from the small village of Lukla, which was located in a small tributary valley at 9,000 feet. They had some land for sale and thought it would be suitable for an airfield. They even suggested that the wind always blew in the right direction! How hill people who knew nothing about airfields could possibly make this sort of judgment I do not know, but when we went up to Lukla we agreed that they were right. And best of all we wouldn't be destroying a lot of arable land. One-third was in rough pasture, one-third in heavy scrub and the last third in terraced potato fields. It certainly wasn't flat, the rise from bottom to top was over a hundred feet, but this wouldn't be a problem to a STOL (short takeoff or landing) aircraft. Even the negotiations for the land were relatively easy. I purchased it on behalf of the Nepalese government for a total of $635— quite a substantial sum in that area in those days.

We had no mechanical equipment, of course, so everything had to be done by hand. Mingma recruited more than a hundred Sherpas and with kukris and mattocks they cut down the bush, dug out the roots and leveled the land. The terraced potato fields required a vast amount of earthmoving, and there were some huge boulders that we were unable to lift. Instead we used the method pioneered by the Sherpas on the Mingbo airfield. We dug huge holes and then rolled the rocks into them and covered them up with earth.

Peter Mulgrew had brought some radio equipment, so we were able to maintain communications with Kathmandu. The airfield was only half-finished when a large Russian helicopter arrived at Lukla and deposited Louise, June Mulgrew and Lois Pearl. This produced a considerable lightening of spirits every evening after dinner. Peter Mulgrew had a remarkable repertoire of Gilbert and Sullivan songs and Jim Wilson was a great singer, too, so laughter and song carried on well into the night. The first Pilatus Porter flight was fast approaching, but I was still not entirely happy with the top surface of the field which was rather soft. I decided to use a simple but practical method to improve this. Sherpa dancing is very vigorous and involves much stamping of the feet. We purchased large quantities of chang and then employed fifty Sherpas to link arms and stamp their way backward and forward across the field. A very festive mood prevailed and the earth received a most resounding thumping. Two days of this rather reduced the Sherpa's enthusiasm for the dance but produced a firm and smooth surface for our airfield. The strip was 1,150 feet long and 100 feet wide and was clearly marked by white painted boards. Altogether I had paid out just over $2,000 for land and labor.

No doubt with memories of Mingbo airfield two Civil Aviation representatives were coming in as observers on the new airfield's first flight and their judgment would be final. It was the sharp ears of a Sherpa who first heard the aircraft coming up the valley and we hastily removed all the children and cows off the runway. I admit to feeling rather tense as the Pilatus Porter circled overhead. Then the plane wheeled, its flaps came down and it swung in to the bottom of the strip. The wheels touched with a puff of dust and next moment it was rolling up the airfield and came to a rapid halt. It took full power for the plane to taxi to the top of the runway and then we were welcoming the clearly delighted crew and passengers. I had an enormous feeling of pleasure and relief. Lukla quickly became the busiest mountain airfield in Nepal and the gateway to Everest.

I was still managing to spend more than half of the year at home and I bought a wooded half-acre section of land in a beautiful position in Central Otago in the South Island. It was a superb camping place, looking down on the magnificent Clutha river not far from its outlet in Lake Wanaka. For five years we spent a month of the Christmas holidays camping in this delightful location. There was so much to do— swimming in the clear fresh water of the river and lake, clambering up modest mountains, floating an inflatable boat down the river, and fishing for rainbow trout. It was an ideal place for the children to learn to love the beauties of nature and they reveled in it.

I was very fond of my children but I was not a demonstrative father. Belinda refused to put up with this. Urged on by Peter and Sarah she would throw her warm arms around my neck and kiss me furiously, while I wriggled in discomfort. But I really loved it. Those camping holidays with my young family were some of the happiest days of my life.

Adventurous activities were not ignored either. My teams reached the summit of the very difficult Tamserku (21,730 feet) and we went to the Antarctic again. We flew to McMurdo Sound in a civilian airliner and to the north again in a ski-equipped Hercules, landing on the rough sea ice at Cape Hallett where we unloaded two Sears snowmobiles and four heavily laden sledges. Across the bay we could see the magnificent spire of Mount Herschel, our major climbing objective. Cape Hallett is the site of an enormous penguin rookery and the sound and the smell was something to experience. At first traveling across the bay to our mountain was quite easy but after a while the snow softened and we had the greatest of difficulty in moving our heavy loads. At times we had to relay the sledges and it was quite a struggle. We passed under mighty icebergs—ominous signs that we were living on an unstable surface which some time in the future would all go out to sea.

To climb Mount Herschel, which is 11,700 feet high, we had to start right from sea level. Base Camp was pitched amongst the tide cracks and we had frequent visits from inquisitive Weddell seals. The bay was surrounded by a vertical icewall with no obvious line to climb it by. We searched the bottom, seeking a safe approach, our legs often disappearing through tide cracks into the frigid ocean. Then we found a way up, a contorted and difficult one, leading in and out of crevasses and over ice pinnacles. When we reached the top of the icewall we were still only 300 feet above sea level and it had taken us three days. Carrying heavy loads of supplies we battled our way up a steep crevassed valley. It was hard going, as the snow was very soft and we perspired freely from the effort. The perspiration seeped through our woollen sweaters and then froze solidly in knobbly lumps on the outside. At the head of the valley it became very steep indeed and with considerable care we climbed the last slope. I hacked a hole in the cornice and we emerged on a saddle on the crest of the ridge at 5,000 feet. It was a broad and roomy place, ideal for a camp. We pitched a tent, left two young strong members of the party well established and then returned down the long valley to our camp on the sea ice. I was forty-eight years old and the top camp was high enough for me.

Next day Dr. Michael Gill and Bruce Jenkinson made a mighty push for the summit. They had 6,000 feet to go, much of it over steep and difficult terrain. From their camp they climbed an exposed slope onto the crest of the ridge which took quite a time. Then a great ice band barred their way and this was a much tougher problem. Hacking steps, front-pointing with their crampons, they made their way up this obstacle, wriggling in and out of crevasses and surmounting icewalls. It is doubtful if climbing of this standard had ever before been carried out in the Antarctic. With the icewall behind them they had an enormous slope to ascend, over a thousand feet high and extremely demanding on leg muscles and balance. With a great feat of agility and strength they forced their way up the slope and emerged on the north shoulder. Ahead of them now was a long ridge leading toward the sharp summit cone. The ridge was demanding and took a long time but, finally, they reached the foot of the summit pyramid. This was steep and got even steeper as they progressed up it. They were protected from the wind here and the work was hard so they perspired freely. The angle grew steeper and steeper and they wondered if they should persist. With determination they pushed on and finally hauled themselves up the last few feet to emerge on top of the mountain. They had made the first ascent of this magnificent Antarctic peak.

Their descent of the mountain became a classic of endurance. It was late and very cold and they had been going for nineteen hours. But it had been a superb effort. We met them at the high camp and happily carried all our gear down the steep slopes to the sea ice and Base Camp. It had been a great adventure.

I was in the United States a couple of months later and Sears took me to Denver to test out various snowmobile models they were considering adding to their lines. I was introduced to a group of young snowmobile racing drivers who, I felt, looked on this old-timer with a bit of scorn. We were all issued with machines and given the task of climbing up some thousands of feet to the Continental Divide. The young men disappeared with a roar of engines, leaving me well behind, but the snow was very soft and deep, just the sort of thing I had been used to. Moving steadily upward I passed one young driver after another, all well and truly bogged down. I reached the Continental Divide before anyone else and most of them simply didn't make it at all. Sears decided after this that snowmobiles were not suitable for their customers.

The following year we did an extensive program of school-building in Nepal and concluded it by driving jet boats up the violent rapids of Nepalese rivers. The jet boat is extremely powerful and maneuverable and can operate in very shallow water. Our main objective was the Sun Kosi river which twists across Nepal in a succession of rapids, deep gorges and abrupt mountain slopes. I estimated there were 250 miles of river to cover from the Indian border to our final destination near Kathmandu, the capital of Nepal. It was the middle of September

1968 when we finally unloaded our two jet boats near the Indian border. To our amazement the river was still in full monsoon flood, rather late for this time of the year. We transferred all our equipment and fuel eight miles up the river to the green oasis of Tribeni where three great rivers meet—the Arun, the Tamur and the Sun Kosi. There we established a comfortable Base Camp in beautiful and pleasant surroundings.

Initially we turned our attention to the Arun, a mighty river, bigger than the Sun Kosi and carrying water all the way from the Tibetan side of Mount Everest. We entered a long deep gorge down which the river foamed with giant waves in the middle. After twelve miles of desperate upstream battle disaster struck! In the lead boat I looked around just in time to see the following boat toss completely over in a couple of great waves that seemed to have risen out of nowhere. We swung around, charged back and picked our companions out of the water, but of the second boat there was no sign. We were a very subdued lot when we arrived back at Base. Our major task was ahead of us and we had only one boat left. But there was no question of turning back. I reduced the numbers in our team and cut down our equipment and off we went.

For day after day we battled upward over giant rapids and amongst huge boulders. We passed many isolated villages and local people brewing spirits beside the bank. They looked at us in astonishment, for they had never seen Europeans before. Rapid followed rapid in succession, and our boat never faltered. We camped at night in beautiful locations, and the Nepalese villagers were always warm and friendly. We were fast approaching Kathmandu when we were struck by torrential rain. The river was stained with red mud and huge volumes of water were plunging down. Even at full speed we had difficulty in making our way against the wild current. Zigzagging backward and forward, seeking every piece of calmer water, we struggled upward. At times we despaired of getting any further. Then, to our enormous relief, we came over the top of a great rapid and raced on through red swift flowing water. The major rapids were behind us. In another hour we turned a corner and sighted the road to the capital and a huge welcoming crowd.

We had successfully completed our journey of 250 miles from the Indian border to Kathmandu.

Our children grew up and became teenagers and Louise and I had the usual problems that all parents experience in this period of family life. But we did make sure though that they learned to appreciate and enjoy the outdoors and they trekked up to Everest Base Camp without any problems. They had probably seen more of the world and experienced a greater variety of cultures than most children at that time had the opportunity to do. Belinda was the closest thing we had to a perfect child—sparkling, bright and loving—or so I used to think as a somewhat prejudiced father.

On 20th July 1969 I was fifty years old and lay in bed thinking of what good resolutions I should make. I knew I could be a better and kinder person but realized it was a little late for that. So I just made two very personal resolutions—I would improve my skiing and I'd do the epic climb of a Grand Traverse of Mount Cook. I'd done a lot of skiing and ski mountaineering over the years, but I'd never had any expert instruction. It was amazing the difference a good ski instructor made to my standard, although I never could keep up with my children who by now were screaming down the slopes. I even succeeded in doing a Grand Traverse of Mount Cook on a superbly sunny day, although I found it rather hard work. The climb was somewhat marred when we discovered that two young people coming up from the other side had slipped and one had fallen a thousand feet to his death. I haven't made any resolutions since then.

They were undoubtedly great years and it was certainly a period of considerable happiness for me. It was really Louise who kept us all going as a successful and tight little team. She fed us, went on our adventures, soothed our sorrows, and played her viola in a first-class orchestra with great flair. She was very kind and generous and we were certainly lucky to have such a mother and wife.

14

Disaster

LOUISE WAS VISITING NEPAL WITH ME ALMOST EVERY YEAR NOW AND was enthusiastically welcomed by the Sherpa community. The Sherpanis (Sherpa women) in particular treated her with great warmth and there was enormous excitement when we brought the children over too. Louise was one of our major fund-raisers, purchasing carpets, jewelry, copperwork and religious statues in Kathmandu and holding highly successful bazaars in New Zealand and Australia. We were working together as a very energetic team. It had long been our ambition to spend a whole year with our family in Nepal, our main objective being to construct a rather larger hospital than we had undertaken before in the village of Paphlu. The New Zealand government agreed to support this aid project and at the beginning of 1975, full of excitement, we rented out our house in Auckland and moved to a smaller home in Kathmandu. We had shipped vast quantities of building materials and medical supplies to Nepal and we had improved the small mountain airfield at Paphlu to enable us to fly the equipment into the hospital site. It was a delightful position for a hospital, a pine-clad slope halfway up the side of the steep Solu valley with a superb view to the north of great Himalayan peaks. With the construction program under way I began to commute between Kathmandu and Paphlu as there was so much to do in both places. It was a very happy period for the family. Louise was learning Nepali and Belinda was doing correspondence classes from New Zealand—she was an excellent student. The other two children were traveling all around India with school friends, so it was a lively and enjoyable time for us all.

Louise and I were invited to the coronation of King Birendra Bir Bikram Shah Dev. We attended many colorful ceremonies and in our formal clothes and decorations mingled with the great in the beautiful palace grounds. For a few days it was like living in a dream. We also attended a private dinner at the British Embassy where the chief guests were Prince Charles and Lord Mountbatten. I have rarely had a more enjoyable evening. Lord Mountbatten claimed to believe in UFOs and questioned me closely about the Abominable Snowman. I had always been somewhat skeptical, but when an Admiral of the Fleet describes how he saw a UFO from the bridge of a battleship, I discovered you just didn't say "What rubbish!" but instead listened respectfully. I was clearly losing the battle on the yeti and I looked desperately across at Prince Charles. He gave me the broadest of winks, so I just relaxed and accepted defeat, but I have always rather liked Prince Charles for that.

Paphlu hospital was the most ambitious project we had ever undertaken as it involved six large buildings. My brother, Rex, who had been a builder by profession for many years now, was supervising things and rapid progress was being made. I concentrated largely on bringing clean water in a one-inch pipeline from a spring a mile up the mountainside and widening and enlarging the Paphlu airfield so that Twin Otter aircraft could use it. The view from the airfield up to the great peaks of Numbur and Karyolung was spectacularly beautiful.

Above the hammering on the hospital roof that day I heard the unexpected sound of a helicopter. I'd been waiting for a couple of hours for a Pilatus Porter to arrive with Louise and Belinda, as we were going to trek up valley to Khumjung. I felt an ominous sense of concern and rushed down to the airfield just as the helicopter landed. Out of it came my good friend Elizabeth Hawley, our Himalayan Trust Executive Officer. She looked very pale and tired.

"I'm terribly sorry, Ed, but Louise's plane crashed on takeoff."

"Are they alive?" I asked.

"I don't think so."

Numb with disbelief I said, "I must tell Phyl and Jim." Louise's parents had been spending a week with me. Phyl just held my hand, obviously more concerned about my distress than her own loss. Murray Jones' partner had died in an avalanche only a couple of months before and he threw his arm around my shoulder in consolation, but I shrugged it off—I still didn't want to believe it. I crawled into the helicopter with Elizabeth and we headed back toward Kathmandu. Looking with sorrow down on the track over high passes and deep gorges that Louise and I had crossed so often before, I told the pilot that I wanted to go to the site of the crash. He tried to dissuade me, but I persisted and he shrugged his shoulders as if to say, it's your decision, friend. We reached the valley of Kathmandu and circled down to a green field below the end of the runway where we landed beside a small stream. I got out and waded across. From the large circle of local people I could tell where the crash was. They parted to let me through and there they were—the battered remains of the two people I loved most in the world.

An American standing nearby said, "Can you identify the bodies?" I didn't know who he represented but I just shook my head. How could I say that body is my wife and that is my sixteen-year-old daughter? I walked back to the helicopter and was flown to the airfield and then driven to our house. I went into our bedroom and just lay down, filled with pain. I don't remember much of the afternoon, but I know that Phyl and Jim were brought back by the helicopter. The British Ambassador, Michael Scott, and his wife, Jennifer, were absolutely marvelous. In the evening they picked me up and drove me to a lonely spot beside the Bagmati river, the holy river of Kathmandu. There were two funeral pyres with bodies wrapped in white cloth on top of them. At a nod from the Ambassador the fires were lit and for half an hour I watched my loved ones go up in flames. Then Michael and Jennifer led me gently away.

To ensure that parked planes don't shift about or flip over in strong winds, locking pins labeled with long red tags were inserted in the flaps. Due to a simple oversight, one of the pins had not been removed before takeoff, turning the aircraft into a flying bomb. The plane had risen briefly into the air before plummeting into a paddy field just beyond the airport. The resulting explosion blew out windows in the control tower. And I knew it was all my fault—Louise had hated flying in small planes, but I had ignored her fears. This feeling would hang over my head forever.

I didn't sleep much that night—all I wanted to do was die. I didn't devote any attention to how I planned to die—just being dead would be enough. But thoughts kept creeping in—what about Peter and Sarah, and Phyl and Jim, and Mingma Tsering and all the Sherpa projects. What would happen to them? By morning I had made my decision. I'd return to Paphlu and complete the projects Louise and I had been working on and then I'd worry about the future. Deeply depressed but quite determined, I flew back to Paphlu to get on with the job. A little altar had been made in the cookhouse with pictures of Louise and Belinda, and every day new ceremonial scarves were draped over the altar, which was strewn with crimson and white rhododendrons, and butter lamps were always alight. I could hardly bear to look at them. In the evenings I walked alone on the airfield with the great mountains behind and tears rolled down my cheeks.

Peter Mulgrew generously brought Sarah over from New Zealand to join me and my son Peter was tracked down in India. He hastily returned to Kathmandu and later wrote, "I met our little green car as it came bumping along the road. Sarah was driving. Phyl was in the passenger seat. Dad and Jim Rose were in the back. The car stopped and the three remnants of the Hillary family reached for each other. We stood there on the road and wept. That meeting was the final affirmation of our loss." It is sad to have to admit now that I was so involved in my own sorrow, I hardly realized what a dreadful shock it had been to my children who concealed their desperate feelings very effectively.

Twenty years later Sarah also reminisced about that awful period. "It was not a time of great family unity. Some families get closer together and that helps. But in our family the people who would have dealt with an accident much better died. Those left couldn't really cope very well and we all spun off in our own directions."

It was time for me to make a visit to Sears in Chicago, so I decided to take the family with me. As we left Kathmandu airport Mingma Tsering asked sadly, "Will you ever return?" Traveling via Europe, we found brief sanctuary with Rhoda and Arnold Lillie in Geneva and then went to Chamonix where the celebrated mountaineer my friend Maurice Herzog was mayor. When he called on us he said, "I express my deepest sympathy. Now let us talk no more about it." I didn't know if Maurice was afraid I would pour my heart out, which was the last thing I wanted to do then. With my good friends from Chicago we canoed down the Buffalo river and camped and laughed as though nothing had occurred. Sarah proved to be an excellent paddler, and Peter displayed his climbing skills on a great rock bluff. Finally, we went home again all the way across the Pacific. Our house was just like an empty tomb without Louise's warm presence and Belinda's laughter and I felt the same way—empty and sterile. I didn't stay long. In August 1975 I returned to Kathmandu. I shared a room with Jim Wilson in Dudley Spain's comfortable residence. After a quiet dinner, Jim and I retreated to our room with a bottle of Scotch whisky. Then the dam burst—we drank and talked and I'm ashamed to say we even wept a little. I have always appreciated Jim Wilson's friendship on that sad occasion.

In Kathmandu the monsoon rains were still pouring down and no flights were available to Khumbu so Mingma and I decided to walk in with a hundred porters. The leeches were really bad and my bites became severely infected. I had bad headaches and backaches and life was so unpleasant, I didn't care too much if I lived or died. For a week in Paphlu I was very sick, then I started getting stronger and eating more. In the middle of September a helicopter managed to sneak in with the construction team and work started again. My companions were very supportive and long-suffering and I deeply appreciated their kindness.

Mingma and Ang Doule were more demonstrative about the loss of Louise and Belinda than I was. I was much more inclined to keep it all inside myself. On the ridge, high above their house in Kunde, they built two chortens in memory of Louise and Belinda and for many weeks Ang Doule climbed up each day to light a fire of juniper brush which sent aromatic smoke up into the sky to commemorate their lives. I have never visited these chortens and never will. As Sherpa men do in times of great sorrow, Mingma began to drink heavily, but he was not alone in seeking solace that way. I don't think I was ever an alcoholic, but every evening I'd probably have four good Scotches which seemed to bolster me up for the rest of the evening, and I needed to take sleeping pills at night. That combination of drink and drugs certainly helped me over that particular period. Yet I still seemed able to think and plan clearly and became even more determined in my fund-raising for activities in the Himalayas. The extra work was no particular pleasure for me but I knew I just had to do it.

By the end of December the Paphlu hospital was virtually finished. My brother, Rex, and his construction team had done a remarkably good job. There was 10,000 feet of floor space in five buildings: an accommodation building for staff, a kitchen, bathroom, classroom complex, a medical center, a large building with several medical wards, and another building where the relations of patients could stay. We had good plumbing, with flush toilets and showers, two solar heating systems, and an excellent X-ray machine. It was now up to our volunteer doctors and the local staff to make full use of the hospital.

We didn't have the official opening ceremony until 1st May 1976. Then we had hired a large helicopter so that the Prime Minister of Nepal could do the task for us. Amongst other dignitaries we had the Nepalese Ministers of Finance and Health and the British and New Zealand Ambassadors. After the formal occasion there was a cocktail party and then a substantial evening meal. The Prime Minister told me that our Paphlu hospital was by far the best remote hospital in Nepal. The following morning we had a simple breakfast and then all the officials helicoptered back to Kathmandu. We were left with a new hospital, quite a few patients and for me a continuing feeling of emptiness and loss.

15

MOTHER GANGA

IN 1977 THE URGE TO TAKE PART IN ANOTHER ADVENTURE RE-asserted itself. This time the plan was to drive three jet boats from the Bay of Bengal up the river Ganges to as close to its source in the Himalayas as we could go. Louise and I had always been enthusiastic about this idea and thought it would be a great adventure. In fact it was one adventure that she had felt she, too, could go on. She wasn't very enthusiastic about climbing mountains but she thought that traveling up Mother Ganga would be a great experience.

Jim Wilson and I began training on jet boats in New Zealand in preparation for this adventure and we had some exciting moments. We did a run down the beautiful Clutha river until we came to the Cromwell rapid which was ferocious with a steep drop. We managed to get our jet boats up and down the rapid but it was an exciting experience. Just for a change we took a small inflatable on a trial run down the same rapid. Gaining speed as we approached the steep section, the next moment the boat was thrown violently around and tossed right over on top of me. The air-bubbly water gave no support at all and I just sank and found myself literally walking on the smooth rocky bed of the river. I seemed to be there forever and accepted that before long I was going to drown.

I'd taken in quite a few gulps of water before I was swept clear of the turbulent area and rose slowly to the surface, in time to see Jim Wilson dive off a jet boat and swim rapidly toward me. By this stage I didn't really need his assistance, but as I was rather waterlogged I was very happy to have him there beside me as I paddled slowly toward the shore. I had certainly misjudged the Cromwell rapid.

My plan was simple enough. Our aim would be to get as high as we could up the Ganges which we knew would involve overcoming vast numbers of very fierce rapids and dodging big rocks. When we got as far as was feasible, we planned to take the boats ashore, walk the rest of the way up to the Holy City of Badrinath and then climb one of the local 19,000-foot ice peaks whose snows contributed to the river's source and epitomized our journey from the ocean to the sky. It would be a journey of 1,600 miles from the crashing surf of the Bay of Bengal to the snow of the Himalayas.

Jet boats are simple enough craft—ours were sixteen feet long, made of tough fiberglass, and contained a powerful V8 engine driving a sophisticated three-stage pump. When lightly laden they could reach speeds in excess of forty-five miles per hour and operate in very shallow water. They were unbelievably maneuverable and excelled in fast-flowing mountain rivers. Our three top drivers were all from New Zealand—Jon Hamilton, Mike Hamilton and Jim Wilson—but we also had Max Pearl, Murray Jones, Graeme Dingle, my son, Peter, and Australian cameraman Michael Dillon. There were also a group of Indian expedition members who made a valuable contribution with their wide knowledge of their country and its customs—Harish Sarin, Mohan Kohli, Joginder Singh, and our very delightful liaison officer, Major Bridhiv Bhatia. For me, no expedition would have been the same without a few Sherpas, so I asked my sirdar Mingma Tsering along and Pemma came as cook.

Our pilgrimage began at the long sandspit of Ganga Sagar that pushes out into the Indian Ocean where a wizened temple priest blessed both us and our boats for the long journey up the Ganges. All India Radio was reporting our progress and we found people lined the banks to watch

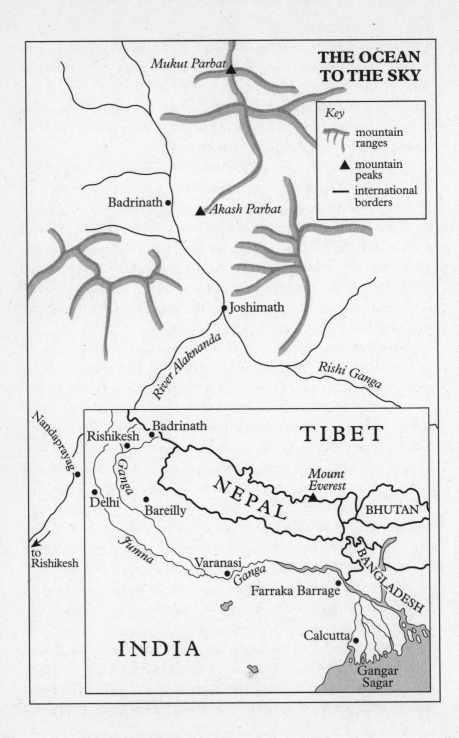

THE OCEAN
TO THE SKY

Key

⋔ mountain ranges

▲ mountain peaks

— international borders

Mukut Parbat ▲

Badrinath •

▲ *Akash Parbat*

• Joshimath

River Alaknanda

Rishi Ganga

TIBET

Nandaprayag •

Rishikesh •

Badrinath •

Ganga

Delhi •

• Bareilly

NEPAL

Mount Everest ▲

BHUTAN

to Rishikesh

Jumna

Varanasi •

Ganga

Farraka Barrage •

BANGLADESH

INDIA

Calcutta •

Gangar Sagar

Mount Cook: (*above left*) Mike Gill, Harry Ayres, my first climbing hero, and I on the way to the grand traverse; (*above right*) the South Ridge, where Harry Ayres and I made the first ascent in 1948; (*below*) I relished the upper reaches of the grand traverse at the age of fifty.

Another first: jet boating from the mouth of the Ganges toward its source, here approaching the temple at Deoprayag.

(*Left*) Offerings float downriver after the blessing of our boats at Varanasi.

(*Below*) Getting to the North Pole with astronaut Neil Armstrong was considerably less sweat than getting to the South Pole.

The work goes on and there's never a draft round your neck. (*Above*) A Japanese helper, my brother Rex and I are garlanded with thanks after the completion of the latest school at Thami; (*right*) June and I receive a warm welcome at Junbesi School.

(*Above*) Well dug in for an advertising assignment with Reinhold Messner in George Band's old Everest gear.

(*Below*) Three of my favorite Sherpas who studied at Khumjung School: Kami Temba, Senior Medical Assistant at Kunde Hospital; Mingma Norbu, WWF representative for the Himalayan region; Ang Rita, Chief Administrator for the Himalayan Trust. With them is Ingrid Versen, Chairman of our German Foundation.

(*Above*) Relaxing with my old and valued friend Mingma Tsering.

Tengboche Monastery, where every Everest expedition went to be blessed, goes up in flames as a result of faulty wiring, but with Trust help it has been rebuilt and lovingly restored (*below*).

Some of my greatest supporters today: (*above left*) the one and only Liz Hawley; (*above right*) June's involvement in the Himalayan Trust has been invaluable; (*below*) Larry Witherbee from Chicago and Zeke O'Connor from Toronto, two of our major fund-raisers, with the Head Lama of Tengboche Monastery after its restoration.

Survivors of the 1953 Everest team meet the Queen on the occasion of the fortieth anniversary of the first ascent. From the left, George Band, Charles Wylie, Gombu Sherpa, Mike Ward, John Hunt, HM Queen Elizabeth, EPH, Mike Westmacott, Alf Gregory, George Lowe, Griff Pugh (*in chair*).

(*Right*) The coat of arms designed for me for the Garter Ceremony.

(*Below*) The Garter procession at Windsor—a great and cheerful occasion for me.

June's meeting with His Holiness the Dalai Lama in Dharamsala was a most memorable experience for her.

Catching up on the news over a glass or three with senior citizens from Kunde and Khumjung, my Sherpa friends Mingma Tsering, Khunja Chumbi, Nima Tashi and Ogchu Lama.

us pass and perhaps share vicariously in the blessing of our pilgrimage. In the cities the crush was almost frightening and I could not remember facing such dense Indian crowds since our return from Everest in 1953. How different the atmosphere was now. At one of our refueling stops, at Nabadwip, a crowd that had swelled to 30,000 surged round a dais protected by a bamboo wall.

I was warmly welcomed by the local magistrate and other senior officials who also had their families along. One child thrust forward an autograph book and rather foolishly I signed it. Immediately there was a sigh from the huge gathering and a small movement forward; it was clear that every one of them wanted an autograph too. The bamboo wall started cracking under the pressure. The police responded immediately, pushing forward their rifles against the mob, which was laughing and cheerful at this stage. Then one of the policemen got rather carried away. In front of the crowd was a large, respectably dressed young man and with virtually no provocation the policeman rammed the butt of his rifle into the man's chest. The reaction was understandably violent—the man was livid with rage and started haranguing the crowd, stirring up their anger against the police.

The situation was looking decidedly grim and I had mentally chosen a path for myself from the dais to the boats if the position should further deteriorate. The chairman of the welcoming committee was also very concerned. He turned to me and politely asked if I would mind going over to the angry man and shaking his hand. Somewhat nervously I crossed to the bamboo wall, tapped the man on the back and when he wheeled round I grabbed his hand and wrung it firmly. Immediately his anger dissipated and he laughed with joy and shook my hand vigorously in return. The situation was eased, but I was glad when we were all back on board and safely out in the middle of the river.

For day after day we pushed on upward. The giant Farraka barrage opened gate 92 of its 102 gates to let us through. We refueled in small towns and camped at night on grassy stretches beside tiny villages. We found it astonishing that in the Gangetic basin with its enormous population there were so many pleasant and open tree-clad locations where tents could be comfortably pitched. The villagers were universally kind and welcoming. In one rather poor village we camped beside a field of ripe sweet corn, and when we asked a village elder if we could purchase some for our dinner he sent a young man off to pick a huge bundle, absolutely refusing to accept any money in return.

On 8th September after covering 800 miles we arrived in Varanasi (Benares of colonial days), the oldest living city on earth and an extremely important religious center for hundreds of millions of Hindus. Once again we were astonished by the warmth of our welcome. We were met at the entrance to the city by a group of dignitaries including the Commissioner of Varanasi who insisted we board his ancient launch to be formally conducted up the river. The vessel was exceedingly unstable and Jim Wilson came alongside and suggested the Commissioner should join me on his jet boat. Next moment we were on board and roaring up the river at thirty miles per hour, leaving the old launch well behind—very much to the delight of the Commissioner.

I had always believed that Hindu temples were prohibited places for non-believers like ourselves, but this was certainly not our experience on the Ganges. The city even insisted on having a special religious ceremony for us so that we could carry on up the river with the bless-ings of Varanasi to guide and protect us. We drove our three boats into an area of steps and hitched them safely to the shore. A large group of smiling Indians gathered around and then the pujare appeared—a tall, slim, muscular young man with tangled hair and a look of wild energy. He started a vigorous chant and a band behind him took up the refrain. It was an incredible scene with flaming butter lamps, the tinkling of bells, and blossoms floating on the water. For half an hour we were transported into a different world, a world of religious fervor, of deaf-ening sound, of the importance of Mother Ganga, and the surprising acceptance of our journey as a sacred pilgrimage. The pujare gestured to us to get down on our knees and then he pressed our foreheads onto the damp sand. I don't know why, but suddenly my feeling of constant depression seemed to lift a little. In my tent that night, with the music and chanting still ringing in my ears, I felt stimulated and revived. For a time at least the sadness of the previous two and a half years had vanished from my mind and life was worth living again.

Our first port of call after leaving Varanasi was the palace of the Maharaja of Benares, an ornate and imposing pink and terra-cotta structure which stands at the water's edge a couple of miles upstream from the Holy City. Just off a marble throne room with crystal chandeliers, intricately woven carpets, and tiger skins underfoot, we sat down for breakfast on a great balcony with majestic views of the river. Our host, the Maharaja, ate nothing for he was of too high a caste to eat with his own family, let alone us. Only half in jest, he suggested we should donate one of the jet boats to him when the expedition was over.

Twenty years later, in April 1997, I returned to Varanasi with a TVNZ film crew and found myself back on the same great balcony waiting for the Maharaja to appear. The palace had clearly seen better days. Stuffing sprouted from the arms of crimson chairs in the gloomy throne room. Dusty rainbow-colored shards of light from stained glass windows bathed rumpled carpets and moth-eaten tiger skins. The Maharaja, when he appeared, bore scant resemblance to the plump younger man greeting assorted world leaders and dignitaries in the elaborately framed photos on the wall. Immaculately dressed in white, with a simple cap, long jacket, and tight leggings, he was almost bent double by arthritis. His eyes though were bright and playful, even if his memory wasn't quite a hundred percent. Spotting the short, fifty-something film director, he shuffled forward, extended a bony hand and beamed, "It's good to see you again, sir." Somewhat embarrassed, John Carlaw explained that he wasn't Sir Edmund Hillary and ushered me forward. I introduced myself explaining, "We met on this verandah twenty years ago."

The Maharaja's eyes twinkled and, in that brutally candid fashion high-caste Brahmins consider their birthright and part of their charm, he looked me up and down and said, "So you have decided to put on weight?"

Not sure if I had heard this properly, I turned quizzically to my companion. "You have put on weight," June repeated cheerfully.

I placed one hand on my chest, waved the other in the air and said apologetically, "I am a little older."

The Maharaja was having none of this. "A lot older! A lot older!!" he exclaimed triumphantly. Pleasantries were exchanged, bottles of cold Coke called for, and then the Maharaja got down to business. "Where is my boat?" he asked keenly.

It was at the renowned town of Rishikesh, where so many famous people had spent time in ashrams, that we met our first severe rapids. The first two looked rather formidable but we negotiated them without too much trouble. Five miles out we could hear the mighty roar of heavy water and turned the corner to see a terrifying sight—great heaps of water pounding down in huge waves with cross currents and flying spray. Could our boats handle something like this? Evening was approaching so we decided to leave this rapid until morning and camp on the white sand beside the river. It was a beautiful place with ample supplies of driftwood and not a soul around. In the chill of the evening we sat around a blazing campfire and talked about mountains and rivers and food—but never about the great rapid above us.

The morning was clear and sunny. We had decided that some of the party would carry loads of gear along the bank to the top of the rapid. Only two of us would travel in each boat. Jon nosed into the bottom of the rapid first but was tossed back by great stopper waves.

"There's only one way to go," he told us. "First into the right bank, then straight across the river and up the left bank and then somehow escape out through the middle."

We watched as he made his run, at times almost disappearing out of sight in the hollows between the waves and then being tossed high, covered in spray. We could hear the scream of his engine above the roar of the water, but then, in brilliant fashion, he was over the top in calm water and speeding easily to the bank.

It was Jim's turn, and mine, and I could once again feel the grip of fear. With a grim face but strong hand Jim took us competently up the right bank. It was time to cross. We headed through the surging waves and were tossed high in the air. Jim's foot slipped off the accelerator and the boat rolled sideways down a huge surge, completely out of control. This is it, I thought, next roll we'll go under! But Jim had quickly recovered, he restarted the motor, got us under way and we were soon in the shelter of the left bank, somewhat shaken but safe for the moment. He turned the boat upriver again, hugging the left bank, keeping out of the giant waves in the center. The water was very fast and the engine was screaming with full power. Ahead of us were big rocks—we needed to get out in the middle. Jim swung right over a huge wave, the bow shot into the sky and we were drenched with spray. Somehow we held on the crest of the wave and then slowly inched our way over. The surface flattened, the waves grew less, and we were at speed again and charging happily into the right bank. We were through.

For four more days we battled up the river, overcoming mighty rapids and narrow rushing gorges. At every small river village there were thousands of people to greet us and our mighty boats—they must have come from several days' walk away. The river became rougher and wilder and on the fourth day we came to the finish of our journey with the jet boats. Only a few hundred yards from the town of Nandaprayag we swung around a fierce corner to be confronted by a vertical waterfall ten feet or more in height that even our powerful jet boats could not overcome. There wasn't too much disappointment—we had gone further than we had ever hoped. We were 1,500 miles from the ocean, every foot of it driven in our jet boats. We had covered 200 miles of wild white water, and were 3,000 feet above sea level.

We had a hundred miles to go which we would do on foot on the pilgrim road. With blistered feet, softened by immersion in water, we walked and camped and walked again, climbing slowly up a series of switchbacks to the sacred town of Badrinath at 10,000 feet. Our journey was nearly over, but we had still to ascend one of the glaciers and climb a snowy summit to complete our journey to the sky. We established our Base Camp at 15,000 feet on a rocky ledge with the terminal face of the glacier only 500 feet above us. We really had plenty of time but we somehow seemed in a mighty rush. Some of us were already showing altitude effects but the fit ones wanted to push on.

I wasn't thinking too clearly so didn't complain when on 12th October we set off to establish our High Camp. The first section was very easy, big rounded red slabs, but then we reached gray steeper rock with rather more exposure. The route now lay up a long snow and ice gully down which we had suspended a 500-foot safety rope. Some of the party picked up loads from the dump and they must have been carrying at least 75 lbs. I was carrying only 45 lbs., but this was more than enough for me. I kept thinking to myself, What's an overweight, broken-down fifty-eight-year-old doing wandering around up here? We started up a steep snow slope and then a long traverse out to the left—it was quite exposed. The slope eased off and ahead of us was a long glacier valley with deep soft snow. It seemed to go on forever and I was having the greatest difficulty in dragging one leg after the other, making frequent stops for rests. It was a tremendous relief to come over a small crest and reach the site of our High Camp at over 18,000 feet. I was very tired but still enjoyed the beautiful snowfield in front of us and the graceful summit of our ultimate objective, Akash Parbat. I had a miserable night, however, and, though I crawled out of my tent next day, I felt very weak and crawled back in again. Dr. Mike Gill gave me an injection of some sort and I promptly passed out.

I came back to life very slowly. The light was dim and I realized I was inside a sleeping bag. But most noticeable was the fact that I seemed to be bumping over rocks and outside I could hear the muted sound of voices. I started mumbling and the movement stopped. The sleeping bag was opened and a face looked in. I don't really know what he said, but I have a feeling it was, "Christ! He's alive!" I wondered where I was and was able to look around. I was below the glacier, below the steep snow slope, even below the long snow gully. I was bumping over the highest of the rocks and that was what had brought me back to life. Stretching up from my bag were two long climbing ropes with a couple of fellows hanging on to each, and below me was another rope. All my companions were smiling—they had certainly given me up for dead.

They continued moving me down and, as my mind got clearer and clearer, I tried to walk on the easier rock, but I was very weak and had to be half-carried. Then we reached a fairly flat place and Mike declared it a suitable spot to camp. It was at about 15,500 feet. Slowly the whole story came out. In the morning they'd found me in my tent, out cold. Mike knew things were pretty desperate and that I probably had a cerebral edema (water on the brain), which meant I had to be got down as quickly as possible. So they left me in my sleeping bag inside my tent, attached the ropes, and started dragging me down the slope. They'd done a marvelous job in very difficult conditions and I was extremely grateful.

Meanwhile Murray Jones had rushed down to Badrinath to organize a rescue helicopter which hovered expertly over to the slope, resting one ski on the rock. The door opened, a hand beckoned, Mike firmly pushed me inside and then jumped in after me. In a few seconds we were floating out over the valley. We circled down to Badrinath and landed beside a big group of army officers and civilians. A line of chairs had been set up and I was put in one of them. It was almost like a formal welcome to some general from down valley. I was feeling much better now at this lower altitude and they asked me if I'd give a little speech about our adventures on the mountain. It was all rather queer—twenty-four hours before I had been nearly dead and now I was being asked to give a lecture. After that I was told I was to be flown to a big hospital at Bareilly down on the plains for a checkup and there was no way I could persuade them differently. By the time Mike and I managed to get ourselves back to Badrinath, the rest of our party had arrived off the mountain with the news that they had climbed to the summit of Akash Parbat and had sprinkled water from Ganga Sagar there, symbolizing the end of our journey from the ocean to the sky.

Despite my problem with altitude it had been a marvelous adventure. We had visited the heart of India and learned much of its culture and religion. We had many exciting challenges, too, and we'd done something that no one had done before and maybe would never do again. It had undoubtedly been one of the most rewarding expeditions I had ever undertaken. I think for a brief space of time, we almost became Hindu in our thoughts. Of course when we all got back home again, we became sinners once more, but for a short period at least, I think we were completely absorbed into the beliefs and the history and the understanding of the people of Mother Ganga.

16

CHAIRMAN EMERITUS

I WAS IN THE HIMALAYAS AGAIN IN THE POST-MONSOON OF 1979 AND my son, Peter, was there too with a small climbing team. Their ambition was to climb the formidable West Face of Ama Dablam (22,300 feet). Why didn't he climb something a bit easier I sometimes wondered? Peter's university career had not been particularly successful—like his father's—but he had quite a lot to show for his life. He was a professional ski instructor in the winter; he had a commercial pilot's license; and in more recent years he had become a very competitive technical mountaineer with many tough climbs to his credit in the New Zealand Alps and in Yosemite. But now Himalayan climbing was his major interest.

I was in Paphlu when a plane arrived with the Director General of Health and I officially handed over the hospital to the government. There was also a message on board from Elizabeth Hawley saying there'd been an accident on the West Face of Ama Dablam. One of the party was dead—she didn't know who—and another badly injured. I had to get up to Kunde and find out if Peter was still alive. Desperately, I asked the pilot if he'd fly me to Syangboche airfield and he generously agreed, in twenty minutes covering a four-day walk. Refusing to believe the worst, I trudged over the hill to Kunde hospital, where I was welcomed with a hug by the volunteer doctor's wife. "It's OK, Ed. Peter is pretty badly knocked around but he's still alive. The chopper will be down in a few minutes."

Ten minutes later we heard the sound of a helicopter as it churned its way up the valley and settled in a cloud of dust beside the hospital. Peter was there, looking pale and frail with a broken arm and several other minor fractures. They'd had a terrible three days descending the mountain. There was room for me on the helicopter and we flew back to Kathmandu, and that night he was operated on at Shanta Bhavan hospital. He had been very lucky to survive—and he still believed the West Face of Ama Dablam could be climbed. It was just the luck of the game, he said. I had no comment to make. Such decisions must be up to him. Peter went on to climb Everest, the Vinson Massif in the Antarctic, and Aconcagua in South America, the highest mountains on three continents. He later nearly died high on K2 when his seven companions were swept away to their deaths in a great storm. But perhaps his most valuable recent achievement has been the hundreds of young people he has taken into the Himalayas to work on our projects and trek up to Everest Base Camp.

Peter Mulgrew overcame his physical handicap and had been climbing the ladder of success in his business activities but he and June had been drifting apart and were no longer living together. June was filling her life by recruiting and conducting trekking parties to Nepal and Kashmir, something she was very good at. I didn't know too much about what was going on, for Peter and I were not on such friendly terms as we had been. He had wanted to go on both the Herschel expedition and the jet boat up the Ganges but I didn't take him. I knew he could do a very useful job, despite his artificial limbs, but Peter disliked some of the members of my team and I didn't want to introduce disharmony in our group. Because of all this it took some time for me to realize the Mulgrew family situation and come to the conclusion that June was having a rather rough time. I was living alone, so was she. So we started seeing rather more of each other. On occasions we pleasantly dined together and we did a few vigorous walks along the wild Piha beach in company with her huge Afghan hound. We were developing a very comfortable companionship.

Air New Zealand had been doing regular tourist flights with their DC10s down to McMurdo Sound, not landing, of course, but just circling around over the sound and then flying back to Auckland. Peter and I were rotated as tour guides describing the absolutely magnificent scenery as the aircraft flew down the coast past the Antarctic mountains and, if we were lucky, seeing Mount Erebus and Mount Terror. It was my turn to do a flight but I had to be in the United States, so Peter took on the task. The date was 29th November 1979. I was in Larry Witherbee's house in Chicago when there was a telephone call from the press saying there had been a plane crash in the Antarctic and there was a rumor that I had been on board. Larry was able to assure them that I was safely in his house in Chicago. But my heart sank with this news— Peter Mulgrew was probably on the plane. I rang June Mulgrew immediately and she confirmed the awful truth. The aircraft had indeed crashed in whiteout conditions on the saddle between Mounts Erebus and Terror and nobody had survived. There was some talk of an incorrect setting on their computers. Despite the fact that we were seeing little of each other I felt great sadness at Peter's death. We had shared so much together in the Antarctic and the Himalayas, and even in New Zealand. Peter had tremendous determination and for many years had been a good and loyal friend. I knew he could never be replaced.

I had known Richard Blum for a number of years. A successful merchant banker, Dick Blum was tall and very fit, a great runner with a considerable knowledge of Nepal and China. He had established the American Himalayan Foundation and was giving active support to our Himalayan Trust and to the Dalai Lama's projects. On a visit to China Dick managed to obtain permission for an expedition to attempt the great unclimbed East Face of Everest—a prize mountaineering plum. Dick invited me to join the expedition as "Chairman Emeritus," hoping, I suppose, that my name could be of some help with the fund-raising.

Because of my bad record with altitude problems I should have unquestionably turned the invitation down but Dick was very persuasive and the temptation to visit Tibet was just too great. Maybe I would be OK this time I thought and anyway I didn't plan to go much over 17,000 feet. So in the end I happily accepted. Some of us never learn and I was later to seriously regret my decision.

In August 1981 I met the team in Hong Kong, a formidable group of experienced American mountaineers with Dr. Lou Reichardt as climbing leader. Lou looked rather like what he was—a very respected scientist—but he had climbed K2 and was renowned for his fitness and ability to acclimatize. This was the first expedition I had been on with a participation agreement stating that "decisions during the actual expedition shall be made collectively with the guidance of the climbing leader." I am a firm believer that all expedition members must be given the chance to express their views but often a final decision must be made by one person, preferably by the climbing leader. I know this is not the popular method nowadays, but as a consequence there are many unnecessary disasters. Our expedition was to suffer at times from a democratic but unquestionably bloody-minded decision-making procedure.

From Hong Kong we flew to the rather uninteresting city of Chengdu and met our Chinese liaison officer, Mr. Wang, and our Chinese cook, Mr. Tsao, before boarding a very unsophisticated Russian aircraft which flew us to Lhasa. Although some of us were affected by the 12,000-foot altitude, we all trooped off to visit the Potola palace whose vast magnificence was minded by a mere staff of eight. So different from the days of Younghusband and the pioneering British Everest expeditions when it was the epicenter of Tibetan Buddhism.

On our second night in Lhasa we had the first of what I called our Democratic Leadership Discussions. Dick Blum was away on the telephone trying to locate thirty loads which were still missing. Lou Reichardt gathered us together and explained his immediate plans and then asked if anyone had other ideas. They certainly did! I had the greatest difficulty in restraining myself from screaming with laughter as a multitude of suggestions were offered, mostly in very dramatic fashion. Fortunately Dick returned with the news that the thirty loads had been located and the heat went out of the discussion. This is the American way one of the young climbers kindly told me. It certainly hadn't been my experience in America—if the president of a company issued an order my impression had been that everyone jumped to it rather smartly. But then I'd probably met more company presidents than most of my young American expedition friends.

I was delighted to find that Tenzing was also in Lhasa meeting various other groups and rather bored with the whole procedure. We had some good long talks and he expressed his sadness at the way his life was developing. He didn't want to be in Lhasa but it was the only way he had at present of earning a decent living. He expressed his envy at the freedom I seemed to have in my life, although I did explain that nearly everything I did was to help support my responsibilities in Nepal. It was hard to suggest to him that I had created my opportunities, while Tenzing had to wait for his to turn up. We parted with the warmth of old and very good friends.

On Tuesday, 18th August 1981, we left Lhasa in a bus and several laden trucks. We crossed high passes and ascended and descended steep winding valleys. Much of the area was the traditional dry plateau of Tibet but we passed through some wide fertile regions too. We entered the large town of Gyantse with a huge shattered monastery perched on top of a great rock. The only major Buddhist relic remaining was a large and very beautiful chorten, regarded as one of the best religious shrines in all Tibet. I don't know why the Chinese had spared it. We drove on through a vast area of arable land, absolutely blinded by dust and gasping for breath until we reached our destination for the night, another large town, Shigatse, where we had to wait a day while our thirty loads caught up with us. In the morning we met the twelve Tibetan porters who were coming with us to Base Camp. I looked at them with considerable interest. They were large, strong and heavily featured young men and looked very tough, but they certainly lacked the lighthearted cheerfulness of my good friends the Sherpas. I soon realized that these young Tibetans didn't like their Chinese masters and as we were being sponsored by the Chinese they didn't like us either. I cannot remember a single one of our Tibetan porters ever exchanging a smile with me.

During the day we visited the Tashi Lumpo Monastery which was the most active in Tibet with 400 monks. It was the seat of the Panchen Lama who was next in status to the Dalai Lama. The Panchen Lama had come to terms with the Chinese and lived for many years in Peking, so his great monastery was therefore untouched. On his death his child successor was approved by the Dalai Lama in the traditional manner, but has since disappeared, while the Chinese have chosen another child to put in his place. Late in the evening our liaison officer, Mr. Wang, arrived with the final truckload of supplies and we were ready for action.

We left Shigatse with four trucks, one bus and a jeep, crossed a pass at 14,813 feet and plunged down into a broad valley which contained thousands of sheep in large flocks. We refueled and had lunch at a Chinese army base where we were treated with great hospitality before climbing uphill again into high mountain pastures, first reaching 15,000 feet in a tight valley with many yaks and yak herders' tents. We carried on through high mountain pastures, dotted with yaks, and then out onto a high brown plateau and a final pass of 17,000 feet. This was what we had expected to see in Tibet, not the fertile flats we had observed further down. This was what we had seen for so long from high on the Nepalese side of the border in the years before China opened some of its doors to the West. We arrived at our destination, Shegar, after nine hours of traveling. It was a real Tibetan town at 14,355 feet with low buildings and everything rather dusty and scruffy. The hotel was very simple but, as I was feeling the altitude, I was glad to crawl into bed.

When we left Shegar on the morning of 20th August our adventures really started. The road over the high pass to Kharta was so rough that our bus could not be used, so we all traveled by truck through the bleak Tibetan landscape for an hour before striking south up an enormous shingle fan. The road was now only a potholed track which zigzagged backward and forward as we gained slow height, mostly in low gear. At first we passed patches of green barley, primitive villages and a couple of dozen mules laden with juniper firewood. Then the terrain became

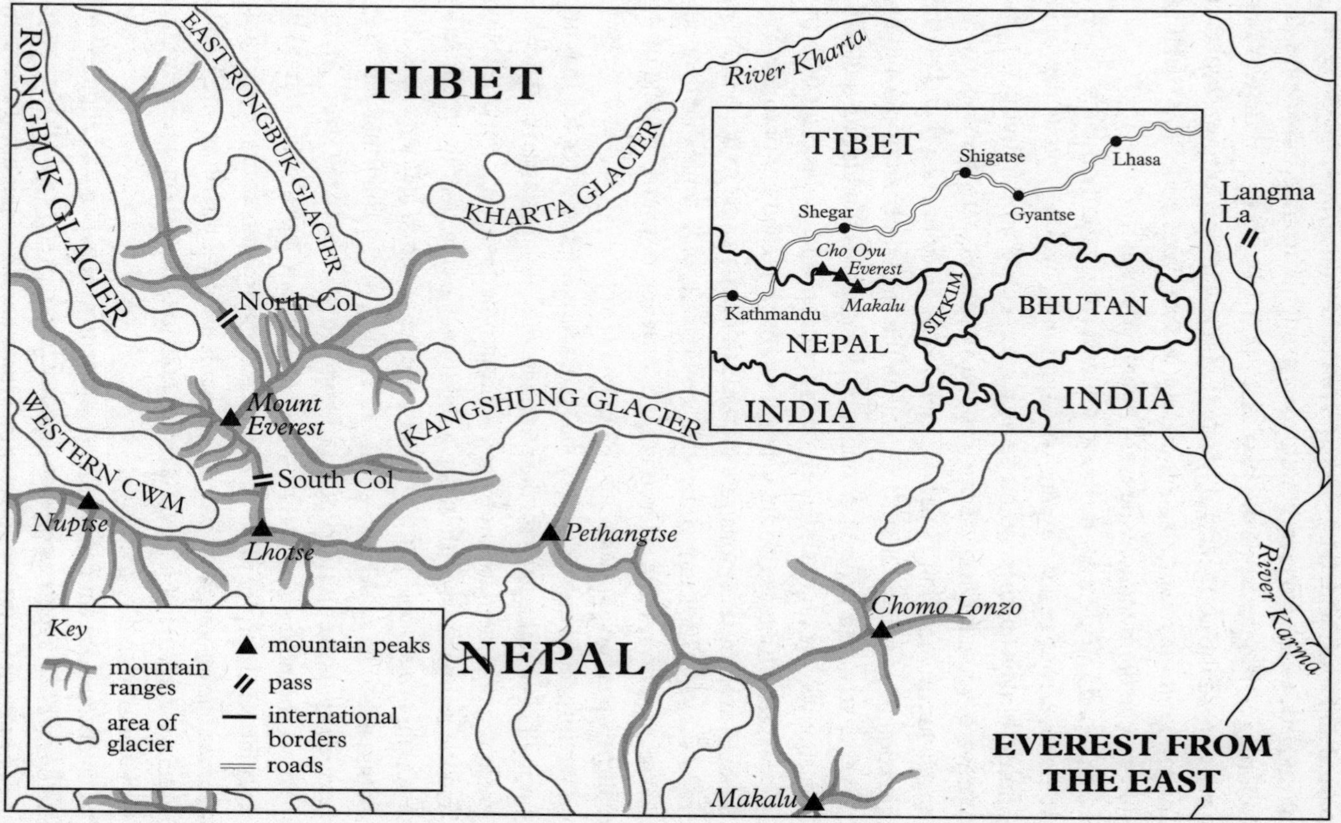
TIBET
RONGBUK GLACIER
EAST RONGBUK GLACIER
KHARTA GLACIER
River Kharta
North Col
Mount Everest
South Col
WESTERN CWM
Nuptse
Lhotse
KANGSHUNG GLACIER
Pethangtse
Chomo Lonzo
Makalu
NEPAL
Langma La
River Karma
TIBET
Shigatse
Lhasa
Gyantse
Shegar
Cho Oyu
Everest
Makalu
Kathmandu
NEPAL
SIKKIM
BHUTAN
INDIA
INDIA
Key
mountain ranges
area of glacier
mountain peaks
pass
international borders
roads

EVEREST FROM THE EAST

barren and steep with only yaks grazing on the thin grass. As we gained altitude we were frequently delayed by engine trouble but we finally labored over the crest of the pass at 17,000 feet. Ahead of us was our first view of the north side of Mount Everest with the summit shrouded in cloud but the lower glaciers clearly visible. We had a brief lunch in this spectacular location and were then ready to go.

The road ahead swept down on dry arid ridges for thousands of feet. We started our crazy descent—rocking and swaying, bouncing over bumps, brakes being jammed on as we screeched around tight corners. We were frequently out of control and I found it a frightening experience. Our drivers didn't ever use their lower gears but just relied on the questionable brakes. Dick Blum was in the truck in front of me and his driver nearly didn't complete one turn, coming to a shuddering halt with his front wheels on the edge of a mighty drop, and it was only with the greatest of difficulty that he was able to back up and get onto the road again. It was an enormous relief when we finally came to the bottom of the 4,000-foot descent and rolled out into a wide valley with green fields, many trees and a large village. Flowing down the middle of the valley was a broad stream, the Rongbuk chu.

We turned down this valley and crossed more barley fields, passing through small villages with the remnants of many monasteries. Then we entered a spectacular gorge on a road jammed between the high cliffs and the raging river with water sometimes lapping over the road. After a couple of nervous hours of this the gorge widened and we alternately bumped across wide rocky flats or crept along a road that had been carved out of the bluffs a couple of hundred feet above the river. At 4:30 p.m. we branched to the right away from the Rongbuk chu and up the smaller Kharta river. The change in the environment was remarkable, from a barren gorge to a beautiful valley with a tumbling stream and green pastures. Half an hour later we reached our destination, the village of Kharta at 12,474 feet.

Everyone was tired and tempers rather frayed when we unloaded our five trucks. Huge piles of equipment were stacked beside the river and tents pitched in any possible spot. Our second Democratic Leadership

Discussion reached a high pitch of intensity as plans were put forward and discarded. Action would begin tomorrow claimed the most energetic group. Yaks, porters and expedition members themselves would carry loads up valley and the push would be on. I listened amazed—what about sorting the gear, issuing equipment, gathering the yaks, storing the remaining luggage? Next day the problem was solved for us—only seven of our promised fifty yaks turned up. I couldn't resist a quiet chuckle.

It was three days later before we really got going. We followed a track beside the Kharta river and then branched to the left up a steep rounded valley. I was the last into camp and came slowly around a great rock and there were the tents in the green grass beside beautiful Tsoa Lake at 15,260 feet. Now that we were under way there was an air of cooperation and even satisfaction within the party. We carried on in unpleasant monsoon conditions with heavy fog and drenching rain over the 16,000-foot pass, the Shago La, and plunged down 3,000 feet to a delightful campsite in the forest beside a river. Another five hours of hard walking next day in the fog and misty rain brought us to a campsite in a broad meadow. At 7:15 next morning Jim Morrissey poked his head out of the tent door and yelled, "Take a look at that!" At the head of the valley were the mighty snow-covered shapes of Everest and Lhotse and soon Chomo Lonzo poked into view as well. The excitement was intense and we were away rather more promptly than usual. Traveling was a good deal more difficult now. We reached the terminal face of the Kangshung Glacier and then had to struggle up the steep and exposed scree slope to the north before we could descend into the lateral trough of the glacier and, after five more hours of walking, reach yet another comfortable campsite at an altitude of 15,000 feet. We called this the Yak Camp and it was a superb location with Chomo Lonzo towering up on the other side of the valley. The sun streamed into my tent, it was like a warm summer's day and I hardly noticed the altitude at all.

28th August was soggy at first and we didn't get away until late morning. It was a very long and arduous day for me. The track was not difficult but the gradual rise in height was decidedly tedious and it was seven hours before I staggered into Base Camp at 17,000 feet. It had perhaps one of the most spectacular Base Camp views in the world. The great unclimbed East Face of Everest was straight in front of us, a horrifying combination of crevassed ice cliffs and deadly avalanche chutes. Avalanches came roaring down with great frequency but we noticed one possible route. Between the avalanche areas a great rock buttress climbed up to more than 20,000 feet, but it looked hard, very hard. In retrospect I have the greatest admiration for my team's efforts in reaching the top of this buttress in most appalling weather conditions.

For several days I suffered from headaches which would not abate and on 1st September our physician, Dr. Jim Morrissey, decided I should go down to a lower altitude, accompanying me for 2,000 feet down to Yak Camp where I certainly felt a little better. I found it lonely by myself and the weather was appalling but now and then one or two of the expedition members would come down to have a walk and a chat with me. On the fifth day Mr. Wang and Mr. Tsao turned up and presented me with a fresh leg of mutton. Mr. Tsao used the limited supplies of condiments I possessed to cook a delicious meat dish, certainly the best food I had eaten for some time, and after a week I felt well enough to climb back up to Base Camp and get up-to-date on what the team had been doing. In extremely difficult conditions they had made considerable progress up the rock buttress but the bad weather had proved quite a problem. There was a certain amount of discussion about persisting with the buttress or traveling around to the traditional North route on Everest first climbed by the Chinese in 1960. Although I was still a little physically uncomfortable, I was able to write a dispatch on the progress of the climb to send to our supporting newspaper in San Francisco.

About midday on Sunday 13th September I suddenly started vomiting. I lay on my bed all afternoon experiencing strange hallucinations which are clear to me to this day. I thought I was perched on a great ice face across from Base Camp and there were avalanches rumbling down on either side of me. I had no particular sense of fear about his but accepted that ultimately I would die. It wasn't until evening that Jim Morrissey realized I was seriously ill and he did all he could for me. All night I had a great shortage of breath and double vision and, although Jim was giving me oxygen, it didn't seem to make much difference. At daylight I crawled out of my tent and it was cold and clear. The mountains loomed above me but I had no idea what they were. I couldn't speak clearly and I had a severe headache. Jim immediately decided I must go down to a lower level as quickly as possible. He asked me if I could walk and I was able to respond that I could.

Jim and I walked slowly off for hour after hour until we reached Yak Camp, after which Jim had decided to take a more direct route to lower levels and we plunged down a huge rubble slope for what seemed thousands of feet. I had no idea where we were and was terrified by the steepness and the big drop to the river. We finally emerged on to a grassy patch beside a stream full of boulders. It was raining and miserable but Jim told me that this was where we planned to meet our porters, so I accepted this. Soon the sun came out and I was feeling much better, although still seeing double. I had the very improbable idea that we were now at the end of the road and that we'd meet our truck here. Down on the riverbed I noticed a movement—there it was, the truck I had been expecting for hours. Gleefully I pointed it out to Jim. "That's not a truck, Ed. It's only a rock!" he patiently explained. "We're three days' walk from the nearest road." But I didn't believe him—I *knew* the truck was coming.

After a long time the five porters arrived and we headed off down valley, following a narrow precipitous track high above the Kangshung Glacier and the Karma river. I felt quite unstable but knew I had to get down if I was to survive. My double vision was receding and, although I still recognized nothing around me, I knew we were losing altitude and that was the main thing. At some stage John Roskelley joined us and we followed a narrow zigzag track down an enormously long shingle slide. Then we crossed a little pass out into a scrubby basin filled with lakes and meadows and here we pitched our tent. I still had a bad headache, but already my vision had cleared and I could talk reasonably adequately. We were now below 14,000 feet. I didn't quite know why John Roskelley had joined us but I really appreciated him being there.

Encouraged by my improvement, Jim decided we would have a rest day in the same camp. I listened as John Roskelley and Jim talked about the East Face of Everest—not the difficulties but the danger. John had a record of fantastically difficult climbs but he felt the East Face in its present condition was an unjustifiable risk. It was hard not to agree with him, even in my befuddled state.

We moved on again. Though I still had headaches and a tightness in my chest, I was moving reasonably well and recognized a long steep hill from the journey in, so my mind was clearing a little. Then we diverted to the left on a different route up a long traverse, entering a beautiful high valley with snow-tipped peaks all around, a sparkling stream running down the middle, a lovely clear blue lake, with nearby the remnants of an old monastery. Camped here were two extremely handsome Tibetan children, a boy and a girl almost godlike in their looks. They had half a dozen yaks with them and they were apparently crossing the same pass as we were. When our porters asked the young people if they could put some of their loads on the yaks they willingly agreed. Jim also suggested that some of his cumbersome load might be put on a yak, but the porters just laughed him to scorn. What bastards they were, I thought, and I pined a little for my always helpful Sherpas.

The Langma La rose steeply in front of us and it never seemed to come to an end. We'd reach one crest in the pass but there was always another beyond. Halfway up there was quite a tricky place over a huge overhanging rock. With his heavy load Jim slipped and overbalanced and slid rapidly down the rock. It was only a desperate grasp at a prominent hold that enabled him to check his fall and probably save himself from falling to his death. Finally we came to the top of the pass at nearly 18,000 feet, so we'd climbed 4,000 feet that day. I couldn't quite understand how I'd been able to reach such a height in my weak condition. For quite a way we crossed a series of summits in deep snow and I noted how the Tibetan children almost danced along in their bare feet. Then we started descending by a steep zigzagging track, first over snow, and then on to slippery mud. We were entering a long steep gully, very narrow, with a small blue lake far down below.

I heard a shout from above and looked up to see a horrifying sight. Charging down the gully with a tent dragging behind was a huge yak with sharp widespread horns. Obviously it had been spooked by the loose tent fly. I looked desperately for somewhere to escape but there was nowhere. I shrank into the right-hand wall and the desperate yak rushed by, knocking me headfirst onto some rounded boulders. Groggily, I clambered to my feet, glad that I was still alive. Something wet was dripping down my neck and I realized it was blood. Jim rushed up and anxiously examined my skull. There was a two-inch split with the bone clearly to be seen. "What next!" said Jim in despair. He had limited medical supplies but sat me down and went calmly and confidently to work, snipping off the hair, putting antibiotic in the wound, and plastering it up. The yaks were reloaded and we continued down, first around the lake, then a plunging descent of a long steep slope, and finally a long rocky traverse to a huge boulder which had obviously been a campsite before. We pitched our torn tent and scrambled inside. About 9:30 p.m. we heard a noise outside. Another porter had arrived all the way from Base Camp—a fantastic achievement—and he had a bottle of Scotch whisky and some fresh potatoes from Mr. Wang, an extremely kind gesture from a very kind man.

Next morning I felt stronger and we carried on for hour after hour down into the Kharta valley. With tired legs and blistered feet I dragged myself into the village of Kharta and the end of the road. Despite my cerebral edema and my cracked head I'd completed a long and difficult journey and I was deeply appreciative of all Jim Morrissey had done for me.

The climbing party overcame the buttress and reached 21,500 feet but it was then clear that in the conditions they were experiencing they could go no further. Two years later another American expedition returned to the East Face with Jim Morrissey as leader. In a superb effort six members reached the summit of Mount Everest.

Dick Blum and I traveled by jeep and bus over the long road back to Lhasa. In Canton I purchased the last remaining seat on a charter flight to Hong Kong with half an hour to spare, two kindly Chinese policemen helping me make it aboard with my 120 lbs. of gear. In Hong Kong the Air New Zealand flight was leaving for Auckland in three hours but the Chinese check-in person said there was simply no room—there were already a dozen on the waiting list. I was very insistent, so he said I'd have to wait for the Air New Zealand agent. When he appeared he was a big cheerful Maori and I knew immediately I'd get a seat.

For ten hours that night I flew south over the ocean and across Australia to land in Auckland on a warm spring morning. For two weeks my head still troubled me but then the dull ache disappeared. The hair on my shaved scalp grew back into place and my split skull mended. I was almost back to normal and starting to think again of other adventures. But one thing was clear—Chairman Emeritus or not, my big mountain days were now definitely over. I was amazed at how much I enjoyed being back with June Mulgrew again. It wasn't surprising really. Neither of us now had a partner and we'd known each other a long time. We had a great deal in common with our affection for the Sherpas. It wasn't as if I was going to forget Louise and Belinda—I'd never do that—but June had known them too and I started getting great pleasure from her company and companionship. My depression largely disappeared and I started a new and happier period of my life. The last six years started to disappear like a bad dream.

17

HIGH COMMISSIONER

IT TOOK ME SEVERAL MONTHS TO RECOVER FULLY FROM THE ALTI-
tude problems I had experienced on the East Face of Everest, but it
was helped a great deal by June and me spending ten days together on
the beautiful resort island of Toberua in Fiji. I seemed to feel much
more energetic and threw myself with some vigor into our various
Himalayan Trust programs in Nepal. June came with me on all these
trips and proved a sympathetic and often astute adviser on any debatable
matters. My brother, Rex, worked extremely well with sirdar Mingma
Tsering and many new schools and clinics were built. Other Trust
members took part, too, particularly Jim Wilson and Murray Jones, and
in our two hospitals we had volunteer doctors from New Zealand,
Canada, the United States and even the Netherlands. It was a great step
forward when we recruited Dr. Mingma Gyalgen Sherpa, who proved
himself extremely competent and carries on to this day as Superinten-
dent of Paphlu hospital and is now the official government supervisor
of all medical activities in the Solu Khumbu district.

In our early days the rate of exchange was 10 rupees to the U.S. dollar,
which was the daily wage for a porter. But things have radically changed
over the years. The rate of exchange is now nearly 56 rupees to the U.S.

dollar and the daily rate for a porter is nearer 250 rupees, roughly $5. Porters, of course, work extremely hard, so they are relatively highly paid, although their employment is erratic, whereas most civil servants and teachers receive a much more modest but regular income. Our need for funds steadily escalated from U.S. $100,000 up to our present level of U.S. $400,000, so much work has gone into the fund-raising side of our activities. Two of our major fund-raisers have been Zeke O'Connor in Canada and Richard Blum in San Francisco. Zeke and his team have been very successful supporters for many years. They undertook the responsibility for financing Kunde hospital and the Sagarmatha Forestry project which meant raising almost $100,000 dollars every year with the help of an annual subsidy from the Canadian International Development Agency.

Dick Blum established the American Himalayan Foundation of which I was also a director. This was a particularly successful operation and the Himalayan Trust benefited enormously from it. Every year they held very large and expensive dinners with distinguished speakers. The Dalai Lama spoke on one occasion which was understandably popular and the Foundation netted a record $150,000. The following year they were having difficulty in choosing a suitable guest, so Dick rang me and asked if I would do it. I had considerable doubts about my drawing power but finally agreed. There was an excellent audience and the Foundation netted $75,000. While the profit hadn't been as good as the previous year, I felt that being half as good as the Dalai Lama was a reasonable recommendation.

Larry Witherbee and our Foundation in Chicago have been steady fund-raisers with the help of Sears, Roebuck and their suppliers. Ingrid Versen was the Chairman of our German Foundation, based in the beautiful area of Bad Weissee near Munich, where the Mayor and some of the Councillors were entertaining and successful fund-raisers too. In the United Kingdom our Foundation was led by George and Mary Lowe and few people worked as energetically for the Himalayan Trust welfare as they did. So with a great deal of hard work and enthusiasm each year we were able to raise the money we required for the operation of our activities in Solu Khumbu.

Most of these foundations relied on one or two visits a year from June and myself to help in major fund-raising efforts, and we found we were soon spending four months each year overseas. It was hard work but we made many good friends and had the satisfaction of knowing that at no stage were we ever short of the money we needed. A constant worry hanging over our heads is what will happen to all these contributions when I am no longer able to play my part. We still don't know the answer to this.

Each year I was becoming more involved in conservation and re-forestation. I became an International Director of the World Wildlife Fund and June and I attended a wonderful international meeting at Assisi. The combination of ancient Italian buildings and important international environmentalists was a remarkable one and when June was invited to sit next to the Duke of Edinburgh at the formal dinner, it was a great occasion for her. A highlight for me was when I was elected Honorary President of the prestigious Explorers Club of New York. I felt I might be turning into a talking head for the environmentally great and the good—which would be OK as long as I didn't get carried away by the media hype.

In August 1984 I was back at my home in New Zealand. There was a ring on the telephone: "This is David Lange. Is Ed Hillary there?" I, of course, knew who David Lange was—he was the newly elected Prime Minister of New Zealand—but why would he want to talk to me? So, rather suspiciously, I said, "Who?" There was a rather peppery reply, "David Lange!" So I gulped and we carried on. The Prime Minister explained the situation. The High Commission (as Embassies are called in British Commonwealth countries) in New Delhi had been closed for several years due to disagreements between the rather grumpy New Zealand Prime Minister of the day, Robert Muldoon, and the very strong-minded Indian Prime Minister, Indira Gandhi. This was a ridiculous situation and David Lange, who had a warm affection for India, intended to change it. He asked me if I would be prepared to go to India as New Zealand High Commissioner. Such an idea had never entered my mind, but it had immediate appeal—it was, in fact, the only country I would have considered as suitable for me to act in. I told David Lange of my immediate reaction but asked him if I could have a couple of days to think it over. He agreed and I hastily rang June with the news.

Two days later I visited David Lange in his modest house in Mangere. I explained to him that I would enjoy being the High Commissioner, but I had a number of responsibilities in Nepal and also in North America that I could not just abandon.

"Keep doing what you have to do," he told me, "but spend most of your time in India."

I couldn't have asked for more than that. "What do you want me to do in India?" I asked the Prime Minister.

"Just exactly what you think is best," he told me.

The only thing that worried me was what to do about June, as I would certainly miss her if she wasn't with me. I was a little scared to ask her to join me in case she turned me down—June has a very close attachment to her family. Finally it was June herself who made the decision. "Why don't I come, too?" she asked me. I was mightily relieved and rang David Lange at once and asked him if I could take June along, to which he immediately agreed. So June came with me to India as my official companion and it proved a most happy and successful arrangement. It actually amused June no end to have the letters OC after her name on official correspondence.

We arrived in Delhi on 4th February 1985 and I went straight from the flight to lunch with a group of Ambassadors and High Commissioners and listened with considerable interest to knowledgeable gossip about the Indian Prime Minister and the ever-present political problems in the vast subcontinent. We finished off the day with a formal dinner at the residence of Sir Robert Wade-Gery, High Commissioner for the United Kingdom. I went to bed that night having said very little during the course of the day and quite convinced that I could never handle such complex diplomatic topics with the devastating experience and aplomb of my peers. I soon learned that, though I might not be very strong on the nuances of diplomatic life, I probably knew more about how the people of India thought than did many of my colleagues. We had rented the very fine residence of my predecessor, but in the intervening years it had sadly deteriorated, so much work was needed to bring it up to respectable condition. In the interim we stayed in a large comfortable suite on the top floor of the Sheraton, with a wide balcony on which we could stand and watch the crimson sun descend over the horizon while all the unique sounds of Indian life drifted up to us mingled with the fragrance of Indian food.

We were not long in Delhi before returning briefly to the Himalayas, trekking for five days over very steep country to the remote village of Bung in Eastern Nepal where I had promised to build a clinic. We worked very hard to complete the building as quickly as possible so that I could return to my new responsibilities in India. The diet was a little different from New Delhi, mostly rice and curried chicken stew, and the refreshment raw and fiery rakshi. But the hospitality was warm, the people lean and tough and I felt far more in control of my life.

Once back in Delhi, my first major task was to present my credentials to the President of India. At the gate to the palace grounds I was met by the Chief of Protocol and ushered into a huge and impressive old limousine. We swept up the gravel drive to the President's palace with a colorful troop of mounted lancers trotting along beside us. I was ushered to a dais, while a platoon of bayonet-bearing Gurkha soldiers presented arms in perfect unison and we listened to the Indian and New Zealand national anthems beautifully played by an army band. I have never been a great flag-waver, but somehow hearing my national anthem played in such impressive circumstances gave me a feeling of warmth and pride and even brought a few tears to my eyes. Then we climbed some great stairs with trumpets blaring and entered the vast reception hall which looked as big as a football field. I had time to note that one huge hand-made carpet covered the whole floor and to wonder about the size of the loom, then I was bowing before the President and exchanging diplomatic notes, in total silence, and carrying out all the other formalities in which I had been well schooled. It was a very impressive occasion which the Indians handled superbly. June was placed in a corner with a group of officials and was not presented to the President. I knew this was a decision by my professional staff and intended to see it did not happen again.

Our residence was still far from complete, but I knew June could handle its supervision much better than I could. So I left her behind and set off on another modest adventure—a trip to the North Pole. The temperature was 45°C in New Delhi when I flew to London and then on to Edmonton in Canada to meet up with my small adventurous group which included Neil Armstrong, commander of Apollo XI, my son, Peter, and a variety of well-to-do Americans. In a Boeing 737 jet we flew north to the Arctic Circle and landed on the frozen ice runway at Resolute Bay. It was extremely cold at Resolute and the buildings had the atmosphere of a construction camp. We were met by a renowned Indian guide (from India) who was the main so-called adventure organizer and he supplied us with all the extra cold-weather clothing we might need and proved extremely hospitable.

Next morning we flew north again in a Twin Otter aircraft fitted with skis, crossing vast areas of pack ice and landing at a weather station to refuel. Soon we were flying on again over the great mountains of Ellesmere Island, all incredibly beautiful in the low polar lighting, to land on the crisp ice of frozen Lake Hazen where another Twin Otter was already waiting for us. Then we struggled up a snowy hill to a Jamesway hut which was warm and comfortable. That evening I talked at some length to Neil Armstrong about opportunity and adventure. I very much liked his relaxed personality and when I rather naively asked him how he had been chosen to be first to stand on the moon he answered, "Luck! Just luck!" I had a definite feeling that it might have been a little bit more than that.

After a comfortable night and an early breakfast, we descended to the aircraft again. Their motors had been heated by hot-air blowers and were ready for takeoff, so we crawled inside one of the aircraft, the second was full of 44-gallon fuel drums. We crossed the rest of Ellesmere Island and then flew out over the pack ice of the Arctic Ocean. After a few hours the pilots picked a large piece of smooth ice and made a comfortable landing, then hand-pumped fuel from the drums into the aircraft tanks. After another hour or two, we approached a large and heavy piece of ice on which some huts and high masts were clearly to be seen. We landed on their rather rough little strip and refueled again. The staff in the base were university scientists we were told, carrying out an important research program under the ice, but one of our pilots casually mentioned to me that their main duties were to identify Russian nuclear submarines.

Our navigation equipment was very sophisticated for such small aircraft and we homed in on the North Pole with no difficulty, our pilots finding a suitable landing place between huge ice pressure ridges. Our landing was a bumpy one, but we scrambled out onto the ice with great excitement. The temperature was -45°C, 90°C lower than the temperature in Delhi only six days before. The pack ice stretched away in every direction to the horizon, broken only by frequent pressure ridges. It was hard to believe that the ice was only twelve feet thick and that underneath was 1,400 feet of ocean. As I walked over the bumpy ice for a mile or so I thought how different it was from the South Pole which was at an altitude of 9,300 feet. I looked back to see our aircraft away in the distance and hastily retraced my steps. Someone produced a bottle of champagne and poured a little into glasses for Neil and for me. Before we could even wet our lips the champagne froze solid. An hour and a half later, we clambered back on board. It had been an exciting experience, if not exactly a great adventure. But I did have a considerable feeling of satisfaction—I believed I was the first person to have stood at both the North and South Poles and on the summit of Mount Everest. As technology had changed, so had my method of travel. I'd used my feet on Everest, a farm tractor to the South Pole, and finally a small aircraft to the North Pole.

I returned to Delhi and for the first time in my life started going to the office regularly each day. It was, in fact, my first 9-to-5 job. It was a busy time, reading and writing dispatches, carrying out requests from Foreign Affairs in Wellington and supervising my modest staff. My diplomatic responsibilities were not on the whole arduous ones—there were few topics of disagreement between India and New Zealand. I also discovered I had certain advantages over many of my diplomatic colleagues. Access to a Minister or a Chief Secretary, I was told, was almost impossible at times, but whenever a matter arose that needed to be dealt with at a high level, a telephone call from my secretary would invariably bring an appointment almost immediately. My Trade Commissioner, Tony Mildenhall, used this to very good effect. He and I made a number of calls on high officials to discuss problems in the importing of such things as coal, wool and timber which he had only been able to handle at a very low official level before. So slowly, but surely, our trade relations improved.

Inevitably, of course, I had my closest diplomatic relationships with the English-speaking Heads of Mission. We called ourselves the Gang of Five and this comprised the British High Commissioner, the American Ambassador, the Canadian High Commissioner, the Australian High Commissioner and myself. We had a leisurely lunch once a month, rotating between our various residences and many interesting topics were discussed. I know that after these lunches I always hurried off to my office to send a fax to my Foreign Affairs Office in Wellington with all the gossip I had accumulated. For all I know my colleagues may well have been doing the same thing.

What I valued most highly was the good fortune of having a very close relationship with the people of India and, if a government Minister or Senior Secretary asked me to do something, I nearly always did it. "We know you are a New Zealander," they would say, "but you are also one of us." Tenzing Norgay and Everest had tied me irrevocably to India. On many occasions June and I were the only foreigners present at important functions and we thoroughly enjoyed this feeling of acceptance by the Indian community. Through it we became involved in some rather unusual functions.

On one occasion I was invited to Saranpur, just a couple of hours drive north of Delhi, to be chief judge at an International Mango Festival. I enjoyed mangoes, but I am certainly no expert on them. However, I had been asked by a Chief Minister so I duly accepted. I arrived at a huge orchard and there were 200 varieties of mangoes laid out on long tables. Despite enjoying mangoes, there are limits to the number I can consume. Fortunately there was a very distinguished Indian gentleman present who helped me out. He was Chief Magistrate of the area, responsible for three million people, but he was a more experienced mango man than I was and picked me out a shortlist of twelve. Eating mangoes is not an edifying spectacle, but I munched my way conscientiously through the twelve large candidates, chose the three I enjoyed most, and they were duly given the prizes. Next morning, back in Delhi, I happened to meet the British High Commissioner, the senior diplomat in Delhi, and a good friend. He mentioned that on the television news the previous evening he had seen me eating my way ad nauseam through piles of mangoes and he didn't quite know if it was the sort of thing that even a New Zealand High Commissioner should be doing. I fortunately realized he was joking—at least I think he was.

I received a message that Tenzing Norgay was ill in hospital in Delhi. I called on him a number of times and was sad to see him looking so frail and unhappy. His lungs were giving him great problems he told me, and he admitted that he was finding life very lonely in Darjeeling. His wife, Daku, was away conducting trekking parties most of the time and he no longer had any responsibilities at the Himalayan Mountaineering Institute. All his younger children were in America, so he spent most of his time in his Darjeeling home doing very little. Several of my mountaineering friends in Delhi whispered that Tenzing was drinking far too much—I could certainly understand that. When I climbed Everest with Tenzing, we were good companions, but not close friends. His knowledge of English was not terribly good and my knowledge of Nepali was minimal, but we could communicate effectively on climbing matters. Over the years Tenzing's English improved enormously and in the five years that we were in Delhi I had many occasions to sit with him and talk about life and the future of our children. He then used to tell me about the things that concerned him.

He was a little sad and he used to bemoan the fact that the government of India had not treated him as Nehru, the Prime Minister, had promised many years before. Of course his expectations had grown enormously. He'd spent so much time overseas, often in an affluent society, that he saw how other people lived and liked the idea of living that way himself. So although the Indian government supported him according to its modest standards, this was not the level of assistance that he believed Pandit Nehru had promised him. Tenzing in his last years was often lonely and plagued with doubts and insecurity. He started turning to me for reassurance. He was still proud of the fact that we had been the first on top of Mount Everest but he agreed with me in deploring the growing commercialization of the mountain. He knew he had done a great deal for the young people of India—training thousands of them in adventurous activity—but he regretted that he hadn't done enough for his own people in the Himalayas—like I had done he would tell me. I did all I could to reassure him but he was now drinking a good deal and just didn't want to believe it.

It was a considerable shock in May 1986 when the news reached me that Tenzing had died in his seventy-fourth year. There were political problems in the Darjeeling area, but June and I were determined to go to Tenzing's funeral, even though we were warned that we might not be allowed through by the disruptive Nepali elements who were trying to establish a state of their own. We flew from Delhi to Bagdogra and were met by an army captain and driver in a somewhat ancient jeep who drove us through Siliguri and then up the steep narrow winding road toward Darjeeling. We came to a village where the road was completely blocked by a large crowd who looked very determined and rather threatening. Our captain proved equal to the task as he told the gathering that Hillary Sahib was coming to pay his last respects to his old comrade. Tenzing was a famous name in the hills and the crowd parted and waved us through. At Tenzing's house we were warmly welcomed by his family with cups of tea and biscuits; then we were taken upstairs to Tenzing's beautiful private gompa where he lay in state, and I looked for the last time on the still, waxy face of my friend who had shared that great moment with me on Everest some thirty-three years before. He seemed so much smaller than the strong and vigorous person I had known. We put our hands together in a formal namaste and then retreated to Mrs. Tendup La's Windemere Hotel, a comfortable, but elderly relic of the Raj.

The funeral was held the next day in the grounds of the Himalayan Mountaineering Institute which had been directed and inspired by Tenzing for many years. His body was placed on a cart and dragged up the hill by men joined together by white scarves. By the time we arrived at the HMI, the body was laid out on the funeral pyre, covered in white scarves and marigolds. June and I were given a place of honor on a comfortable sofa beside Tenzing's wife, Daku, and the family gathered all around. I believe we were the only foreigners present. Norbu, the very handsome eldest son, stood at his father's head throughout. There were many Buddhist monks present, marking the ceremony with a constant chanting of prayers and clashing of cymbals. In many ways it was a happy occasion with an almost picnic atmosphere of laughter and tea-drinking. As Buddhists, they all believed in reincarnation and that ultimately Tenzing would return, but now they must celebrate the departure of a great hero with both joy and sadness.

The moment came for Norbu to light the funeral pyre and as he commenced doing this the rain started falling in earnest. It was only by pouring large quantities of ghee on the funeral pyre that it burst into flames. The thousands of onlookers all stood perfectly patiently in the rain while the ceremony continued for several hours and finally there was a dull crack as Tenzing's skull split open and the chanting rose to a crescendo to symbolize his spirit being released from his body. It had been a sad occasion for us but June and I also felt it had been a great honor to be present at this farewelling of our old friend. The Sherpas are always practical people; as the ceremony concluded, Daku produced a bundle of airmail envelopes containing money and handed one to each of the monks.

In April 1997 June and I returned to Darjeeling to the grounds of the Himalayan Mountaineering Institute for the unveiling of a statue dedicated to my old friend. I concluded my speech as follows: "I have never regarded myself as much of a hero but Tenzing, I believe, undoubtedly was. From humble beginnings he had achieved the summit of the world. I think it is appropriate that this magnificent statue should stand here forever in front of the mountains he loved where he introduced so many young people to the joys and challenges of the great outdoors."

Being Head of Mission in a place such as Delhi was a very pleasant experience we discovered. Although India is regarded by some as a hardship post, we were very comfortable there. Under June's determined supervision, our residence became an extremely comfortable home with a central courtyard, wide verandah, beautiful carpets and furniture, and pleasant air-conditioning. We had a huge lawn which was wonderful for entertaining. In the winter we erected a huge decorated Shamiana tent with charcoal heaters and invited large numbers of guests to special functions. For someone who had never had staff before, June handled her large team very expertly, but then she looked after them well, supervised the health of the children, made sure their accommodation was adequate and that they were well paid according to local standards. We bought June a small Honda car and she obtained a license so was able to drive herself around Delhi and survived for four and a half years relatively unscathed.

At first we had much to learn about handling our guests. The New Zealand cricket team was touring India and we invited them all to the residence for drinks. We were advised that twenty-four people would be coming and that their favorite drink was New Zealand beer. I checked our supplies and found we had 140 cans of excellent New Zealand

Steinlager Export. That made six cans per person, which seemed to me a more than adequate supply. The young men and their coach duly arrived after a hot day in the field. Within an hour all the beer had gone and, although we offered them ample supplies of chilled white wine, this was not acceptable. They politely expressed their apologies and departed to more fertile pastures.

On one of our visits to the fine city of Jaipur we were entertained by the Minister of Tourism who had an outstanding musical group playing colorful Rajasthani music with great skill. We had a very important function coming up on our wide lawn in Delhi, so we asked the Minister if we could hire his musicians for that occasion. He very kindly agreed and they duly arrived on time. We placed them in a corner of the verandah and for two hours they played superbly, much to the pleasure of our guests. June's eight-year-old granddaughter Rebecca, who was a very friendly soul, went to the musicians and asked them what they would like to drink. The leader was quite positive. "Whisky, no Coke," he advised Rebecca and that's what they duly received.

Each Christmas we had a party at the residence for the children, not only of our family, but for all our residency staff, too. We always tried to produce something a little different for them. One year we had a large camel arrive carrying great bags of presents which were enthusiastically received by the children. We went even further the following year when we had all the children of the office staff present and a large elephant strolled in the gate and gave rides to dozens of children. It seemed strange that in a land of elephants almost no ordinary city child would have ridden on one.

The trips June and I really enjoyed most in India were visiting the vast number of remarkable old forts, palaces and temples, and we loved the tiger sanctuaries, too. December and January was wintertime in India, so the climate was very pleasant. It was also the summer holidays in New Zealand, so on a number of occasions we brought June's family over to spend six weeks or so with us. These were great holidays—we stayed in the beautiful Lake Palace Hotel in Udaipur, crossed the desert to the superb walled city of Jaisalmeer, swam in the warm surf at Goa, and looked with wonder at the great carvings in the caves at Ellora and Ajunta. I found the fort at Chittogarh absolutely fascinating and wandered around inside the great walls, reliving in my mind the tale of Rajput courage. At the beginning of the fourteenth century the fort was attacked by a Moslem ruler who wished to secure the hand of Rani Padmini, said to be the most beautiful woman in the world. As the city collapsed under the onslaught, a funeral pyre was kindled in a vault and Rani Padmini led her 13,000 women into the flames. All the conqueror found on entering the city was a few wisps of smoke ascending from the silent vault. This was the sort of dramatic story I had dreamed about as a child—and still found fascinating. Another amazing experience for all of us was in Khanna Tiger Sanctuary when we were riding around on elephants searching for wild game. We reached a small bank and looked straight down onto a magnificent tiger that had clearly just eaten so was resting and fully relaxed. It was barely twenty feet from our elephant and we watched and admired for some time while it ignored us. There can be nothing more beautiful than a great tiger free in the open forest but heavy poaching has reduced the numbers substantially, which makes the work of India's tiger sanctuaries so important.

One year I accepted an invitation to present the prizes and give a short speech to one of the important boys' schools in Delhi. I had not been feeling well for a few days but I had made the commitment. We arrived at the school to find its large hall crammed with parents and pupils. June was placed in the front row of the audience and I was conducted up onto the stage. First I was asked to present the school prizes and this went on and on forever. I was starting to feel slightly dizzy and the heat was tremendous. I was then asked to make the congratulatory speech, so moved in rather shaky fashion to the lectern and started talking to the gathering. June immediately realized I was leaning heavily on the lectern, wasn't speaking very clearly, and was sometimes turning over three pages at a time. With some courage she moved up onto the stage and asked clearly if there was a chair available. But it was too late as I

282

subsided dizzily to the floor. There was immediately a great uproar and, as half of the parents seemed to be doctors, they all converged rapidly onto the stage. My tie was removed and so were my socks and shoes. I came back to clear consciousness to see my very large bare feet outlined against a huge concerned sea of faces. A wheelchair was produced from somewhere and, with a couple of people holding up my feet, I was wheeled out to my car and driven to the residence. I staggered to my bed and was given a check-over by a handsome young Sikh doctor. "I don't think there is much wrong with you," he said. "You'll probably be OK tomorrow." And he was right. One of the nice features of this incident was that I received a very pleasant "Get Well" note from Prime Minister Rajiv Gandhi.

We enjoyed any time we had with Rajiv Gandhi and appreciated his quick wit and easy manner. When he visited New Zealand at the invitation of David Lange he was completely relaxed and I think thoroughly enjoyed himself. When we first saw him stepping off the plane in Auckland both June and I thought he must have lost weight, but then we realized it was the first time we had seen him not wearing a bullet-proof vest. All of us in Delhi knew that Rajiv Gandhi's life span must be limited for, despite his formidable array of security guards, he was just too easy with people and there were too many political factions who wanted to see him dead. When later he was blown to pieces by a female suicide bomber in Tamil Nadu, we were not surprised, but terribly distressed.

In February 1989 an urgent message came through that the famous Tengboche Monastery at the foot of Mount Everest, the main religious and cultural center of the Sherpa community, had been burned to the ground. June and I immediately flew to Kathmandu and helicoptered up to Tengboche to view the still smoldering ruins. An old lama whom I had known for many years threw his arms around my shoulders and wept. "Tengboche must rise again," said the Sherpas. "Will you help?" The Sherpas themselves raised U.S. $50,000, a fantastic sum for people who are far from well-to-do. I traveled around the world, encouraging people and organizations to contribute to the monastery and great generosity was shown. Zeke O'Connor and I lectured from coast to coast in Canada and raised a great deal of money. Funds poured in from Japan and France and the United Kingdom. The Swiss supplied a magnificent copper roof at great expense and altogether we raised $400,000. The American Himalayan Foundation in San Francisco had been particularly generous. It took four years for the building to be completed, all the work having been done by hand, both with the timbers and the squaring of the rock for the walls. Our Sherpa master builder proved to be extremely skilled.

On 22nd September 1993 we helicoptered in again for the opening ceremony to be met by a line of monks carrying welcoming scarves. There was June and myself, Dick Blum, Zeke O'Connor and Larry Witherbee, all of whom had been deeply involved in the fund-raising. But of course we had to have the politicians, too. There was the Prime Minister of Nepal and other Ministers, plus many senior officials and even the international press who had managed to get a seat on the large official helicopter. I noticed one pressman bustling after the Prime Minister and bumping the Rimpoche (head monk) off the path with careless arrogance. We entered the new outer door into the courtyard which was crammed with hundreds of people. The main door of the monastery had a spectacular curtain and the inside door was superbly painted. We listened patiently while the Prime Minister of Nepal and the other Ministers gave speech after speech, though they had contributed nothing to the building. I noticed many of the local Sherpas dropping off to sleep—they knew very well who had done all the planning and carried out the work. I gave a few brief words of pleasure that Tengboche Monastery was once more able to function.

In the last few years, the inside of the monastery has been carefully redecorated. The religious ornaments not destroyed by the fire have been restored. The ceiling panels have been repainted, and a great Buddha, two stories high, has been molded. The large dramatic panels to line the walls were repainted in Kathmandu and helicoptered in. On the crest of its spur, the new Tengboche Monastery is quite magnificent. It has indeed risen better than ever before.

In July 1989 June and I said our farewell to India. It had been a remarkable four and a half years, but although we could have stayed on longer, we felt it was time to go home. We arrived back in Auckland and June returned to her house and I returned to mine. Even though June was only a mile away, it seemed a rather lonely existence. It was our children who solved the problem for us. "Now that you are home why don't you just get married," they told us. June had only one proviso—she must be able to redecorate and improve my house. It was a small sacrifice to make as the house had needed improvements for some years.

In November 1989 it was a superb sunny day when June and I were married on the deck of my home in Auckland by an old and good friend, Cath Tizard, the Mayor of Auckland, now Dame Cath Tizard. We had known Cath for many years and she was soon to become the Governor General of New Zealand. It was a very happy event with all our children, grandchildren, relations and friends gathered around. I was now seventy years old and June was twelve years younger. My life would have been very empty without Louise and June. For the twenty-two years after Everest Louise was responsible for the happiest and most productive period of my middle years. After her death I had five years of depression and misery. When my long friendship with June blossomed into a much warmer relationship, I learned to live and love again. Louise and June are different in many ways, but they have each given me a feeling of unchanging security and happiness. They both have had sound judgment and their advice has been kind and prudent. What a fortunate person I have been!

Being married didn't seem to make a lot of difference to our lives. June and I had already established a strong supportive friendship that we knew would last. But now we had become respectable—and all the old squares in the community must have nodded their heads in approval. As if to give its official seal of approval, New Zealand established its own award system and I had the honor of being granted its highest decoration, the Order of New Zealand, in the first group of twenty-four recipients. June also received the highly respected Queen's Service

Medal in recognition of the excellent work she had carried out in re-establishing our High Commission in New Delhi, a well-deserved honor in my view.

My daughter, Sarah, has established a good life for herself. As Chief Conservator of Art in the Auckland Art Gallery she travels frequently around the world on art conservation matters. She loves her small but comfortable home which she shares with her son and daughter. I am greatly relieved that she seems to have renewed a modest fondness for her father.

In fact June and I have a large extended family who all seem to fit in very well together. Between us we have nine grandchildren ranging from three years old to twenty-three and each with their own very particular individualities. With sisters, cousins and good friends, we have thirty people or more who gather at our Christmas dinners and very happy occasions they prove to be. My contribution is little—mainly pouring the drinks—but the women in the family from younger to older work like Trojans to make the happy event successful. I have even learned to enjoy family birthdays, something I ignored before.

18

Worlds Revisited

I N MAY 1990 I WAS SITTING IN MY STUDY AT MY HOME IN AUCKLAND when the phone rang. I picked up the receiver, said "Hello!" and the voice of my son Peter replied, "Oh, hello Dad."

"Where are you Peter?" I asked him.

"On top of Mount Everest!" he told me.

Peter had a walkie-talkie on the summit which operated down to a dish antenna at Base Camp and then the message bounced from satellite to satellite around the world and arrived at my home in Auckland as clear as a bell. Peter and I had the longest talk we'd had for some time and he even expressed admiration for the difficulty he had experienced in climbing the Hillary Step—something I had done more than thirty years before. For some reason you don't expect your son to be impressed by something you've done a long time ago, but I have to admit I experienced a slight glow of pleasure. Peter finally admitted his feet were getting a little chilly, so we duly said good-bye and hung up. But it does show the changes that had taken place in technology over the previous thirty-seven years. It is very appropriate that Tenzing's youngest son, Jamling Sherpa, also climbed Everest in 1996 and his grandson, Tashi Sherpa, did the same in 1997.

I am fully aware that I push things to the limit as far as altitude is concerned. In 1953 I had been an exceptional acclimatizer, but as the years passed I have become increasingly prone to cerebral edema. In 1991 I suffered an attack after spending a week at Kunde which is at 12,700 feet. So in 1992 I based myself at Namche Bazaar, which is around 11,000 feet. I didn't sleep well there, although nothing desperate occurred. Now I don't sleep any higher than 9,000 feet and this seems satisfactory at present. Fortunately, with the increasing number of helicopters that are available in Nepal I can now fly readily from Paphlu airfield to Tengboche Monastery and Khumjung school and spend several hours at 13,000 feet, feeling short of breath, but with no major discomfort. It will become very distressing for me if I am no longer able to visit my good friends in the Solu Khumbu even for a few hours.

Every year without fail we are approached by a number of villages requesting assistance with some project or other. I can pick a group of mountain people waiting to present a petition from some distance away. They will be serious village elders who will formally welcome us with a namaste, sit us down on a comfortable rock or bench, place scarves around our necks and finally pour us a drink of the local alcohol. Only then will the petition be presented, maybe written in English by the local school headmaster or in Nepali to be translated by my executive Sherpa, Ang Rita. In response to such requests over the years we have established twenty-seven schools, two hospitals, twelve clinics, many bridges over difficult mountain rivers, piped fresh water to villages, and assisted in the rebuilding and maintenance of the Sherpas' greatly loved monasteries. Probably the greatest strength of the Himalayan Trust has been its continuity. We have been going for over thirty years now and the local people know that if we promise to do something we can be trusted to carry it out. We are proud, too, that most of the time we are responding to the wishes of the local people.

The nature of petitions has changed. In the early years they were nearly all for community projects but nowadays the requests are frequently for personal assistance. June is a vigorous advocate on behalf of young girls who, like women all across Asia, usually have a harsher life than their brothers. Some of the petitions are heartrending. Cute children, their huge brown eyes moist with sorrow will whisper "No Mother having! No Father having!" but when a modest sum is given to them for school expenses their faces break into a flashing smile. Decision-making is very hard and I suppose at times we are led up the garden path—but not too often! We have a considerable respect for the mountain people of Solu Khumbu. They are hardy, bright and cheerful, with an urge to better themselves, and there is a great deal of satisfaction to be gained from working on a worthwhile project with friends who may well have contributed greatly to everyone's enjoyment in the great mountains of the Himalayas.

I realize I personally get much of the credit for Himalayan Trust activities, but nothing can be achieved without vigorous support. Our Trust volunteer builders, like my brother, Rex, have worked hard and long to build the schools and hospitals. Rex believes that the plans for any structure must be capable of being drawn out on the back of an old envelope, and I suppose some of them look that way, but they have been surprisingly effective. Trust members like Jim Wilson, Murray Jones and Murray Ellis combine their mountaineering skills with a deep affection for the Sherpas and a solid practical sense. Our many doctor volunteers have climbed mountains, helped build schools and hospitals and treated the enormous variety of ailments that afflict the people in these remote areas.

But great though the efforts have been by all these incomers, nothing would have happened without my friend sirdar Mingma Tsering Sherpa. Almost completely illiterate, Mingma had an astonishing memory and an executive ability that was unequaled. His rigid standards and complete understanding of the thoughts and wishes of his people brought enormous respect and maybe even a little fear. It was a brave man who tried to deceive Mingma. All of us in the Himalayan Trust relied on Mingma for his sound judgment. I could certainly have done little without him. It was a very sad moment in 1994 when Mingma Tsering passed away. It left an enormous gap.

Over the years methods and technology have changed, and it became important for our Sherpa executive to be fully literate, respected in Kathmandu as well as in the hills, at home with computers and senior government officials alike. Fortunately, we had the right man for this task—Ang Rita Sherpa. Ang Rita was one of the first pupils at Khumjung school; he gained the highest marks in the School Leaving Certificate for the whole of Nepal and then carried on to obtain two degrees at university. Nevertheless, Ang Rita still retains his close relationships with the Sherpa people and is greatly respected by them all. He has been able to replace Mingma Tsering efficiently in a new and more complicated world. The Himalayan Trust has had much to be thankful for in its Sherpa leadership over the years.

When I first visited the Khumbu in 1951 the forests were superb—big trees up to an altitude of 13,000 feet and extensive areas of azaleas and juniper shrubs covering the rocky valleys up to 16,000 feet. In 1952 the Swiss Everest expedition cut vast quantities of juniper to burn at their Base Camp and there was still much of this left in 1953. We in our turn burnt the remainder of the Swiss firewood and cut extra ourselves. So the higher valleys after a succession of expeditions quickly became devoid of virtually all shrubs and it is only in more recent years, when the use of firewood in the high valleys has been prohibited, that there has been a modest resurgence of the high-altitude flora. In building Lukla airfield we were partly to blame for the tremendous increase in the number of trekkers that visit the Khumbu, now exceeding 17,000 each year. There are only 3,000 Sherpas living in the region, but probably 20,000 porters and workers from lower altitudes carry loads into the Khumbu or work in the fields. This has put tremendous pressure on the forests, both to supply timber for many hotels and firewood for cooking and heating.

When the Sagarmatha National Park was established as an aid project by the New Zealand government, a small tree-replanting program was begun. (Sagarmatha is the Nepalese name for Everest.) The Himalayan Trust has carried on this program now for many years, establishing a number of nurseries, and we have now planted out more than a million seedlings. Initially we enclosed extensive areas of steep barren hillsides with rock walls and filled them with seedlings, but at this high altitude growth was very slow. Now suddenly in the last few years the trees have shot ahead and most are three feet high, some even ten feet high. Growing trees is a very long-term business, but at last we are seeing signs of real improvement. Following the advice of professional foresters who visit our tree projects every year, we no longer fence in the new areas. We plant seedlings in open areas amongst the remaining forest and this has proved much more satisfactory. It operates more like natural regeneration. I have asked our forestry experts if we are indeed making progress in the re-establishing of the forests and their answer is encouraging. We are not increasing the amount of timber available, because big trees are still being cut for building purposes, but the actual number of trees has increased considerably, so in twenty or thirty years the forests in the Khumbu could almost be as impressive as they were forty years ago—or that is indeed my hope.

A number of other foreign aid projects have been undertaken in Solu Khumbu, notably the massive Austrian hydroelectric scheme in the Khumbu and the very effective Swiss one in Solu. These are both playing an important part in the upgrading of the standard of living and also in reducing the pressure on the local forests. There have been many other smaller projects carried out, too, usually very worthwhile in themselves but often with short-term finance. On many occasions the Himalayan Trust with its long-term programs is requested by the local people to complete a task or take over the burden of further financial support, and this we are usually prepared to do.

We have also received many offers of support that have just appeared out of the blue. In 1994 I had a telephone call from Peter Gschwind of the Swiss company Global Marketing and Design. He told me a rather surprising story. Two large Swiss insurance companies, Helvetia and Patria, had decided to operate more closely together. They had a total staff of nearly 6,000 people and planned to merge their offices and general agencies, but, as each company was handling different types of insurance, it was important that the combined staff learned to work together. So Peter Gschwind had made the suggestion that all of the 700 people in higher management should spend a day together, first listening to well-known and adventurous types such as Reinhold Messner and myself, and then spending the rest of the day working together in constructing two buildings which would later be transported to Nepal by the company and erected at the Junbesi and Khumjung schools. As there would be no cost involvement to the Himalayan Trust, it sounded quite a useful idea to me, although a mighty expensive way of obtaining a couple of buildings in a remote area of Nepal.

So I flew to Switzerland and in a village near Lucerne there were a series of huge tents crammed full of modern machinery with a large number of carpentry instructors in attendance. After the motivational talks the 700-strong group in upper management entered the tents in very orderly fashion and were soon constructing windows, roof trusses, floor and wall panels, chairs, tables and bunks. By the end of the day one building had been fully completed and erected and it certainly looked much more sophisticated than any school we had built in Nepal. In the evening with their task completed, all the upper management team shook hands with great friendliness and departed to their homes all over Switzerland. Then in efficient Swiss fashion the buildings were dismantled, shipped to Bombay, trucked to Kathmandu, and ultimately helicoptered in to Junbesi and Khumjung where Jim Wilson and Murray Jones joined the Swiss construction team to erect them. These structures were certainly a very useful addition to our two schools, though I still have no idea what cost might have been involved. It would also be interesting to know if the combined insurance companies found the whole project advantageous to their staffs.

Mention of speaking with Reinhold Messner reminds me of another occasion when he and I worked together, this time doing a commercial for Rolex watches. We were driven to a large tourist resort in the German Alps below which there was a wide snow-filled valley surrounded by snow-covered mountains. It could have been anywhere in the Himalayas. The advertising agency had obtained from George Band, one of our 1953 Everest expedition members, his ancient set of down clothing and I wriggled into these bulky garments. Reinhold was dressed superbly in all the latest modern mountaineering equipment. We plodded down into the snow valley and stood side by side—this was just the picture they wanted—a famous ancient climber in ancient clothes wearing a Rolex and an equally famous modern climber dressed in all the state-of-the-art modern equipment, but still wearing a Rolex. There was only one problem. Reinhold is a superb physical specimen and very handsome, but he just happened to be about six inches shorter than I was. The advertising agency was equal to the task. Very politely they asked me to step aside while they dug a six-inch hole in the snow. I then stepped down into this and there we were—the old and the young at precisely the same height. This advertisement was printed in magazines all over the world and every time I see it I have to chuckle.

In April 1995 June and I were back in the village of Junbesi to check on the new Swiss school building. It is a lovely spot with pine-clad slopes, a rushing mountain stream and the great white Himalayan peaks above. There is no road access to Junbesi, only tracks, but a few months before a telephone line had been established. We were staying in headmaster Kazi Sherpa's small but comfortable hotel, resting after an energetic day, when we heard someone approaching our door and there was a sharp rap. "Telephone call for Burra Sahib," said a Sherpa voice.

It was quite a way down to the telephone box so, with a groan, I asked June if she would mind answering the call. Very agreeably she descended the hill and talked to the caller—it was the British Ambassador with a message from the Secretary to Queen Elizabeth II. Would I be pleased to accept the award of the Order of the Garter? Somewhat shaken, June started back up the hill and then stopped abruptly—maybe it was a hoax? Down she went again to the telephone box, rang up the British Embassy in Kathmandu and was able to confirm that it was indeed no joke.

Panting somewhat with the altitude she joined me in our room and conveyed the story. To say we were surprised was no exaggeration— we were amazed. We knew very little about the Order of the Garter, except that it was for the Queen to decide who would receive it and it was regarded as the highest of all the knightly orders. I hadn't received many invitations from Her Majesty the Queen and as this was clearly a great honor we agreed I must accept. This time we both went down the hill to the telephone box and conveyed our warm appreciation to the British Ambassador.

In June we arrived in London for the installation. First we visited Buckingham Palace where we were brought to meet the Queen standing at the end of a small throne room. We bowed, walked forward and bowed again, but then informality took over and a very friendly Queen Elizabeth showed us the bejeweled decoration I would receive in Windsor Castle in a couple of days' time, and then we sat and had a pleasant talk about the America's Cup (in which New Zealand had a strong presence), World Cup rugby and the Queen's own forthcoming visit to New Zealand. The big day was Monday 9th June. It was a beauti-ful morning as we drove to Windsor and everything was superbly organized. At the Castle I met my distinguished fellow Knights of the Garter—mostly Dukes and Earls and Lords—who all welcomed me in to the Order in extremely friendly fashion. Among them was John Hunt who had been a Knight of the Garter for some years and was very proud that now two members of his expedition had achieved this distinguished status. I didn't get the impression that my new colleagues had a similar background to mine—a New Zealand beekeeper from Papakura—but I thought we all fitted in rather well.

I was not the only new member being admitted to the Order on this occasion. The other newcomer, and my processional partner from then on, was none other than Lady Thatcher, former Prime Minister of the United Kingdom. We were formally accepted into the Ancient Order of the Garter by the Queen in a simple private ceremony in the presence of the other members of the royal family, the other Knights and our spouses. Afterward we gathered to sip sherry while the Queen and the royal family circulated before a splendid lunch at which I had the good fortune to find myself sitting between the Queen and the Queen Mother who proved very pleasant table companions. After lunch it was time for the great procession from the Royal Apartments down to the final cere-mony in St. George's Chapel. Clad in my great cloak and feathered hat and bedecked in all my finery, I escorted Lady Thatcher down the hill with thousands of people lining the verges, shouting and cheering. The service that followed was overwhelming, with a magnificent choir, and the final words from the Queen which accepted Lady Thatcher and myself into the Order. It combined the present with ancient tradition in a remarkable fashion. I have never had an experience quite like it.

With the departure of the Royal Family in horses and carriage our limousines drew up in the correct order—mine was the last—Number 21—and June and I drove up to the Royal Apartments for a very pleasant cup of tea and a jolly good cucumber sandwich. Then it was disrobing, back into our limousine, and through the rush-hour traffic to our hotel in London. It had been an astonishing occasion—one always to be remembered.

I am now seventy-nine years old, and still leading a busy life. In January 1997 I joined the party of the New Zealand Prime Minister, the Right Honorable Jim Bolger, and flew in an RNZAF Hercules aircraft to McMurdo Sound to celebrate the fortieth anniversary of the first raising of the New Zealand flag at Scott Base—a task I had supervised when we commenced building the Base in January 1957. Scott Base is completely different now—much larger, more comfortable and a great deal more sophisticated, though at the time we felt that our original Base was pretty comfortable, too. I feel some satisfaction in knowing that our establishing of Scott Base precipitated New Zealand's activity in the Antarctic and I am delighted that the New Zealand government has continued to support its Antarctic program vigorously.

We had a film team from Television New Zealand with us recording footage of my return to the Antarctic. The day after our arrival we boarded an American ski-equipped Hercules aircraft and flew to the South Pole, soaring up the great Beardmore Glacier and over the Polar Plateau to land at 9,300 feet. There were buildings everywhere, the Pole Station had grown enormously. The film team borrowed a chair and I sat out in the polar waste in a temperature of -35°C, shivering in the latest thermal clothing, as I narrated the story of my first journey by tractor to the Pole. Over the next few days we helicoptered all over McMurdo Sound filming areas like Butter Point, the Skelton Glacier and even down a great crevasse. We landed at Scott's Hut at Cape Evans and I admired the recent work that had been done by the Antarctic Restoration Trust to get this historic site back into the order it must have been in when Captain Scott last saw it. Then we carried on to Shackleton's Hut at Cape Royds. This was my first visit and as Sir Ernest Shackleton had always been a hero of mine it was a very special occasion for me. On entering the simple building I believe we all had the same sensation. It was as though Shackleton himself was coming forward to meet us—a most eerie experience indeed.

At the end of March 1997 June and I flew into Paphlu for our annual visit to Solu Khumbu, calling on a number of the schools we had established and discussing problems with the headmasters and the village elders. We were welcomed warmly at the new Salleri Monastery which we had helped build as both a religious and cultural center for the local Sherpa people. A little further on was the Solu Khumbu Multiple Campus which, at the request of the Nepalese government, we were financing as a Junior University. Here we are starting a new project. The government-appointed teachers in our primary schools lack formal training and our young students are consequently disadvantaged. After discussions with the officials in the Education Ministry in Kathmandu we have agreed to undertake at the Solu Khumbu Multiple Campus a new primary-teacher training program which we believe will be one of our more useful activities.

Using the helicopters which have made traveling through the mountains so much easier for me, we flew up the great valley of the Dudh Kosi and landed at Tengboche Monastery where we were warmly welcomed by the Rimpoche and his monks and looked up the valley with awe as ever at the great peak of Mount Everest with its long plume of icy cloud sweeping across the summit. Inside the monastery the wall paintings had been completed and were a most spectacular sight. In three minutes we soared across the valley to Khumjung school, normally a more than three-hour walk, and were energetically garlanded in welcome scarves by the 400 students who entertained us with traditional singing and dancing. Then at the small but effective Kunde hospital we discussed plans with the volunteer New Zealand staff before flying back to Kathmandu. That was duty but duty of the most rewarding and satisfying kind. The rest of the year demonstrates the variety of our lives these days, as fund-raising mingles with pleasure, from attendance once more at the Garter ceremonies at Windsor Castle to visits to Tokyo, Korea, the States and to see the amazing moies, those great stone ancestral statues on Easter Island.

Life has given me an amazing variety of experiences. Perhaps nothing can surpass the opportunity of being first in the world to reach the summit of Mount Everest; to be first to drive a tractor overland to the South Pole or to make the first journey by jet boats up the mighty Ganges river to its source in the Himalayas. But there have been many other lesser adventures. I have been seriously afraid at times but have used my fear as a stimulating factor rather than allowing it to paralyze me. My abilities have not been outstanding, but I have had sufficient strength and determination to meet my challenges and have usually managed to succeed with them. I've had many exciting moments, too, that have not been life-threatening—even lecturing to several thousand people can be rather terrifying and I have done this many times.

I would not be human if I did not have regrets in my life. Louise loved mountain walking but was very afraid of flying in small aircraft. But I persuaded her to do it, so she and Belinda died. I have never forgiven myself for this. On one occasion I arrived back home to find that my mother had been rushed to hospital. I hastily went to her ward and she, as always, greeted me with a warm smile. I held her hand and for ten minutes we talked gently about family matters. Then I started getting restless, as I have a habit of doing, and my mother kindly suggested I should return home. I kissed her on the cheek and left. During the night she died. Why couldn't I have waited, even another miserable ten minutes, I kept asking myself? I have not always been thoughtful and kind, I fear.

I sometimes wonder what lies ahead for me. I can look back on seventy-nine years of challenge and adventure. I have experienced much joy and a share of sadness, too, and there have been many times when I have been close to death and yet survived. I am glad that my major Himalayan climbing happened more than forty years ago when almost everything we did was a first. We worked together as a team, established new routes and overcame most problems as they occurred. We climbed roped together, as we believed this was a safer and more responsible method. Procedures are very different nowadays, particularly on Mount Everest. Increasingly the mountain is littered with scores of aluminum ladders and thousands of feet of fixed rope. Deep tracks are beaten up the mountain by dozens of eager feet. Even on the Hillary Step near the summit there is usually a choice of three ropes to ascend. If the weather is kind, the standard routes on Mount Everest are far easier now with the advantage of modern technical equipment. Many inexperienced people have been conducted to the summit by expert professional guides. For some years I have been forecasting disaster in this area if the weather should deteriorate, and, unfortunately, this has happened. Everest must never be treated lightly—it is still a formidable challenge. Guided climbing has proved successful at alpine levels but it can be very dangerous above 26,000 feet. The unpredictable factors of altitude and weather then play their parts and life can be balanced precariously on a knife-edge if team members are inexperienced. At 29,000 feet no one, not even the best of them, is fully mentally balanced and can be relied on to make correct decisions all of the time.

Everest has also become an appalling junk heap with masses of empty oxygen bottles, torn tents, tin cans and even a few bodies as well. Regrettably our expedition was one of the first to set this miserable example and it is not much of an excuse to say we didn't know any better in those days. Fortunately, matters are slowly changing. Quite a few expeditions make considerable efforts to remove their rubbish off the mountain. Some even remove other people's rubbish. So a sense of environmental responsibility is slowly creeping in.

When climbers die on a mountain, the understandable reaction of family and friends is to say that they died doing what they enjoyed most and their bodies rest on the mountains they loved. This approach must certainly help the bereaved and, as such, is a positive attitude to take. However, I've never had any desire to end my days at the bottom of a deep crevasse—I've been down too many of them for that to have much appeal: I'm a somewhat fearful person and would prefer to go peacefully if that were possible. I should even like my ashes to be spread on the beautiful waters of Auckland's Hauraki Gulf to be washed gently ashore maybe on the many pleasant beaches near the place where I was born. Then the full circle of my life will be complete.

It was the mountains that introduced me to the adventures that I had dreamed about as a youngster. They just seemed to fit my frame of mind. Sometimes solo, sometimes with inexperienced friends, and finally with formidable companions I climbed many peaks and became more and more competent—competent enough to finally stand on the summit of Mount Everest. I have visited many countries and admired places of great beauty. But I feel fortunate to have been born a New Zealander. With a modest population it is so easy to visit the ice-clad mountains, the forests, the lakes, the wild rivers and the ever-present ocean. Adventure is always near at hand in New Zealand.

In November 1998 the sad news arrived that John Hunt had died aged eighty-eight years. I felt great sadness for his family but it was a time of deep sorrow for me too. John had been such a brave and good man and I had come to admire and respect him enormously. So many of my mountaineering and polar friends have died over the years and this has left a huge gap. But I have been very fortunate to establish close relationships with many members of younger generations around the world—so life goes relentlessly on.

Nobody can forecast when their life may come to an end. But there is still so much to do. With June's help and the support of my Himalayan Trust Members, I am hopeful that our work in the Himalayas will continue for some time yet. I have had my sorrows but, on the whole, life has been very good to me. I have enjoyed many adventures, supported many worthwhile causes and benefited from the generosity and love of wonderful companions. I can hardly ask for more than that!

INDEX